Managing
the Message

Managing
the Message

Peter Hobday

LONDON
HOUSE

First published in Great Britain in 2000 by
LONDON HOUSE
114 New Cavendish Street
London W1M 7FD

A catalogue record for this book is available
from the British Library

ISBN 1 902809 18 1

Edited and designed by DAG Publications Ltd, London.
Designed by David Gibbons. Edited by John Gilbert.
Printed and bound in Great Britain by
Creative Print and Design, Wales

Contents

Acknowledgements, 6

First – some messages, 8

1 Here is the news, 9

2 The Sultans of Spin, 21

3 The battle for public opinion, 31

4 The widening credibility gap, 47

5 The data game, 63

6 Mad media disease, 67

7 What the news media demands, 81

8 News that shocks around the clock, 89

9 Who's who in the news business, 101

10 Defining the message, 115

11 The five questions every reporter asks, 127

12 Controlling the message, 135

13 Messages in a time of crisis, 141

14 Watch your language, 153

15 Tricks for the memory, 173

16 Ourselves as others see us, 179

17 In the eye of the camera, 189

18 Hold the front page, 205

19 Now is the time, 215

20 And finally ... 221

Notes, 230

Index, 235

Acknowledgements

A long career, first in newspapers, then mainly in broadcast journalism at the BBC, incurs so many professional debts to friends and colleagues that there is not space enough to list each and every one. I worked under some notable editors: Vincent Duggleby was the force behind Financial World Tonight and Moneybox – and taught me how to tackle the most complicated story in the world of finance in a minute or less; Paul Ellis took me into TV at The Money Programme and patiently explained the difference between reporting for radio and television; George Carey appointed me one of the original four presenters on Newsnight, where I sat alongside John Tusa, Peter Snow and Charles Wheeler – a trio of top-class broadcasters who were inspirational. Carey encouraged me to move outside my specialist role as an economics and financial correspondent into politics and foreign affairs. Julian Holland, my first editor at Today on Radio Four, was a demanding task master, and left you in no doubt when he thought you had been less than perfect; I spent fourteen happy years on the programme, learning how to interview all and sundry, from the highest in the land to the modest and retiring, thanks to such masters of the art as Brian Redhead, John Timpson, John Humphrys and Sue Macgregor.

Down the years I have met some maestros in the world of public relations – and I've learned from them, too. Phillip Pettifore has one of the most ingenious of minds; while Basil Towers was always thought-provoking when we discussed the art of public persuasion. A lifetime friendship with Jim Dunne and Arthur Wielden, who built one of the country's most successful travel PR consultancies, gave me the inside track on how the business really works. In politics, the briefings from Harvey Thomas, while he was with the Tory Party, and Des Wilson, while with the Liberal Democrats, helped my understanding of Whitehall; Ann

Dillon took me into the world of agriculture and its special problems when she was head of public affairs at the National Farmers Union, and food and health issues afterwards.

Among the younger generation of PR gurus, John Hobday, my son, and his business partner, Mary Longhurst, are growing a successful business together. It was John who cured my techno-phobia, took me into cyber-space and on to the Internet.

Then of course there are all those senior executives in so many companies in the top 100 who have given insights into the corporate mind as they submitted themselves to relentless questioning in one of my media seminars. I think I have learned every bit as much from them as I hope they learned from me. I'm sure they'd prefer not to see their names here. But there is one name – Brian Johnson, who was a director of the worldwide advertising agency JWT and developed a two-day presentation training course which took us all over the United States, Europe and even the Far East – I should really have paid him for the knowledge it gave me of advertising in particular and media in general.

We are planning a second edition of Managing the Message: if you want to comment, contribute or criticise, please e-mail me at **pjhobday@aol.com**. Your views can be on or off the record – between us, I'm sure, we'll be able to manage the message even better.

First – some messages

'No one means all he says, and yet very few say all they mean, for words are slippery and thought is viscous.'
Henry Brooks Adams

'If it falls to me to start a fight to cut out the cancer of bent and twisted journalism in our country with the simple sword of truth and the trusty shield of British fair play, so be it.'
Jonathan Aitken, who spent eighteen months in prison for perjury and perverting justice

'As you know ... I was asked questions about my relationship with Monica Lewinsky. While my answers were accurate, I did not volunteer information. Indeed I did have a relationship with Ms Lewinsky that was not appropriate.'
President Clinton on national TV

'Now is not the time for sound bites, I feel the hand of history on my shoulder.'
Tony Blair, when he signed the Northern Ireland Peace Agreement

'Sound bites are the equivalent of chicken nuggets.'
Richard Hoggart in The Way We Live Now

'Mass democracy, mass morality and the mass media thrive independently of the individual, who joins them at the cost of at least a partial perversion of his instinct and insights.'
A. Alvarez writing in The Listener in 1963

Here is the news

For fourteen years I led a monk-like existence as one of the main presenters of BBC radio's Today programme. The daily routine was not unlike that followed by any closed monastic order, because I had to observe a number of set rituals. My day began with the early call at around four a.m. when I tuned into the BBC's World Service to get the latest news. Then to the office, where I scanned the agency tapes and wrote a script, before broadcasting 'live' for up to three hours. Back home around ten a.m., I would begin to listen to or watch all the main radio and TV news shows; I read most of the daily papers, from red top to broadsheet. And as the technology began to change, I began to 'surf' the Internet for an international perspective on any stories I was following. There were press conferences, lunches and receptions to be attended. Last thing at night, after News at Ten, I would put out the light and go to sleep. Wherever I was, whatever I was doing, the Great God News was with me. My church was Broadcasting House, in the West End of London. My pulpit, where I publicly professed my faith, was studio Four A. The congregation was a large one – around six million people every morning.

Before I joined the Today programme, I had spent an equally challenging time as one of the four original presenters of the late night TV news programme, Newsnight. Before that I had anchored TV's The Money Programme for three years. Before the move to television, I helped launch Financial World Tonight and Money Box on radio. I began my career in newspapers with the Express and Star Group in Wolverhampton. There is an unwritten and unbreakable rule for all broadcasters – indeed for all journalists. It is that the programme (or the paper) comes first, regardless of the cost to oneself or one's family. When I look back to those days, I now realise how little of the time I spent doing 'normal' things

– like the school run with my son and daughter, having a drink in the pub with a neighbour, or even watching a cricket match at any level, though I professed to love the game. I was a news junkie – and like anyone with an addiction to feed, everything else just got in the way.

Nowadays, life is more sedate, though no less full. I still make and present programmes for radio and television, but no longer for the mass audience that was attracted each morning to the Today programme. And I've moved outside the cloistered world of broadcasting into a more real environment. I spend a great deal of time talking to business audiences about the media, how it works and why. They seem both repelled and fascinated at the same time. As a Visiting Professor at de Montfort University, I get the chance, from time to time, to talk to the next generation of broadcast and print journalists about current trends and the impact information technology will have on their professional lives in the years ahead. Once a year I spend a day with the MBA students at the Cranfield School of Management talking about the media to Britain's future business leaders. And I seem to be building a second career chairing, or as the business jargon has it, 'facilitating' business conferences – from the Institute of Directors' Annual Convention in the Albert Hall to international jamborees, in such exotic places as Disney World outside Paris.

Wherever I go these days, and whatever company I find myself in, the same questions about the media are put over and over again. Top of the list is: Why does the media lie? And so it goes on. Why does the media demand total transparency in everyone else's business but its own? Why does the media feel it must report intimate details of an individual's sex life? Do we really need to see pictures snatched by the telephoto lens of the paparazzi of a duchess having her toes sucked by a financial adviser? Was it really in the public interest to show us twelve-year-old pictures of Prince Edward's then fiancée Sophie Rhys Jones's breasts? Why does the media set out to destroy people's careers, hound the innocent, and, when the victims complain, the media seemingly feels no responsibility for its actions?[1] These questions are usually asked with an aggressive finger jabbing one in the chest to emphasise the questioner's revulsion. 'How can anyone read the details of what went on between the President of the United States and a White

House intern', they wonder? Yet mention the merest detail, and you find they have read every last word, and could pass an A level exam in the subject.

This book is not a defence of the media, but an explanation of some of the pressures that drive it. And because I was trained in the old-fashioned BBC tradition of balance and fair play, I also suggest some possible strategies to survive a world where it seems the media sets the agenda, and the rest of us must bend the knee. To survive, it is essential to understand the media world in which we live. You can't survive in the Arctic unless you've had cold weather training and are aware of the dangers; nor can you survive the attention of the media world unless you know and understand the dangers. It's an equally hostile environment in Medialand.

The hostile environment

We all live in this hostile environment. There seems to be no hiding place. We are bombarded with words and images every minute of every day of our lives. We probably have more words thrown at us than any previous generation at any other time in the history of mankind. Most used to bounce off us, like rain off a waterproof coat. Some of the more persistent might eventually penetrate and make their presence felt – to depress us, cheer us up, or prompt us into action. But it was all a bit haphazard. An essential ingredient in the history of the twentieth century is the way in which the battle for public opinion has become more necessary than ever before. And because of that, it's becoming much more professional and targeted than ever before. It is no use, any longer, just saying something and hoping that you are listened to. Sam Goldwyn, the legendary Hollywood mogul, once remarked that 'you throw your bread on the water and hope it comes back a peanut butter sandwich'. These days it is better by far to make a proper peanut butter sandwich before you cast it on water.

Words as weapons

In the hands of the expert practitioners, words and images are now used more like weapons. And this war of the words has opened up an arms race to go with it. That's why these days you should always remember that famous

World War Two slogan – 'Careless talk costs lives'. These days it would be more relevant if it read 'Careless talk costs careers'. In the public arena words can no longer be spoken or written without any regard to the impact they will have. Words today are verbal smart bombs, laser guided, to make sure they hit the target. If we miss the target, then we could be part of what the military like to call 'collateral damage'. We have added massive technology to help give us more range and fire power. It's becoming harder and harder to find a place to shelter from the impact. People are no longer content to have just one TV set, or one radio – they have several. The Sony Walkman radio gives them access even when they are between home and job. The car radio can be tuned to any number of stations. And now you find more radio and TV sets in public places – shopping malls, restaurants, rail and air terminals, almost anywhere that people congregate. You would think we had reached saturation point. Yet still the electronics industry goes for the hard sell to get you to update, to receive more channels, to 'go digital' and acquire the ability to surf up to 200 channels. Rupert Murdoch even offered the public free set-top boxes to try to spread the coverage of his digital television channels. And if all that were not more than enough, now comes the explosive growth of the Internet, with millions, it is claimed, logging on every minute of every hour of every day. The Internet has taken us into what's called 'cyber space', a mysterious place full of incredibly small bits of data flying around in ways that are beyond the imagining of mere mortals. The good part is that some of this information technology is essential – for example the programmes that make sure that computers will pay our bills and our wages on time. Some of the data in cyber space is dangerous – there seem to be a growing number of computer anoraks who like developing viruses that will eat up the data on someone's hard disk. Seems hardly worth the bother. And there's a lot of data that just clogs the system. Everyday, I find junk e-mail in my in-box. The advertising and public relations industries are becoming very adept at directing their messages on to your screen almost regardless of what you are doing at the time. And when it comes to getting your message across, you ignore this new dimension at your peril.

Strategies for survival

This book sets out some strategies for survival in this hostile environment. It is aimed primarily at the business reader, although, in fact, many of the strategies can be adopted and adapted by any individual who wants to communicate with society at large. There comes a time in most people's lives when they are caught up in events which become part of the daily news. It could be the directors of a large public company fighting a hostile take-over; it could be the ad hoc committee formed by a small village to save the village green from property developers; it could be a charity raising funds to fight some disease. It could be the lone individual fighting what he or she perceives to be an injustice; or the individual who has become a victim of medical or professional misconduct. It could be someone who has suffered because of a tragedy such as the Hillsborough disaster or the Paddington train crash. All face the same challenge: putting their point of view across, and making a case. In the din of battle it can sometimes seem impossible to make oneself heard. Over the years I've done my share of what is generally called 'media training' – a short course to familiarise small groups of individuals with the media and advise them how to manage and target their messages more effectively. The one-day seminars usually involved talking to scared executives at the highest level and listening to them rant on about how much they hated the media. They hoped that they would learn some tricks of the trade about how to cope with 'hostile' interviewers like the BBC's John Humphrys or Jeremy Paxman. Note that I have put the word 'hostile' in quotes. What is usually meant by 'hostile' is that the interviewer has asked the interviewee a question that the interviewee doesn't want to answer. I always told them that there are no tricks that can get them off the hook.

The BBC has now banned all its news and current affairs producers, presenters and correspondents from giving any media training or advice. It argues that to provide such services in some way diminishes or calls into question a staff member's editorial independence.[2] The argument from the journalists' side is that a well-prepared business executive means that it is more difficult to get the real story. Yet surely journalists have a second sense when someone is being evasive, or is lying. In my opinion the better the person you interview, the better the story. The more robust the relationship, the nearer to the truth you get.

Business often misunderstands what media training is all about. Executives think they are going to find some easy panacea for all their media woes. They assume that they will be given a slick method of being able to deny whatever they want, and foist whatever they want on some unsuspecting reporter. If they believe that, they are living in never-never land. I think everyone should operate on the basis of knowing that if they do anything wrong or illegal, or are simply withholding uncomfortable facts, sooner or later they will be found out. If you start to lie, as President Clinton discovered, sooner or later, no amount of 'wriggle room', as his advisers called it, will stop the truth from emerging. The other awful phrase to come out of Washington was 'plausible deniability'. I may be naïve, but in the end honesty really is the best policy. Many executives believe that the less said the better as far as the media are concerned. Sadly, silence is no longer an option. Some believe that being 'economical with the truth', as one British senior civil servant rather quaintly described it, will get them off the hook. That is even less of an option. As President Lincoln once observed, 'You can fool some of the people, all of the time, and all of the people some of the time – but you can't fool all of the people all of the time.'

The media, because of its experience of the world in which we live, tends to think you guilty of lying unless you can prove otherwise. You have to prove your innocence. Just think how many times we have all read of someone in the public eye admitting that they lied. Jeffrey Archer is the most recent example. No wonder the media – and the public – mistrust people in authority. This climate of mistrust explains why the relationship between business and the media is fraught with difficulty. The journalist does not believe the executive – the executive does not trust the reporter. Each is so suspicious that neither really pays attention to the other. So each plays the role they believe has been allotted to them. Defensive and evasive on the one side, probing and disbelieving on the other. I shall set out some strategies to minimise that mistrust.

For example, there's an accident in your plant and, tragically, someone dies. I've heard it asked, 'Why do the media concentrate on the bad news?' One senior executive in his defence actually said, 'But it was only one fatality.' Tell that to the bereaved. I shall explain what it is that moves the media to behave in the way that it does, and why it asks what people see as awkward or accusing questions.

Awkward questions

The most effective way to avoid awkward questions, as any good public relations guru will tell you, is 'not to get it wrong in the first place'. That's easier said than done in a world where everyone's attention span or boredom threshold is getting shorter day by day. In an age where even the most difficult concept is reduced to 30 seconds of air time on national radio and TV, there are huge risks. Part of the problem, these days, is corporate jargon, which is a useful shorthand between colleagues but often meaningless to outsiders. By using such language, interviewees either fluff the message,[3] or fail to explain a situation properly. This business-speak can also make something sound more complicated than it is, or so mangle the language that the public is given a totally wrong message. Too often people will 'focus on the key issues to be addressed, install a help line and make counselling available'. The increasingly common use of such phrases means that your messages are instantly forgotten. If the audience is confused, or gets the wrong idea, you may never be able to put right the first mistaken impression. A mistake can haunt you for ever more. Ask those railway companies that blamed 'leaves on the line' for the lateness of the trains![4]

Radio and TV may seem the most ephemeral of media, yet modern technology means that what's said on air now has a very long shelf life. Long after you've uttered a phrase into a microphone, the tape can be taken down and used in evidence against you whenever the media sees fit. Jonathan Aitken's publicly announced and self appointed task of 'cutting out the cancer of bent and twisted journalism with the sword of truth' was quoted ad nauseam before, during and after his trial for perjury.

In the sections about interviews in radio and television, and statements at press conferences, I shall be looking at what one could and should say, and how

15

to say it. There is, of course, a special challenge in the broadcast interview. The executive is in a foreign environment. He or she is doing something of which that they have little experience. Not just the words, but the body language speak volumes. You cannot deny what you said. It's no use claiming that the editing was unfair. I'll be explaining the editing process, and the difficulties involved in keeping your defence within the time limits imposed by the programme makers.

Perhaps I should rephrase that. It's not the programme makers who impose time limits. They know their customers, and they know the attention span for a 'talking head' on the box is about 30 seconds or so – any longer, without interruption, and the interest begins to waver. Here again I shall be explaining the hows and the whys of broadcast journalism. It's no use berating the media at every turn for its faults, real or imagined. It exists and it is expanding all the time. Yes, standards have fallen in some areas, and I'll explain why in the sections on the media. Ironically, the pressures on the media are those which any business manager would understand. The owners want higher productivity, with fewer people and with smaller budgets. They want a bigger market share, and new products that will beat the competition.

Honesty and truth

So the message is simple: if you act honestly, produce safe products, market them at a competitive price, and do nothing that you would be ashamed to tell your children about, there is nothing that the media can do to you. All too often, in my experience, business people ignore their image until it is too late. They keep the media at bay, and stay silent. Then when a crisis happens, as it will, they believe some slick PR guru is going to get them off the hook.

One of the most recent examples of what I'm talking about is the mis-selling of pensions. People were told that if they gave up their current pension they would get something better. In some cases it was true, but in many, many other cases, the poor client got something worse. It came about because the industry was pushing for results from its sales teams – who cut corners to push up their strike rate. At first it must have seemed like Eldorado. Then the truth began to emerge. Pensioners had been duped. The whole sorry saga has cost the industry untold billions, it has damaged its reputation, and it will be a long time before anyone really trusts it again. It has given a wonderful stick to politicians to beat the City with. And anti-business groups can have a field day. In a wider context it has further undermined the standing of the financial services industry, and confirmed the suspicions of many that the Square Mile is a place for the unscrupulous wheeler-dealer. And just to add insult to injury, they are now linked to Robert Maxwell, fraudster extraordinaire – even though what he did was very different. I will be generous in suggesting that the insurance companies did not set out to gull the unsuspecting public. Some of them may have been victims of corporate jargon, which is a language that seems to have little foundation in reality. They were probably following an 'aggressive' marketing plan, designed to 'grow the business'.

Beware of jargon

Corporate jargon is the single biggest problem for anyone with a message to put across. Let me give you but one example. Not so long ago a company that made photocopiers decided they needed to sack some people because the competition had become so tough. The resulting announcement said that 'the company needed a more rapid integration of the organisational structure so as to provide a seamless global organisation'. As an afterthought they added that there would be 600 redundancies. I will be discussing the dangers of jargon and following fashion by using words just because everyone else uses them. And you'll find more in the section on Mission Statements – more vacuous or useless pieces of managerial mischief. They all seem to want to be 'the best', 'leaders', 'global', 'satisfying their customers'. As one BBC colleague remarked, 'We should avoid clichés like the plague.'

So can you manage the message better? The straight answer is 'yes'. There are a few caveats to be entered to that – because no one can manage totally. Every dictator in the world – from Ozymandias to Ceausescu has discovered that sooner or later the people will break free. There will always be the unexpected. But there is no secret ingredient, nor magic formula. What you'll find in this book is, I believe, only common sense about the information-led world which we inhabit. We live in a society obsessed with data rather than knowledge. It's a world obsessed equally with brevity, speed and simplicity. I believe that instead of fighting the media, if you study it, you can operate more successfully – as the Royal Family found after Diana's death. The public is telling Them what they want in the First Family; and the public is no longer prepared to tolerate the old-fashioned approach of keeping One's distance and doing One's own thing. When the Royal Warrant was withdrawn from the tobacco firm Gallagher, which makes Benson & Hedges cigarettes, anti-smoking groups were quick to praise what they saw as a move to help stamp out smoking in general. It was seen as a modern move. 'A symbolic breakthrough,' said a spokesman for Action on Smoking and Health – or ASH. Somehow I feel that the Royal Family had not thought of it as a 'symbolic gesture', they had just given up smoking. But this is the world of today – where every gesture by someone in the public eye causes comment and provokes reaction.

It may be that as the new all-embracing world of instant communication, propelled ever faster by information technology, becomes more deeply embedded in the human psyche, we will all be able to manage our public image better. Indeed the gap between the public and the private may even disappear. What could happen in this new century, as all sides begin to understand one another better, is that we end up with what diplomats call 'a free and frank exchange of views'. And that should work to everyone's benefit. It might have helped the former Welsh Secretary Ron Davies after his night out on Clapham Common. It might have stopped Glenn Hoddle, England's former football coach, from talking about Karma, reincarnation and people with disabilities. In short, every message can be managed better.

Like the game of football, this is a book in two halves. The first looks at the world we now inhabit – what's happening to the media as it expands day by day; what's happening to the audiences you want to reach; what's happening to language. I examine the effects of around-the-clock news, and introduce you to the people who manage the news and make the key editorial decisions about which story runs, and which, to use old-fashioned newspaper jargon, ends up on 'the spike' – today I suppose it's the office shredder. It's well worth reading this section before you tackle the practical second half.

This second part is a step-by-step guide to using (or should I say working with) the media in the most effective way. The chapter titles are to the point – 'Defining the Message', 'The Message in Time of Crisis' and so on. I deal with radio, television and press interviews, as well as what's called in the trade 'non verbal communication' – in plain English how to sit, dress and move when you are in front of an audience. Your body language often speaks louder than the words you use. In each section and in each chapter there are cross-references to other pages and sections should you want to know more about a particular subject at that moment. Rather like hypertext on your computer.

I have tried to make each chapter stand alone so that it can be a quick and easy reference point. You can read this book from beginning to end, you can dip in and out of it, as the need arises. At the end of each chapter is a list of the key thoughts and action points (around 200 in all). There's a full index, so that you can get to the subject you need as quickly as possible. I've also given the names of a few books which are interesting to read for their own sake – and which develop some of the ideas in my book in more detail.[5] As I said, in the relentless and pressured world in which we live, everything has to be and can be abbreviated. At the same time, the need to know more has never been greater. I have tried to meet those two mutually incompatible objectives in this book.

In Chapter Two, 'The Sultans of Spin', I trace the rise of that mysterious creature the Spin Doctor – and spell out the dangers of spinning out of control. I quote many examples from the world of politics, and the business reader might wonder what politics can teach. Politics attracts more journalistic scrutiny than almost any other aspect of the modern world, so it provides some essential lessons on what to do and what not to do. Business is having to become much more political these days, so what is happening in the political world has greater relevance than ever before.

2

The Sultans of Spin

The phrase 'spin doctor' has a surprisingly long history. It was first heard in the United States in the earliest years of the twentieth century. Baseball was the national game, and the search was on for pitchers who could destroy the opposition. What was needed were men with the ability to spin or 'curve' the ball. Experts, called 'spin doctors', soon appeared out of the woodwork, and the phrase was born. It was much later that the word began to apply to the art of 'spinning' a message. This time the spin was needed in the political arena, as television began to replace print as the prime source of information for the American electorate. Inevitably the idea crossed the Atlantic, but, at first in Britain, it made little impact. That was because a certain lady, Margaret Thatcher, was able to dominate through force of conviction and personality. And although her spin doctors got her to deepen the voice, soften the hair, and fix her teeth – in the end she was her own best spin doctor. She may not have thought of them herself, but phrases like 'the lady's not for turning' seemed freshly minted when she uttered them.

It was the Labour Party that really brought 'spin doctoring' to public notice. The party had lost four general elections on the trot (the last to a grey man called John Major). They knew they needed to change their appeal to the electorate. Tony Blair had been impressed with the way the Democrats fought the last presidential election – and how Bill Clinton was able to handle himself in front of the media, no matter how difficult the situation. Britain's Labour Party needed all the spin they could muster.

Staying on message

The Labour Party leadership knew that the public was cynical in the extreme about politics and politicians. As a noted American investigative journalist, I. F.

Stone, once observed: 'Every government is run by liars and nothing they say should be believed.' So it was not enough to say that the party had changed, or was changing; the leadership had to prove it. And it had to do so in the toughest court of all – the court where public opinion is both the judge and the jury. First the party set about developing policies which were voter-friendly. In doing so they faced a great deal of opposition within their own ranks, but they persevered and finally came up with an agreed set of policies with which the vast majority of their supporters agreed. As the business world would say, Labour supporters 'bought into' these new policies. Before the Labour leadership could begin communicating those policies, it set about acquiring the necessary communication skills in the most professional manner possible. In the end, just as business goes about launching a new product – Labour had identified the market, developed the product, and then set about marketing that product effectively. They had, however, a product that needed to be controlled, just as the quality of any branded product needs to be protected. This is easier said than done because, in this case, the product was essentially a set of ideas or messages. These messages were wrapped up in words – and, as Henry Brooks Adams once remarked, 'words are slippery and thought is viscous.' The message needed managing every bit as rigorously as, say, quality control in a food plant.

The man mainly credited with making Britain's Labour Party electable, Peter Mandelson, coined the phrase 'on message'. He was backed up by Tony Blair's spokesman, Alastair Campbell. In the run-up to the general election of 1997 they were determined that everyone would be 'on message'. In plain English that meant that everyone who spoke up on behalf of the party knew exactly what they should say in public. The 'message' or 'issue' was decided on a daily basis by an inner core – depending on how the campaign was going. Once decided, they knew it would be political suicide to deviate from the agreed party line. That had happened all too often in the past. Labour – old and new, plus its union supporters – had to sing from the same hymn sheet.

All the key party workers were given bleepers which kept them up to the minute on what the message was. The interviews were carefully allocated to the best spokesperson on particular policies. Some individuals were more favoured than others. Harriet Harman was thought the best person to appeal to women; as a professional mother, with children and a full-time job, she presented the perfect image of 'New' Labour. Clare Short, dumpy and not the most fashion conscious, was seen as 'Old' Labour; she still believed in Socialism, and so she was kept out of sight. Robin Cook, the brainy Foreign-Secretary-in-waiting, looked, as it was rather cruelly put, too much like a 'garden gnome' to be taken seriously by voters. Frank Dobson was told to shave off his beard; beards, it was believed, were not appealing to the voters.[6] Tony Blair backed the system to the full, and Peter Mandelson and Alastair Campbell soon became the most hated men in the party because of the way they managed the message. Yet it worked, and there is no gainsaying that.

Spinning for Britain

Once Labour had won, Alastair Campbell, the former political editor of the Daily Mirror, was appointed head of the government's communications service, and the Prime Minister's official spokesman.[7] Very quickly he cleared out long-serving civil servants, and replaced them with outsiders. This was the beginning of the fall. At every opportunity the media made much of 'government spin'. Soon the main story was how the government put across its message, rather than the message itself. It's not surprising that the media would adopt this attitude. The idea that spin doctors were able to place any story in any paper and ensure that it was favourable to the government was an insult to the independence that the media rightly claims for itself. As the famous American journalist H. L. Mencken remarked early in the twentieth century: 'Never pick a quarrel with someone who buys printer's ink by the barrel load.' The 'sage of Baltimore's' advice holds good these days – though perhaps we should add – 'or video and audio tape in bulk'.

Even if Alastair Campbell had known that line by Mencken, I don't believe it would have stopped the Prime Minister's press secretary picking a quarrel with the BBC. He said of Jeremy Paxman and Newsnight, 'What is the point of traipsing out to TV Centre late at night so that Jeremy can try to persuade the public that I am some kind of criminal?' Some argue that Campbell is too partisan to be a good press officer – he lets his belief in the message get in the way of the necessary professionalism needed to put it across effectively.

Nor was the government's reputation helped by some of its lesser 'spin doctors' who, it was reported, were now spinning against each other – Charlie Whelan from the Chancellor of the Exchequer's office against Alastair Campbell at Number Ten. In fact, Whelan became famous in his own right, first coming to public attention in a documentary made about his boss, Gordon Brown. In the film he is seen 'spinning' and boasting that he could control the media. Later he was at the centre of a row over leaked information when he was overheard in a pub not far from the Treasury talking loudly into his mobile phone to a member of the media.

Later on, another Labour supporter came to the public's attention in a row over lobbying – Derek Draper. The Draper affair seemed to underline everything that the critics were saying. There was something sleazy about the government and its supporters; they would say anything to win. It was said he was peddling influence in government at some of the highest levels in exchange for cash. The story first appeared in The Observer, a paper which supported Labour. Then came the classic counter-spin. Attack the messenger, not the message. It was pointed out that the man who wrote the story, an American named Gregory Palast, was allegedly a liar and a cheat. It subsequently turned out that this was a phrase used in a court case, subsequently thrown out by the judge.

The most extreme example of spin control was the story that emerged about Robin Cook and the end of his marriage. It was said that when the story was about to be printed in a Sunday newspaper that he had a mistress, who worked in his private office, Campbell told Cook to make a choice – to dump either his wife or his mistress. Cook chose to dump his wife, and told her the marriage was over in the departure lounge of Heathrow Airport. No one involved has commented directly.

All spin and no substance

The situation was beginning to worry a number of old hands in the party. Even the Deputy Prime Minister, John Prescott, a man who was sufficiently Old Labour to see the danger in the spin, warned that they were getting out of control. He had long held this position. Back in 1992 he attacked what he called the 'beautiful people' in Neil Kinnock's campaign team; and in 1996 he said he wanted a campaign built on 'substance, not sound bites'. But in January 2000 he was advertising for a spin doctor 'who wanted a challenge'. And another minister, Clare Short, observed that 'the trouble is it's often not about anything specific. It's "X isn't doing any good. Y is for the chop. Z has fallen out with so-and-so. The Prime Minister doesn't like" ... This constant briefing against people is wicked and wrong. It's cruel. It's mean, it's nasty and it hurts people.' All this was said in an interview with a former Tory MP on Radio Five Live – Edwina Curry – someone who would have known exactly what Ms Short was talking about, having been the victim of some notorious slurs when she was a health minister.

Is there a spin doctor in the house?

Such reservations, even though expressed in public, still didn't stop some senior members of the government reaching for their own personal spin doctor when the media declared open season. The most notable was Lord Irvine, the arrogant Lord Chancellor who had his apartments redecorated at public expense, but somehow did not manage to persuade the media that it was done, not for personal comfort, but on behalf of the nation. It had been a disaster, with stories about £20,000 spent on carpets, wallpaper at £15,000 a roll, and so on. Out went his Whitehall PR and in came Alan Percival, seconded from Number Ten.

Inevitably spin soon became the dominant political issue to be exploited by the albeit depleted Tories, still suffering from post-traumatic stress syndrome after their record-breaking defeat in the election. Then the Select Committee on Public Administration started to look into the whole business of how the government managed its message – the Tories were beginning to acquire the ability to counter the government's popularity with spin of their own. Of that committee's deliberations more later. Mandelson's enemies quickly labelled him a 'spin doctor', who practised 'the black arts'. It was meant as an insult. One of the BBC's political correspondents, Nicolas Jones, wrote a book about the 1997 election in which he seemed to find Mandelson, Campbell and their cohorts somehow undermining democracy with their bully-boy tactics. And a former prime ministerial press officer, Sir Bernard Ingham, who was not above a little bullying in his day, also wondered whether Labour had taken the system of managing its message to extremes.

In the end Peter Mandelson was driven from office over a mistake that the great spin meister should have foreseen would be impossible to defend if it became public. He borrowed money from a millionaire colleague to buy a house and did not tell his building society. Technically he was found to have done no wrong; but the perception was that somehow it was all very sleazy. And as I shall point out many times in these pages, 'perception' is everything, no matter what the reality. Mandelson went, and his enemies rejoiced. Next to depart was Charlie Whelan who was said to be implicated in Mandelson's downfall. He denied the charge vigorously, but he still had to go. Once again the 'perception' that he had been 'spinning' against Peter Mandelson was enough. Mandelson came back into office ten months later.

From time to time the question is asked, 'Can Alastair Campbell last much longer?' As I write, he seems more than capable of fighting his corner – but as the national media begins to question the government's record, he has turned his attention to getting the message across in the regions and on what are called 'sofa' interviews on morning television. And he has definitely lowered his profile.

As ye spin, so shall ye reap

I believe that some lessons can be learned from Mandelson's and Campbell's initial successes. The foremost is that the system shouldn't be quite as rigid as the message management system they imposed. Indeed it was the rigidity which contributed to many of the subsequent difficulties that the Labour government encountered. While there surely needs to be a strategic overview of what the messages are that you want to get into the public domain, you have to allow some flexibility in the way individuals cope. The biggest lesson to be learned, though, is that once people notice the spin, then you are in danger of losing the battle for public opinion. While the government's information service still does a very credible job, people now look for spin. And those who are being controlled begin to try to free themselves from the shackles.

Perhaps the final blow was the leaking of two faxes from Alastair Campbell's office to the two ministers in charge of Health and Social Security, Harriet Harman and Frank Field.[8] 'I would urge extreme caution in relation to lunches,' said one. 'I should be grateful for an explanation on why the interviews with the Guardian, Woman's Hour and The World at One were not cleared through this office.' A second fax read, 'I see from today's press that no matter how much we urge silence, continued briefing goes on about who is responsible for what ...'

The fact that these faxes were leaked just goes to show how much they were resented – although, such is the nature of leaking – we will never know who did the deed. Joe Haines, a man who held Campbell's job when Harold Wilson was Prime Minister back in the 1960s, put his finger on the problem now facing his successor. 'The reason he hits so many headlines is that from the beginning he has been seen and heard instead of being not seen and heard.' Haines tells the story that while in opposition Tony Blair introduced his press spokesman as follows: 'This is Alastair Campbell. He gets more publicity than I do.' Haines said that in his day you will find some, but not many photographs of him and Mr Wilson. 'Members of my staff caught on camera with the Prime Minister were fined a bottle of wine.'

Once the internal workings of the system become public knowledge, and once the way the spin is being done and by whom is part of the daily round of media gossip, then the system has severely damaged itself. Take the example of spin bowling in cricket. Ask any spin bowler who will tell you that the way to get the batsman out is to disguise the spin so well that he thinks it's a straight ball. When he plays at it, the spin deceives him, so he misses the ball and is bowled.

Spinning for crown and mitre

Notwithstanding the critics of this disciplined approach to the presentation of policy – and there were as many inside as outside the party – soon the most surprising people wanted their own spin doctor. The Church of England, riven by faction, was said to be looking for a top spin doctor to put across its message. The Guardian reported that a secret memo, written on the eve of the General

Synod, said that 'We are a hostage to fortune on many issues; our agenda is terminally tedious; we have become a refuge for the pedant, the bureaucrat and the bore ... and much of our agenda panders to the concerns of the small minorities.' Since then, as far as I am aware, nothing more has been heard of the Guardian's story, but, a couple of months later, after a huge debate about whether to recognise the rights of homosexuals to full membership, the Church seemed in even greater need to find someone who can try to manage the messages it wants to get across. And it still does.

The House of Lords, battling to save the rights of hereditary peers, called in an American body-language expert in the summer of 1999 to help them improve their communication skills. Richard Greene, who advised both Princess Diana and Tony Blair, said he hoped to make the peers 'a little more Clintonesque'.[9]

To crown it all, the Royal Family, hit hard in the public's esteem by the way it reacted to Diana's death, wanted a spin doctor. The Royals were even prepared to spend £200,000 a year on a top man. The Queen is said to have chosen a Labour Party member as her communications secretary. Derek Lewis is his name, and he is on secondment from Centrica, the supply arm of British Gas. And the heir to the throne, also a victim of the public's falling esteem of the Royals, has made a similar move. Prince Charles regularly met Peter Mandelson and seemed to be moving closer to Labour as he tried to win public support. In the end, however, he acquired the services of Elisabeth Buchanan from a lobbying firm run by Sir Tim Bell, who had been a key adviser to government in the Thatcher years. Ms Buchanan had been a press secretary to Mrs Thatcher.

The deal, for the Prince, has not been cheap. It will cost him £200,000 over three years. It has to be said that the Prince's new PR team seemed to have learned the lessons of not having a high profile – they are content to remain very much in the shadow. And surprise, surprise: slowly the Prince is being seen not so much as the hateful husband who destroyed a beautiful young woman, but as a caring father. Even his relationship with Mrs Parker Bowles is being treated differently – and one senses a much surer touch about the way her appearances are handled. The best example was allowing the media a photo-opportunity of the royal 'couple' leaving the Ritz after a birthday party.

The business of spin

The business world, of course, can never dominate the news agenda like the politicians. Politics creates news because it is seen to affect all our lives. Politicians make themselves endlessly available to the media. You stumble over them round at Millbank House near the Commons, where the main networks have based their political correspondents. Somebody rather unkindly said that politicians were like prostitutes plying their trade, hoping to pick up some custom. 'Psst – want a quick quote for the Nine O'Clock News, deary?'

Business has to work harder to get its messages across – and it is an unfortunate fact that usually it only gets the media's full attention when something goes wrong. This is why in the main it is so re-active, rather than pro-active. But business is spending more and more on the PR function. Some 7500 people work in PR consultancies – those are outside agencies that work on a retainer basis. And there are at least twice that number who work 'in house'. That means that all in all at least 21,000 people could be called 'experts'. Be sure to beware of anyone who claims complete expertise. As Dr David Butler, the psephologist, once said: 'The function of the expert is not to be more right than other people, but to be wrong for more sophisticated reasons.' Turnover in the agencies, according to a survey by the accountants BDO Stoy Hayward, is about £300 million pounds a year – and possibly one could 'guestimate' that at least twice that is spent in house. So a billion pounds a year is being spent in the corporate sector – and it's probably growing. One other significant fact is that public relations is the third most popular career choice.

There are lessons to be learned from politics by business. Above all, the climate in which business works is created and to some degree controlled by the political agenda. And politics exploits propaganda techniques to the full. Therefore the way that agenda is set must be of direct interest to business if it is to make its views known if not prevail. It's no use saying, 'But that's politics, I want nothing to do with it.' That is no longer an option in the modern world. So the other vital lesson is that the PR function needs to move nearer the centre, and higher up the organisation, in order to achieve an Alastair Campbell kind of position in the hierarchy. Moreover, to be effective, such a key person must be discreet, self-effacing, yet committed totally to the job in hand.

TEN KEY POINTS ABOUT SPIN DOCTORS

1   A good spin doctor should be heard, but not seen.
2   If your spin doctor is more famous than you, you have a problem.
3   Don't put all your faith in the skills of a spin doctor – you need to contribute as well.
4   It's the message, not the way it is managed, that the public should know about.
5   Discipline in managing the message works, but it can be counter-productive if it's taken to extremes.
6   When you manage a message, make sure your messengers don't sound like Daleks.
7   Always remember that while you spin, others are spinning faster.
8   H. L. Mencken said, 'Never pick a quarrel with someone who buys printer's ink by the barrel load.'
9   The business of spin in the corporate sector is getting on for a billion pounds a year – and over 20,000 practitioners work in the sector.
10 Remember (in the words of psephologist David Butler) – 'the function of an expert is not to be more right than other people, but to be wrong for more sophisticated reasons.'

3

The battle for public opinion

Government, because of its central position in public life, will always dominate the news agenda. But there is no guarantee at all that it will win the battle for public approval or support. Government can try to be pro-active – announcing new policies, launching initiatives – and these moves will be fully reported. But news always brings comment, and comment encourages public debate, and public debate is never easy to control. Public opinion is shifting all the time, blown first this way or then nudged that way by events that are outside government control. Nor can government always choose the ideal moment or place where it will stand and fight. Often its opponents have forced government into retaliation. Such moments almost invariably come at the wrong time. As often as government seeks to control events, events more often than not will in the end control government.

It's exactly the same in the world of business and commerce. Something will always happen when it is least expected. A new survey about the danger in some of the foodstuffs we consume, or an aggressive take-over bid, will inevitably catch some of the interested parties on the hop. Then battle is joined, as the key players try to defend their positions. Generals talk of the 'Fog of War'. In the battle to win public approval, there is fog 'a-plenty', with confusion and noise all around. Everyone is shouting at the top of their voices to make themselves heard, and the world itself is changing minute by minute, so that one fashion is quickly superseded by another. In this chapter I want to look at some of the developments that have been taking place which have led to a babble of voices trying to make themselves heard by fair means or foul.

The clamour of events

It is worth staying a little longer with the challenge facing government spin doctors regardless of political affiliation. There are more lessons to be learned, and more pitfalls to be avoided. Politics used to be a secretive business, but transparency is being forced on it by the media which itself is egged on by the electorate. This need for greater transparency is now spreading to the business world.

The boardroom tries very hard not to wash its dirty linen in public. It also likes doing business behind closed doors and then announcing as a fait accompli its latest decision about products, plant closures or take-over bids. This is still possible, and business still can do many things away from the glare of the public spotlight. It still has places to hide. The boardroom, of course, would always argue that much of its work is commercially sensitive – and that the competition must not get its hands on it. That is a perfectly tenable position. But the world is changing, and the transparency of the political world may soon become the norm in the business world. I question seriously whether a culture of secrecy helps business reputations. There may be a short-term benefit, but there is always the longer-term danger that what the boardroom has been hiding will eventually come into the public domain. And if politics is any guide – it will emerge at the worst possible moment.

The people who have the most challenging communications job in a democracy, are the civil servants who try to put across a government's message. There are some 1500 of them in Whitehall alone.[10] But they are not left to get on with the job. The fact that they have won so many column inches, or minutes of air time for their political masters does not mean that their jobs are safe, or their reputations enhanced. Far from it. Parliament is obsessed with its role, jealous, as always, of its rights and privileges, and the fear that what should properly be announced first in Parliament is leaking into the public domain before MPs have the chance to scrutinise it.

It is worth reading some of the reports into how civil servants have managed the government's message. One of them coined a useful phrase which sums up the challenge: 'The clamour of events'. The Whitehall press officers' job, said the

Mountfield Report, was to ensure that the government's messages got through, no matter what was happening, despite the 'clamour of events'. 'Clamour' is the perfect word to describe the world today and the challenge of making your voice heard above the constant hubbub. That 'clamour' is there because of the speed at which the world now moves. People in power always get distracted when the unexpected happens. Or, as the newspapers usually headline it, 'Government Blown Off Course'.

Harold Macmillan, when he was Prime Minister in the 1960s, was asked what was the most difficult thing he had to deal with. His one word reply, uttered in his much imitated patrician voice, was 'Events'. That was some four decades ago. Since then, the computer has entered our lives. We now live in a digital age, and 'events' are something that all of us have to deal with in one way or another. More is now crowded into a shorter time-span than ever before. Information technology has changed the world in ways that would have been impossible to imagine when the early computers made their appearance. If you have a message for an individual or for the whole nation, the modern means of communication allow you to deliver it instantly. Nothing seems too far away, or too remote to be reported. And what is reported – be it the latest scandal to engulf President Clinton, or violence in some small country fighting for inde- pendence, or the new single from Madonna, or the latest fashion from Milan, it melds into a series of images and words that blur the mind.

As business goes global, so the coverage of its activities goes global too. How you pay your workers in the Third World can be front-page news back home. Your links with Latin American or African dictators will surely be reported – remember Lonrho. And as Mohamed Al Fayed, the controversial boss of Harrods found, his business career before he came to Britain has been put under the microscope – so much so that he finds it hard to shake off the nickname that the satirical magazine Private Eye has given him: 'The Phony Pharaoh'. And his evidence at the Old Bailey in the Hamilton libel case hasn't helped either. The Asian economic crisis of the late nineties has only underlined the fact that the 'global village' is now a fact. It was predicted in the 1950s by a little known Canadian media guru, Marshall McCluhan. And he was mocked for his ideas. As business has gone global, so has the media –

thus reinforcing the trends and almost obliterating national frontiers. There's more on this last point in Chapter Eight 'News that shocks around the Clock'.

Minimising the risks

One of the few certainties in this life is that if the unexpected can happen, it always will at the most inconvenient time. And as Britain's New Labour government has learned, you can put too much faith in control. Management of anything can only take you so far down the track. All you can do is minimise the risk of getting it wrong and getting into trouble. In the end, success depends on whether what you are trying to achieve is really possible. So the watchword is – be realistic in your plans. Remember the example of Lady Thatcher who sought to deny Sinn Fein what she called 'the oxygen of publicity'. The voices of Gerry Adams and their other spokesmen were banned from the British broadcast media. The media got round the ban by using actors' voices to read what was said. Some of these actors became so good at imitating Ulster accents, and speaking at the same pace, that it was impossible to tell the difference, were it not for the caption on the screen which said that it was an actor's voice. Not only did Lady Thatcher fail in her aim, but every time a Sinn Fein representative appeared in vision, the audience was reminded of that failure. It was what you could call a 'double whammy', to quote an advertising slogan used by the Tories in an election campaign poster suggesting higher inflation and higher taxes if Labour came to power.

And there are now new ways in which the media can 'inform' the public. With more pages to fill, and more air time at their disposal, media these days have a passion for long background reports reconstructing events by talking to the key players involved. It could, for example, be about the thalidomide scandal which did little for the pharmaceutical industry.[11]

In broadcast journalism, the extension of this idea is the docu-drama, as it is called, in which significant moments are dramatised. Actors play the key roles and are usually more persuasive characters than the people who were actually involved in the original event. As we shall see later, this is a growing trend because most stories these days are about people, personalities or celebrities – and this applies to the business world as much as the political. In fact, the media in many ways reports business in much the same way as it reports politics – stories are based on the individual, rather than the ideology, or the company name.

The audience is now in control

While it is to be applauded that so much information is available, the amount can lead to confusion. The consumers of this vast and torrential outpouring of information try to make sense of the news as best they can. Their attention span, though, is getting shorter all the time, and so news summaries and updates are the order of the day. And new technology now works more in their favour than ever before. Via the Internet it is possible to get summaries of world news from the news agencies or the leading newspapers in selected countries. There will be some who can get a radio version or even TV clips. And British Telecom and Microsoft have announced that they want to increase the use of broadcast technology to access the Net. Digital technology enables the service providers to give the public even more.

OnDigital was the first of the new digital channels in Britain in the late nineties – giving the audience access to up to 200 channels when the system was fully up and running. The ad said, 'Wanted, a new programme controller – no experience required.' The point was that, with digital TV, the individual viewer could actually programme what he or she wanted to see that evening and when they wanted to see it. This means that the media product is fast becoming like those sweets that Woolworths sell loose in their High Street stores – the 'pick and mix counter'.

But this control has gone even further. Audiences can now go to the source of news – by watching channels such as CNN or Sky which cover events from start to finish. The O. J. Simpson trial was the prime example of what is called in America 'gavel to gavel' coverage. Audience reaction also quickly shows you how a story is playing – the very low viewing figures for the Senate impeachment trial of President Clinton served as a warning to the Republicans that they were on a hiding to nothing if they dragged out the process any longer. It is possible to argue that in the case of Clinton's impeachment, the American electorate had reached a verdict months before the formalities of the trial even started. Backing all this up, of course, is the increasingly sophisticated use of public opinion polls, which are reported as fact. These polls gave President Clinton personal ratings ranging from the high 60s to the low 70s.

As if that were not enough – personal websites, and chat lines on the Internet mean that the new technologies allow individuals to put their own personal 'spin' on to the subjects or the personalities of the day. Monica Lewinsky jokes were a rich source of material in inter-office e-mail. Unlikely people can figure on the net. One of the BBC's arts correspondents, Rosie Milward, has had a website created about her by a fan. She is said to be pleased, but her permission wasn't asked before it happened. Even Buckingham Palace has a website. New websites are springing up on the net all the time and total strangers from around the world begin exchanging their views. My son John created a website devoted to a blues singer called Wynonie Harris, not a name that crops up all that often in conversation, unless you are a fan of early blues music. Within months a few hundred people had 'visited' his site, including Ike Turner who wanted to 'set the record straight' about his treatment of his former wife, Tina.

There's at least one documented case of a couple 'meeting' via the net and subsequently getting married. Sometimes these websites will give you uninterrupted coverage of someone's sitting room. Sometimes the views and opinions that are exchanged are irreverent, sometimes downright lies. It was on the Internet that the story about Bill Clinton's relationship with Monica Lewinsky first saw the light of day. It was put there by a certain Matt Drudge who has now become famous for his website. The traditional news media seem to have known about the affair but were unwilling to report stories about oral sex in the Oval Office. All this activity is the authentic voice of the computer-literate Joe Public. The Internet has become the most effective weapon in the armoury of the growing number of single-interest pressure groups who want to achieve change in a specific area. It has global reach, the audience is expanding all the time, you can make new contacts and win support around the world for the cost of a local call. The street battles in Seattle at the end of 1999 at the WTO summit are a prime example of rallying support. It is also very difficult to control – as the merchants of Internet pornography have profitably discovered.

The global notice board

If the global village now exists, the Internet is its notice board. In both London and Washington government is harnessing the power of the Internet to disseminate its message. So too are the media. I was on holiday in central Italy, yet within minutes of Bill Clinton talking to the nation about his relationship with Monica Lewinsky, I had got the complete text of his remarks from the Internet.[12] And here's an even more significant statistic. It was said that within the first sixty minutes of the Starr Report becoming available, the Congressional website received over four million 'hits'. In plain English that means four million individuals around the world wanted to go directly to the source of the news, rather than wait and see how their local news media handled it. The audience is increasingly taking control. You could say the inmates have taken over the madhouse.

Democratising the control of knowledge

The Internet has done for the end of the twentieth century what the invention of printing did back in the fifteenth century. It has democratised control of knowledge. And it has the ruling establishments floundering. Up to the fifteenth century the Church controlled – or managed – the images and the messages that the faithful were allowed to see. Then printing allowed dissenters like Martin Luther to challenge the received wisdom of the age, and by appealing directly to the faithful in print, let people decide for themselves what they believed. It led to huge upheaval, undermining the Church, allowing the spread of new religions and destroying the unquestioned power of the clerics. In the twentieth century the Internet has taken that process further. And there are uncanny parallels with five hundred years ago. Until the Internet, governments used to be able to control quite effectively what people thought. Society was hierarchical, and social obedience was the norm. How otherwise could Britain, Germany, France or America have sent so many men to an almost certain death in the First World War?

Absolute control versus relative control

In the old Communist world, and under any dictatorship, there is almost total control. It is a necessary part of maintaining power. That control is backed up with state violence. Which is why that control only lasts as long as the dictatorship, of course. Come the revolution, the new spin doctors can damn you for all eternity. History is written by the victors. Among the most recent examples was the uprising in Romania against Ceausescu. One story I came across, though, neatly illustrates the short-term benefit in news management when you control all outlets. The Romanian dictator was worried about energy consumption and the strain it put on the economy. So he apparently instructed the weather service always to say that the weather was a few degrees warmer than it really was. People, despite the frost and snow, took the official version as gospel truth. After he had been executed, the truth came to light. In the first few weeks, after his violent removal from office, Romanians often remarked how the weather had changed for the worse!

Such is the porous nature of frontiers in a world of satellite communication – the people only do as they are told because of the dire consequences if they resist. In Iraq, today, the total control of the media by the ruling clan of Saddam Hussein seems on the surface to be working. And during the Kosovo campaign, Slobodan Milosevic appeared to be keeping his people fully behind him with total control of the media. Yet in the outside world, his boast after the bombing ceased that 'we have shown that our army is invincible' will start to wear very thin as the truth about the economic devastation his nation has suffered is recognised.

In the democracies, obviously, control is a relative term. But democratic government always gets more air time, more page space, than any other single group in a country: therefore more chances and opportunities to put its message across. Of course, in a democracy, opposing ideas can be debated openly. Now the Internet has undermined even more the power of the ruling class in a democracy, and people can have unlimited access to information that may or may not be approved by the powers-that-be. When the British government under Lady Thatcher tried to ban the book Spycatcher by a former member of the British security services, it failed. People ordered the book from America via the

Internet, and it was sent to the UK under plain wrapper. When the British authorities were worried about the effects of a male potency pill called Viagra, British consumers just ordered it on the net. The most vigorous invaders of our air space seem to be foreign TV channels devoted to pornography – a startling example of, dare I say it, the growing impotence of national governments to police the airwaves.

So, if you want to manage your message, you can't afford to ignore the net. Every moment of the day zillions of messages are being flashed around the world in less than a nano second, moving markets, shaking governments, creating or losing jobs, helping to make peace, but more often causing war. It means that if you want your voice to be heard above the 'clamour', you have to learn how to manage your message in a more effective way than ever before. The days of the simple press release and nothing else are numbered.

Demystifying the media

For the past thirty years as a broadcaster and journalist I have been part of this information-based world. I've watched it grow and change. There's a wonderful film clip in the BBC archive of a reporter asking the Prime Minister, 'Is there anything you'd care to say, sir?' I particularly like the use of the word 'sir'. How times have changed – it's the reporter who gets the respect (even if it's not meant) and the politician who usually gets the raspberry. I began work as a reporter in the days of hot metal and printing presses, and stayed on through film and video tape, from disc to audio tape and on into the digital age. I've covered world summits where increasingly governments have deployed huge forces to try to make sure that their message made it to the TV and radio stations in ways that benefited them. And I have come to the conclusion that the relationship between media and public needs to be demystified. That is especially true in the relationship between business and the media.

Business in the front line

Business leaders are convinced that all that is needed to win public approval for what they do is to increase market share, make ever bigger profits and keep the shareholders happy. Just to make sure, they spends billions on advertising their products, and sometimes themselves as good corporate neighbours. Naturally they try to do this while obeying the laws of the markets and countries in which they operate. They spend equally vast amounts on market research, including focus groups, consumer panels, product sampling and testing – and on whatever new marketing ploy is fashionable. Yet in many parts of the world, the image of business has never been lower. Why?

I think the answer lies partly in the fact that they over-complicate their messages, and seem to say less, even when they are saying more. Their main critics and adversaries are the growing number of single-interest pressure groups. These non-elected, self-appointed and usually obsessive groups seem to be taking big business to the cleaners. And, as I said earlier, with the Internet at their disposal, they can spread their messages far afield, garnering support and building up global opposition.

An interesting case in point is the sudden emergence in Britain of the issue of genetically modified (GM) foods. The pressure groups already have a relatively willing audience. A Mintel survey showed that almost 60 per cent of people believe they can never be sure that the food they buy is safe. Mintel said that consumers remain sceptical following the salmonella, BSE and E-coli crises. The report said that 78 per cent of consumers wanted better food labelling. One person in three was specifically worried about GM foods. The report's author, James McCoy, was quoted as saying: 'The issue of GM foods will continue to hit the headlines as we go towards the millennium and beyond. It is likely to become an even more high profile subject as pressure groups and biotechnology companies expound their respective views on the subject.' But McCoy went on to say that 'It remains to be seen whether the current concerns of consumers and lobby groups will deter full-scale implementation.' When Prince Charles added his twopenny worth, and discomfited the Prime Minister into the bargain, it seemed that GM food production in Britain was doomed. (Now an equally strong movement has started in the USA, and one company to date, Monsanto, has pulled out of GM foods.)

Often these movements begin with a small single-interest group who have an obsessive need to persuade the public to their point of view. In many ways the modern world and the new information technologies make it easier for them to get the message out. But the prime reason why the single-interest pressure groups have an easier time of it is the fact that they have little responsibility, save to themselves. They have no shareholders to worry about. They are not driven by market share or profit. They have a single issue and can create compelling slogans. With food issues they already have public opinion ready to be persuaded. It's said that there are nine million cases of food poisoning a year in Britain. Anything that raises concern about food finds a willing audience.

The compelling slogan

Take another example. A dental health pressure group argues that 'Sugar rots your teeth', and at every opportunity they repeat the phrase like a mantra, until it is seen as the absolute truth. Dr Goebbels would have been proud to see how the latter-day business of propaganda still uses some of the techniques that he developed. He, too, used to try to reduce everything to a simple, easily repeatable formula, or set of images, until it had been seen and heard so often that even the most horrific and repulsive ideas became the norm. Goebbels told absolute lies. His propaganda would be banned under any number of laws, especially those concerned with inciting racism. Yet in his day, the unsuspecting public believed what their masters were telling them. The safeguard today, though some may not agree, is that we live in a much more cynical, less reverential age, so that people are less prone to believe everything they are told. Rather like baby food, everything has to be pre-digested and easier to swallow. If the public have to make an effort to understand, they will not make the effort.

Back to sugar. There is enough truth in the idea that 'sugar rots the teeth' to make it acceptable. These 'experts' don't tell you how much sugar you need to make sure your teeth rot. Nor do they tell you what happens if you regularly clean your teeth after eating sweet products. The partial truth is often better in an argument than the whole truth: it's better because it takes less time to say, it's easier to remember, and does not distract the audience with too much information. The whole truth takes much longer to tell, and the audience have to work harder to understand and appreciate what is actually being said. These

41

days heavy intellectual argument is a no-no. What people want is easily absorbed data. There is a cult of superficiality.

Scare tactics

Before the anti-sugar lobbies try to get their (obviously perfect) teeth into me, let me explain that I cite them as but one example of pressure groups using mild scare tactics to win the battle for public opinion. There are plenty of other examples I could use – about milk, eggs, fat, meat and a whole range of other food products. In the case of alcohol or tobacco, the pressure groups feel able to use much more threatening scenarios to drive home their message. In the case of government campaigns against drink-driving, some of the images used in TV commercials are extreme. The most notorious recent case of a scare tactic being used in Britain was a claim by one group that eating meat causes cancer. The Advertising Standards Authority finally banned the campaign after there had been complaints.

I think, nonetheless, that there are significant lessons to be learned from the way these single-issue campaigns work. They really do know how to manage the message. And because the opposition to business has learned how to win the permanent battle for the public's hearts and minds, business is left playing catch-up. Like your average England Test eleven, business always seems to be trying to save the game in fading light against hostile bowling. By keeping their messages simple and understandable, any non-elected, self-selecting single-interest pressure group, with access to a fax and a phone, seem to be able to get more air time and more page space. They have learned that when it comes to putting over information, less usually means more. Let the audience finish the sentence. You don't have to spell everything out.

The human angle

The single-interest pressure group also understands what it is the media want and need in the competitive marketplace of the news business. Part of the problem is that individual media have to shout to be heard above the clamour. In order to be noticed, the human interest story has been developed – so there is always an actual person at the centre of every story. By giving the disgruntled a voice, the population will take their side. A lot of it is to do with the media's mindset, always seeing themselves as the champions of those without a voice or power. Partly it's because we live in a world where, despite every claim to the contrary, the individual counts for less and less, and is not listened to. Force comes in numbers. The single-interest groups appeal unashamedly to this constituency.

Beware the sound bite – it has teeth

Another reason why the single-interest group wins out is that it also knows that the public quickly gets bored. It fashions 'sound bites' which last no more than 20 seconds. That's the challenge that has to be met. Can you sum up your key messages in 20-second sound bites? In the section on the sound bite I set out what works and what doesn't when you are debating in 30-second phrases. For better or for worse, sound bites stay around for ever. Who doesn't remember, for example, Jonathan Aitken's carefully planned remark that he would use 'the simple sword of truth and the trusty shield of British fair play' to defend his honour? It led to a complete downfall of a man who was once tipped as a future Prime Minister – he lost his fortune, his wife, his house and his reputation – and was the first minister of the crown in the twentieth century to end up in prison. That is the most extreme example. Others tend to illustrate a state of mind that can damage the individual politically. Who doesn't recall Mrs Thatcher's remark, 'We are now a grandmother' or 'There is no such thing as Society.' In all those brief phrases we hear something about the person, in all cases more than they ever intended. Beware the sound bite, it can bite back.

But if you can get your sound bites right, if you can put your case in such a forceful way and in few words, then you may win at the bar of public opinion. Norman Lamont coined the devastating remark that John Major's government 'was in office, but not in power'. A phrase of less than ten words, but which seemed to say everything you needed to know about the standing of the government of the day. I have met many business leaders who deplored this shift to a sound bite culture. They argue that the world is increasingly complex, and to reduce the public debate on serious issues to an exchange of sound bites only makes matters worse. The public is not informed, and therefore will not be able to make informed choices. Yet these same people see nothing odd in spending millions of pounds on advertising their products, using simple catch phrases – 'OMO washes whiter' – and yet not seeing that what has happened is that the techniques used by Madison Avenue have now been applied to the messages they wish to disseminate in other circumstances.

Is the public better informed?

It is no use fighting the trend. It's what the public wants and it's what the public responds to. There are those who believe that far from confusing the public, the public is better informed than ever before. Why give it a 1000-word explanation of something, which it will ignore, when you can get to the nub in 100 words, which it will read or listen to. At least it begins the process whereby the public thinks more for itself. And if it is interested enough, then and only then will it begin to seek further information. It may even want to find out more, because its curiosity has been stimulated by the arguments that have been batted back and forth.

That of course is the claim that all politicians make. An informed electorate will see the virtue of their policies. In opposition Labour talked of devolving power, of a freedom of information act, of a modern, well-educated Britain. We still wait to see whether that is possible. It was all part of the 'message' that Britain should elect Labour. It is to Peter Mandelson's credit that he recognised that government is too often (some might say always) seen, alongside big business, as public enemy number one. He exploited that fact while the Tories were in power, by arguing that Labour would be different. He's now learning that being in power is not at all the same as when you are in opposition. Then Mandelson was part of a pressure group, so people were more ready to believe him and the party. They wanted change. They were tired of the Tories. But now his party is in power and taking the decisions. They are now 'them', no longer 'us'. Now his very skills, and those of his colleagues like Alastair Campbell, the Prime Minister's spokesman and head of the government information service, so highly praised, are deemed deeply worrying, as I outlined in the previous chapter. The knives are out. You can't have 'spin' at the heart of government. When the Select Committee on Public Administration was asked to enquire into the 'spin doctor' phenomenon that had invaded Whitehall, the spin master general, Alastair Campbell, denied that he had any special power to influence the media. Then, as Mandy Rice Davies had observed, 'He would say that, anyway.' At issue was whether Mr Campbell and his chums who had been brought into government were working in a party way, or for government when they spoke to the media?

That is a debate rather like discussing how many angels could dance on the head of a pin. Yet what we did learn in evidence to that select committee was that, in the words of Sir Richard Wilson, the head of the Cabinet Office, 'There is a more systematic determined effort to co-operate in a strategic way, presentation of the government's policies and messages in a positive light across the whole of government, than I can remember since the time I have been in the senior civil service.' The business of democratic government is largely the management of its messages so that it can gain support for its policies, and enough votes to stay in office when the elections come round. I would suggest that business – and anyone else who wants to make their voice heard – could do worse than watch the politicians and their advisers in action. Imitate the skills where they work, but above all avoid their mistakes. Because the media is obsessed with the way government works, you get a free public relations tutorial every day in your newspaper.

TEN KEY POINTS ABOUT
THE BATTLE FOR PUBLIC OPINION

1   You can never have total control of the message. Be flexible –
     don't press on regardless.
2   The 'clamour of events' will soon force you to change course –
     be ready to change.
3   Learn from the politicians – study their successes, avoid their
     mistakes.
4   The arrival of the Internet has speeded everything up – and is
     increasingly democratising the control of information.
5   The single-interest pressure group always has the edge – and it
     keeps that edge by making sure its messages are simple, easily
     understood, and above all brief.
6   Beware the short-term sound bite created for the moment – it
     can bite back, as Jonathan Aitken found.
7   Don't believe everything the experts tell you – test it with your
     own experience.
8   Remember to talk about people as people, not as statistics.
9   In an age where the individual feels more powerless, the
     media's appeal is to write only about individuals.
10 Whatever you say, however you say it, it must be true – be
     sure your sins will find you out.

4

The widening credibility gap

Given all the choices that are now available, it's not surprising that audiences are now in charge. They have the power of the on/off switch or the channel zapper to help them stay in control. It means that if you want to say something to the public, the way you communicate has to be much more carefully planned and those plans skilfully executed. Managing the message is as much about marketing as anything. 'Know your customer' is one of the most widely quoted marketing mantras. So let's have a look at these customers.

In this increasingly sceptical age, I think I'm on fairly safe ground when I say that the first law of presentation is to expect the audience not to believe you. You have to prove what you are saying is the truth as you understand it. There's a huge and widening credibility gap between those in power and those who have no power. There is a huge 'them and us' syndrome, which undermines every message that comes down from on high. It is breeding cynicism among audiences.

The most extreme example of this was watching President Clinton squirm under harsh questioning by the lawyers representing Special Prosecutor Starr before the Grand Jury. The more Mr Clinton nit-picked over words, and the meaning of words, the more it seemed he was lying. Yet subsequent research showed that even though the audience may have believed the President was lying, they still wanted him to be President. What's more, despite his tarnished reputation, they still felt he was doing a good job.

What Mr Clinton had going for him was that the American economy was experiencing a golden era of growth, with rising living standards and falling unemployment. While Mr Clinton presented one face to the Grand Jury, he presented an entirely different face when he talked directly to the American people every day about the job he was elected to do. Here he was confident, full of positive messages, looking America directly in the eye. Mr Clinton has the lucky knack of being able to talk his audience in an open and direct way. He is never condescending.

Every book I've ever read on presentation skills always stresses the point that you should know your audience and talk to them in the most direct way. You are probably nodding in agreement and thinking, 'But that's basic.' 'Everyone knows that,' an inner voice is saying. In my experience, the reality is very different. Watch carefully, and you'll soon notice how too often people in the public arena seem only to talk to each other, rather than to the audience. It's in the eyes – are they looking directly at you, or are they avoiding eye contact?

The private conversation

It's as if the people in power inhabit a private world which they generously allow the rest of us to observe, but to play no part in. They seem to have no interest in who's listening to them, as long as the 'right' people are listening. I will never forget those TV pictures of the last hours of the reign of President Ceausescu of Romania on the balcony of the presidential palace, trying to talk to the people in the square below. They were booing and catcalling. He could not believe that he was the target of their anger. Within hours he was on the run, within days he had been shot by a firing squad.

No such fate awaits the company executive who has to face a hostile public when there has been an accident at the plant which has put lives at risk. Yet, all too often, the statement, which has probably been prepared by a committee, shows that the executive is more concerned about what colleagues think than how the public will react. Rarely is the focus on what the audience thinks, or whether the audience understands. Indeed it's very rare that they think of the audience at all. I once watched a man at a conference come up on stage with his head down as if he were walking in a rainstorm. He set out his speech very carefully on the podium. Both hands gripped the edges very tightly – the knuckles turned white. Then he began without a single glance at the audience. At one stage in his preamble he read carefully, 'It is for me very ex—', and then turned to the next page, '—citing to be here to have this chance to talk to you directly.' The head-down, white-knuckle approach is too often the norm in my experience.

This is not an attack on the executive under pressure. Public speaking is not their main occupation. That is not what they were hired to do. Many have taken a short course in presentation skills or public speaking, but few are really comfortable speaking in public. All too often they rely on bullet points on a slide, which allows them to look more at the screen behind them than at the audience. They need the comfort of a tele-prompter in case they forget their words, and a podium to grip until their knuckles are white. And quite often someone else has written the speech. Or at least someone has written the first draft – and the person delivering it will have only seen it a day or two before.

At the Institute of Directors' Convention one year, when I was involved, I watched as PR executives or PAs ran through their boss's speech just to make sure that the slides came up on time. The boss was too busy to be able to attend. Company executives are not the only culprits in this regard – ministers often turn up just in time to deliver a speech written by their private office. Yet these days more and more we are judged by our public performances – whether it's making a presentation to our bosses, to new clients, to financial analysts or to shareholders.

Some companies take it seriously. I was involved over a number of years with JWT, the biggest advertising agency in the world, which ran regular two-day courses for people who had to pitch for new businesses. The courses ran throughout Europe and North America. They were developed by the then new business director Brian Johnson who knew that just one mistake in presentation could cost the agency millions in billing fees. He told me once that he and his team had worked hard on a presentation – they had rehearsed and rehearsed, they knew they had a winner. On the day the presentation went perfectly. As the potential client and his team left the building in central London, they said they needed a cab to get to their next appointment. It was raining hard, and not a cab was to be had for love or money. All the agency cars were being used. The potential client waited and waited with increasing frustration. JWT did not get the business. Brian told me that after that they always arranged transport on stand-by for visitors to the London headquarters. 'The potential client had thought to himself,' Brian told me, '"if the biggest agency in the world can't get a cab on a rainy day, what else could go wrong?"'

So nothing must be left to chance to make a good impression. Yet even so, it always amazes me to see how some quite senior executives behave on television. I've seen people with a mentally prepared script in their head gaze into space while they try to remember what it is they want to say. They look ill at ease, with their hands clasping and unclasping. They try not to look at the interviewer; and when they speak, out comes jargon. A confectionery company executive was talking about one of their top sellers – and called it 'a two-bar proposition with instant taste gratification'. I can't tell you the name of the product, because they didn't even give it a name.

For the audience, a broadcast interview is still thought of as a conversation between two people. Too often for the embarrassed interviewee, the main hope is that their colleagues aren't watching, because of the stick they'll get when they get back to the office. Such interviewees forget that they are watched not only by colleagues, but also by the competition and the general public. And of these, the public should be the audience you concentrate on convincing. If that audience responds, what your colleagues or the competition think is beside the point. So the first requisite for a would-be good communicator is to see the world as it really is, not as you would like it to be. And to study the audience you are addressing. Do not fall into the 'them and us' syndrome.

The way we live now

We all need to understand the way the modern world lives now.[13] Most of all, the good communicator needs to understand what makes people tick. These are truths that most people would hold to be self-evident. Yet what happens in reality? Too many people in the business world try to understand the way the world works with endless market research surveys, focus groups, random interviews, feedback from consumer surveys and so on. One marketing man I know read what I've just written and said that I was attacking the very core of the modern business world. It showed, he said, that I did not understand the way that modern business functions now. The point I want to make is that there is a danger that too much reliance is put on research, and that sometimes you need to see things for yourself, at first hand. As a reporter I can rely on press clippings and agency reports. But when you cover the story yourself in the field, you get a very different 'feel' for what is happening. A successful BBC TV series put chief executives back on the shop floor with some surprising results.

The research tools used by business and government seem to multiply remorselessly as both seek the holy grail of communicating effectively to their chosen audience. On Madison Avenue, the home of American advertising back in the 1950s and 1960s, they tried it all – with motivational research, and other now largely discredited techniques. It's all detailed in Vance Packard's classic book The Hidden Persuaders. Little of it seemed to be the magic ingredient that they were seeking to make an ad persuasive, so that no one could resist the chance to buy. People resolutely remained people.

Yet modern management cannot face the possibility of life without research. It's a crutch they use because they are so scared of falling down. Even the BBC, which used to pride itself on its ability to spot talent and develop it, carried out a survey to find out what the audiences thought of its key presenters. Former DJ Nicky Campbell scored highly because he had 'the common touch' – the 'magic ingredient' as far as the BBC is concerned. Justin Webb was said to be 'snooty', as was Anna Ford. To be dubbed 'snooty' by the masses can now end a career. The new controller of BBC Radio Four, James Boyle, carried out a huge exercise in public consultation (which is a snootier way of saying market research) before he rejigged the network.[14]

More often than not this kind of research gives management nothing more than a built-in excuse when something goes wrong. 'Don't blame the manager, blame the research.' And since the research is usually carried out by outside consultants they can be fired, while the staff keep their jobs. Despite the millions of pounds invested in these exercises, what the purchasers don't seem to have spotted is that they are getting second-hand information. And all too often the research carried out on one day is quickly contradicted by research carried out by someone else the next day. In the end research can only provide guesstimates. But they have a scientific gloss which makes them believable.

The 'them and us' syndrome

Another part of the problem is that senior people live in a world that is increasingly cut off from the sort of reality that the majority have to contend with. The pressures on busy directors and senior executives have them racing from one meeting to another. They have PAs to help shift the work load; and that work load is growing all the time. So is the travelling, and so is the time spent away from the family, and so are the hours spent in the office eyeballing the new spread sheet on the laptop. Many of these executives just don't have the time to do personal chores like the rest of the population.

What takes the rest of us a great deal of time and causes immense frustration, just happens for our leaders, because they and their companies have created expensive support systems so that they can concentrate on the job in hand. The restaurant table or the theatre seats are booked for them, the plane tickets arrive at their desk, the PA deals with all the little distractions like the partner's birthday cards and flowers. The hairdresser comes to the desk; so will the tailor for a fitting. Cars are ready to whisk them to and from each appointment, airport or station. When the office day is over, the reception, the dinner or even the box at the opera is a chance to meet people with exactly the same lifestyle.

All of this gets in the way of being able to survive once they leave the support system, and find themselves alone in front of an audience, or in a television studio, or in a radio studio. They know how hard they work, they know about the pressures they are under and they know they deserve the remuneration they get. But now comes the problem of public perception. It's how the public perceives the senior executive that is the challenge. Take the money issue. The public thinks that they pay themselves huge increases, and yet they tell their employees that there is no more money to increase wages. Executives would argue that their salaries are not in the same category as pay rates on the shop floor. Executives have responsibilities – onerous responsibilities. I've heard some executives argue that the problem is all to do with envy, and the sheer lack of understanding by an envious public. I've not met a business person who doesn't hate the phrase 'fat cat'. The general public would answer,

'Just look at what your boss is paid, what you are paid and what the lowest paid person in the organisation gets. Look at the boss's pay rise, and look at the shop floor pay rise.' Seen from that perspective, they are not just fat, but extremely obese animals. Let me stress we are talking about perception, not necessarily reality.

Many, many business people do not fit into any of the categories that I have just described. The overwhelming majority of companies in Britain today are small to medium-sized, where managers live and work alongside their few employees. But there are enough of the highly paid high flyers for the perception of a privileged existence to have taken a firm hold in the public's mind. People may even know it's not true, but they want to believe it, because it feeds their own prejudices about the unfairness of life. If there is a perception of greed, there is also a perception of white-collar crime to go with it. Once again, let me stress, we are talking about public perceptions. But there's enough truth to sustain that perception.

Corporate crime – image and reality

There have been too many corporate scandals for comfort. A recent book[15] gave some shocking statistics about corporate crime. For example, one academic established that the total cost of fraud reported to the Fraud Squad in 1985 was over two billion pounds, twice that of theft, burglary and robbery in the same year. In 1996, the authors say, 22,400 citizens suffered from serious life-threatening assaults. In the same year major industrial injuries involved 29,475 people. And you can find figures from the United States which tell the same shocking tale. So audiences listen to you with suspicion – and wonder, no doubt, why you employ so many lawyers to get you out of trouble? The single-interest pressure groups are indefatigable in finding examples of corporate wrong-doing, and disseminating the information as widely as possible – and with the Internet, that's globally.

What this all adds up to is that despite the best endeavours of business, the public is more likely to think the worst than the best of it. Unlike politicians, the heads of companies aren't elected by universal suffrage. They suddenly emerge as the head of a public corporation as if by magic. There is always the public belief that 'the old boy network' is working again. By the time they rise to this prominent position many will have been formed by the internal culture of the group. They will be steeped in company lore. They will speak the internal language as fluently as anyone. They will be adept at company politics. These are essential skills. But they are the skills needed to survive and prosper in a very closed environment. As they move up the corporate ladder, the distance grows between the everyday world and the corporate world they now inhabit. By the time they get to the top and face the public for the first time, all their skills have taught them to play their cards very close to the chest. 'Safety first' is the motto. Even at the top of the very biggest companies there is always the danger that the company chairman or woman is surrounded by people who always say 'yes'. Like kings and queens of old, they have a court and courtiers, and while they rule, no one says anything that they don't want to hear. The PR department gives them a set of press clippings every day, and tells them what was on radio or television the day before, or what might be coming up. At most, all they've heard is the BBC Radio Four Today programme – on average twenty minutes of it. So when they venture out into a studio, they are like children who have barely learned to swim suddenly finding themselves in at the deep end. No wonder they think all reporters and interviewers are rubbish. These people have the temerity to ask them questions, and then frankly disbelieve the answers which they give.

Politicians, like business people, don't come very high in any popularity stakes either, but the saving grace as far as the public is concerned is that they occasionally get fired, and are thrown out of office. When politicians are not in power, they make a point of keeping in touch so as to better gauge what the voters want and offer it to them come the next election. Ken Livingstone has never learned to drive. He says it was the best decision he ever took as a politician; travelling on public transport keeps him in touch without really trying. But when politicians regain power, it's back to the Red Boxes, and the Private Office and the same thing happens to them as happens to the people who run the biggest corporations.

The 'real' world

So on the one hand you have people who lead lives that are believed to be markedly different from the voters or the customers they seek to win. And you only have to watch the standard 'Question Time'-style TV show to see the gap. The audience participation programme always reminds me of the stories about the Colosseum in Rome where the Christians were fed to the lions with the crowds baying for blood. The most direct example was when I was on Newsnight, and we planned just such a programme in a working men's club near the Longbridge plant. The British motor industry was once again in the news for all the wrong reasons. Newsnight in those days went on air at 11 p.m. We planned the panel carefully – Tory and Labour MPs, a trade union leader, and the inevitable expert on the car industry to tell us what had gone wrong and how to put it right. We set up shop in the club, while the customers filed in and got down to some serious drinking. We were so busy with our programme running orders – who sat where, whether we would get make-up on time, the line to London, the script and all the other complications of an outside broadcast – that we failed to notice the alcohol-fuelled enthusiasm of the members of the club. When we went on air, behind me was this raucous audience, who saw it not as a 'serious' piece of television, but as a free 'floor show'. It taught me a vivid lesson – your audience doesn't sit in respectful silence while you discuss its future, or anything else for that matter. An audience has its own agenda – and you'd do well to get to know it.

Same view, different perspective

So much for the broad perceptions about life at the top – or what's thought to be life at the top. What about the view from below? You don't need a survey to tell you that most people worry about their jobs. Too many feel that redundancy is just around the corner. They are working harder than ever before, often for less money. Stress is a common affliction at nearly all these levels of society. At its lower levels it is endemic. Public services let them down. They queue for hours in the day to catch buses and trains that usually don't run on time. The newspapers these days seem to enjoy telling us how the newly privatised rail companies fail to deliver on their promises. Travel costs always seem to be going up. They are showered with bills, produced on computers which are less than friendly. Prices always seem to go up, never down. They live a long way from the job. Both partners work. They have to go and shop when everyone else is shopping. The kids can cause concern even if they don't take ecstasy or hard drugs. The annual holiday takes a lot of cash, so they don't take kindly to being fobbed off with easy excuses when the hotel turns out to be only half built. The papers they read tell them they have rights. Consumer programmes are watched so that big business is made to squirm. When business complains of unfair reporting – as they often and rightly do – the audience is prepared still to believe the programme rather than the company. When Gerald Ratner remarked at the Institute of Directors' annual Albert Hall conference that his jewellery had about the same value as a prawn sandwich, it got a huge roar of laughter from his peers. But outside the Albert Hall, it only confirmed the public's view that business doesn't care as long as you part with the cash. And they voted with their feet and shopped elsewhere. Soon his business was on the line, and he was out of a job.

Not anger but rage

The public now seem to delight in taking this sort of revenge, when given the opportunity. It is told it has 'rights', and given half a chance it will exercise those rights. Yet too often lawyers have written in so many caveats into the small print that business wins.[16] When something goes wrong, there always seems to be small print. One of the new words these days is not 'anger', but 'rage', as in 'Road Rage', and everywhere we hear of other examples of this rage – the pensioner who shot a man on a neighbouring allotment; the elderly man who got a black eye when his supermarket trolley bumped into another man's trolley. Everywhere the politicians and the business leaders are telling them that everything is working well, life has never been better. The groundlings do not believe a word.

Given the gap between the haves and the have-nots, is it any wonder that neither side finds it easy to communicate? One side speaks the language of the balance sheet, of dividends, of human resources, of productivity increases, of the need for savings, and then jets off to Vail, Colorado for a skiing holiday that costs the equivalent of a half a year's salary for the shop floor worker. The other half asks why can't we have the good life that we keep reading about, why do taxes go up for us, yet the rich seem never to have to pay any? What's wrong with being a single parent living off the state, while no one censures the rich for their affairs, divorces, multi-million-pound settlements financed by buying and selling of companies without any regard for the people who are employed in them. I'm exaggerating a little – though not really all that much. The point is that it will never work if the powerful communicate in a patronising or supercilious way; nor will it work if they try to pretend some kind of humility or knowledge of what most people's lives are like. It took a long time for Tory leader William Hague to live down the image of wearing a baseball cap to the Notting Hill Carnival as if he were just an ordinary guy.

Vox populi

What makes these differences much sharper is the growth in the number of groups fighting for a bigger share of the national cake. And the motives are always economic. These days, such groups are demanding to be consulted or reassured. In history these people were called 'trouble makers', and were put down without a second thought. At least society has moved on from then. Nowadays the public has not only been given the chance to have its say, but is positively encouraged to speak up, without any real fear of arrest or a writ arriving through the letter box. And the trend is gathering momentum all the time. What's more, the phone-in or public access programme is cheap to put on. It's another way, too, of getting to know the broadcaster's audience, what they like and what they think. Increasingly they have an e-mail address to get viewers to vote on the news of the day. Did the nanny kill the baby? Was Clinton lying? Should Scotland become independent? It usually makes for interesting if one-sided programmes. And another reason the public gets air time is because too often the powerful disdain the chance to debate or put their side. So the media, which needs as large an audience to sell air time to advertisers to make money, courts the popular view, pushes the consumer angle, and seeks at every turn to be closer to the people it serves. And that's why business and politics see the media as a rabble rouser, a barrack-room lawyer. The closer it tries to get to the audience, the further it shifts from the establishment view. The broadcasters need to be noticed every bit as much as the people they put in their programmes.

The disappearing audience

Despite all this, however, audiences are drifting away, and with it, advertising revenue. The worst-hit area has been news and current affairs programmes. There has been something of the order of a 30 per cent drop in viewing figures for ITV's News At Ten, and the BBC's Nine O'Clock News. In fact ITV were so worried about the falling figures that they successfully persuaded the TV watchdog to allow them to move News At Ten, so that they can run uninterrupted films or special programmes in order to keep their audiences higher. They then launched a massive ad campaign suggesting that 'The news is getting better'. The high-minded and the highbrow see this as part of a trend called 'dumbing down', by which these critics mean appealing to the lowest common denominator. On the other hand, it means making something more popular and more accessible to catch mass audiences.[17] In business terms it's repositioning the product to take account of changes in the market place – a business move and nothing more. Market forces drive the media. Market share is what counts. In the end the audiences fell even further for the new early evening news.

So instead of lambasting the media, maybe other businesses should look at what it does in the context of their own business – they are, after all, getting and keeping customers. We may not like the way it's being done – but there is little we can do to reverse the trend. Phone-in programmes, public access programmes – and confessional programmes like Jerry Springer's awful show from Chicago – are the manifestation of this world in which the voiceless have acquired a voice. Those at the top are less and less likely to watch such popular television – indeed not only do they not have the inclination, they don't have the time. And their tastes are or have become more refined: they can afford the hundred pounds and more for a lovely evening at Glyndebourne or Garsington opera. But every chief executive should find time to watch Blind Date or Jerry Springer or 'Oprah'. This is not because the people who appear on these shows are more or less authentic examples of their customers, far from it. But they do represent popular culture at its most advanced. They are part of the current zeitgeist.

The haves and the have-nots

Sadly the gap between the haves and the have-nots, the powerful and the powerless, is widening all the time. From the way people dress, to what they eat and how they spend their leisure time – the gap between the hard-pressed majority and the favoured minority seems to grow day by day. The man in the dark suit or the power-dressed woman are at odds with the generality of what's on our screens. Sometimes their accents show up the difference when we hear them on our radios. They are 'them'. From the moment they appear in public, and then open their mouths, the general audience has them identified as 'them'. So the first rule of managing the message has to be – know your audience as people, not as statistics. That means knowing what makes them tick. This will help shape the messages you want to give because you will be more likely to address them in a language that they understand.[18]

I am not suggesting that one should imitate Tony Blair who went on a television chat show to talk to Des O'Connor, and started to speak Estuary English,[19] as it's called. He had all the glottal stops you could wish for. His spin doctors told him that it would show him to be a man of the people. What's more, it would attract a huge audience not normally reached by politicians – the so called Cs and Ds. In their millions. In the view of the media, it showed him to be condescending and insincere. Another piece of advice is don't do a William Hague and wear a baseball cap at a public event to prove your man of the people credentials.[20] It does not show that you have street cred, but that you are street dead. True, American Presidents can and do wear baseball caps, and are seen in clothes that the rest of us use on our free days. British political and business leaders, however, still have to work their way towards being seen in such outfits. At the moment all they do is take their jackets off and show their braces.

Some might ask, has Richard Branson got it right then, only wearing a sweater, never a business suit? Yes he has, but he thought of that first and he's always done it. The lesson from Branson is that he has managed, despite his wealth, to give the impression he is one of us. Princess Diana had a way of dressing for the occasion, especially when she was in public with her young sons – they could wear baseball caps, and t-shirts. Now they've been put into suits by their father.[21] 'Apparel oft proclaims the man …' said William Shakespeare. I'll be dealing with clothes and style later.

So don't place all your trust in advisers, market research or focus groups. Sometimes it may pay huge dividends to dress like ordinary people, and go out and see how the other half lives: preserve the common touch. Look, listen and learn about the real world beyond the boardroom on the top floor. I've seen it suggested that senior executives ought to spend some time every day answering the phone to hear what the public, their customers, really think and what they say about it. One company who has actually tried this is Iceland, and it worked wonders for the company's relationship with customers. It gave them some great stories to tell about the business, I discovered, when I chaired a conference at which two of their executives were keynote speakers on 'customer care'.

The dangers of the ever widening gulf between those in power and those who will never have it should be self-evident. The changing nature of society, though, is not all negative. In this information age people are hungry for knowledge. They may not be seeking knowledge as dispensed in our great universities, but useful information to enhance their lives. They want to keep up to date, to know what's going on. There are more people out there willing to listen to what you have to say than you realise. But you have to say it in a way they can understand.

TEN KEY POINTS ABOUT
THE WIDENING CREDIBILITY GAP

1 Know your audience.

2 Be aware of the gap between the haves and the have-nots.

3 Don't put all your trust in market research; think people.

4 Don't worry about what colleagues say in private about your public performance.

5 Talk to your audience, not at them.

6 Don't patronise your audience.

7 Say what you mean, and mean what you say.

8 Don't use numbers, when words will do as well.

9 Put yourself in the listener's place – what would you want to hear?

10 In the court of public opinion, it's the people who decide.

The data game

One of the most dreadful words in media jargon is 'Factoid'.[22] You see it flash up on the TV screen – the worst offender is CNN. It is usually a fairly useless fact that you can drop into conversations to show that you are well informed. This has replaced knowledge with data. In America, after you've said 'Hi' to someone, the next line is 'So what's happening?' Americans are obsessed with keeping up to date and on top of the news. They know that if you can't join in a conversation about the latest gossip from Washington, what the score line was in last night's game, or the name of the latest movie and what it grossed on its first weekend, then you are socially dead. Britain, inevitably, is following where America leads. Even the most ardent football hater had to know how England were doing in the World Cup in France in 1998. We all knew why Glenn Hoddle had dropped Gazza, and that he was wrong not to pick young Michael Owen. Equally we all knew why in time Glenn Hoddle was sacked by England after some injudicious remarks about reincarnation and people with disabilities. In fact it became such a topic of public debate that it drew in the Prime Minister, the Minister of Sport, and every possible shade of opinion.

There was no escaping the Hoddle story. Yet it's more than just having something to say while you're in the pub, or waiting for a bus. Even though the gap between those in the top jobs and the rest of us is getting wider all the time, people are seeking to know more about the world in which they live. There is a growing appetite for news and information. It's become a cliché to talk about 'lifetime learning', but it is increasingly a fact that many skills which once lasted a lifetime quickly become obsolete in this day and age. The certainties that were once a feature of life are no more. People are seeking information about what is happening so that they can have some control over their lives – and they want that information in an accessible and digestible form, be it house prices, job opportunities, cheap summer holidays, skill courses and a whole host of subjects. They are also aware that they need to know more about the world in which they live if they are to be able to compete effectively in the job market. There is a growing need to feel informed.

Information anxiety

Information Anxiety is the title of one of the most compelling books[23] about the media-driven world that I have come across in many a year. The author, Richard Saul Wurman, says that 'information anxiety is produced by the ever-widening gap between what we understand and what we think we should understand. It is the black hole between data and knowledge, and it happens when information does not tell us what we want or need to know.' Wurman paints a picture of a world-glut of data getting bigger by the minute, leaving people anxious that they can't keep up, but afraid to admit that they don't know. 'There is,' he writes, 'more information available in the average edition of the New York Times than was available to an individual in a lifetime in the 17th century.' The result is that more and more people become news junkies – hooked on 'news', without defining what they mean by it. But the news media oblige with updates, every hour, on the hour. I remember when I worked in New York one radio station offered the following deal to its listeners: 'Give us twenty minutes and we'll give you the world.'

Information overload

While the appetite for news increases, and the need for information grows, there is a new condition we need to worry about. It's called 'information overload'. There's more data than ever before, but somehow we seem to recall less of it. Surveys show that viewers of a nightly bulletin often cannot remember the stories that they watched, or what was said or in what order they were screened. Many of these stories have no direct relevance to their lives; and they are power-less to affect any change. Yet still they watch, so that by being up to the minute and up with the news, they won't get caught out at tomorrow's meeting. Now suddenly one word becomes the story. 'What about Clinton?' says someone. Since this could involve the declaration of World War Three or an admission that he 'had an inappropriate relationship' with Monica Lewinsky, you prevaricate. 'Uh huh', is the answer while you hope that another key word will tell you which 'story' the person is referring to.

This brings us back to that loathsome word 'factoid', which I define as a useless piece of information that seems very important at the time. Let me give you an example: it takes 33 rabbits one hour to eat three tons of grass. Sounds good enough to be true; I don't know. I've just made it up. But use it at some moment in your next conversation and I doubt whether anyone will question the truth or otherwise of that statement. Your messages are being sent out into an anxious world awash with data. Its most likely fate is that no one will notice. On the other hand it might become part of the moment and gain a life of its own.

That was a fact made up to suit the occasion. Here's another. 'Read my lips,' said the presidential candidate George Bush. 'No new taxes.' It was a great slogan on the campaign trail and was repeated time and again. Sometimes he did not actually say the second part of the phrase, but mouthed the words as the audience chanted them. The phrase came back to haunt him when he became President, and, yes, raised taxes. Six words which at first did him a great deal of good, but in the end dogged his presidency. After the taxes went up, people used to say, 'Watch my lips, I lied.' But those six words, which took two to three seconds to say, seemed the perfect sound bite, attuned to a world which doesn't have time for deep thought or long-winded explanations.

The media is very aware of this new world. It knows that boredom is the great enemy to communication. To increase its appeal and win audience share, it does everything it can to grab the public's attention. So headlines become snappier; stories get shorter; drama and excitement are the watchwords in this battle for attention. Since the media – in all its guises – is the conduit through which your message to the world is piped, then you need to understand what makes the media tick.

TEN KEY POINTS ABOUT THE DEMAND FOR NEWS

1   There is a huge public appetite for information.
2   There is more information in the average daily newspaper than was available in a lifetime in the seventeenth century (Richard Saul Wurman).
3   If it takes too long to say, you've lost the debate.
4   Broadcasters reckon no one pays much attention beyond 30 seconds.
5   People want simple facts that will be easy to remember.
6   People don't want too much detail.
7   If you have something to say, make sure it is relevant.
8   Sound bites may seem transitory – but they have a long shelf life.
9   Don't just say something to satisfy the demands of the moment – it will come back to haunt you.
10 George Bush said, 'Watch my lips ...' We did, and he lied.

6

Mad media disease

Some people see the exponential growth of the media as a plague visited upon the modern world – the virus is spreading in the most alarming way. You can't escape it, you can't inoculate yourself against it. It's the communications equivalent of BSE – once infected there seems to be no known cure. I call it Mad Media Disease. It is now so invasive and persuasive that we forget that it's a very recent event – pushed on by the advances in communications technology which makes instant 'news' a reality. When I was a young reporter in Wolverhampton in the 1960s, my family was rather ashamed that I had decided on a career in something that was not really the sort of thing a well-brought-up young boy did for a living. There was something rather grubby about it – enquiring into other people's lives, and reporting things that were best left unreported.

How the job has changed. People may still malign it, hate it, rail against it, but parents these days are proud that their offspring work 'in the media'. At the moment what's called 'media studies' is one of the most sought-after university courses. As for the media itself, it is now one of the fastest growing industries in the world, and an industry with truly global reach.

Just look at the most recent example of what can happen – the dissemination of video evidence given by President Clinton to the Grand Jury, which was seen in every part of the globe. Of course it was a rare event, and many might claim of dubious value, but it was there on your TV if you wanted it – from a huge screen in Times Square in New York to the local hairdressers in a local high street. The same happens with sport which seems to have become a truly global language. The downfall of Communism had a worldwide TV audience; indeed, some suggest that media attention helped the revolution to succeed. Now I'm not suggesting that your message will ever have the global reach of that event

– but there are some lessons that we need to learn in this world of instant global communication.

One of the results of this almost exponential growth in the business is that cultural differences in the developed West are beginning to disappear. A new all-purpose international language is beginning to emerge. We see young French or Italian pop singers these days singing 'rap' music in their own language. English is now firmly established as the world language – even though some regional forms of it, be it accent or vocabulary, or both, can still confuse.[24] The media seem to be reinventing and reshaping our world on a daily basis. It's become a confusing, competitive, compelling marketplace of ideas. In Italy you often find British or American TV spots dubbed into Italian and the consumer urged to buy a product with a foreign-sounding name. Few concessions seem to have been made to the local culture. But that is not always the rule, and what might be seen as mildly suggestive in a commercial in one country could be banned as pornographic in other markets. Yet still the general proposition holds true – the broadcast media is tending to create at least the veneer of a global culture. If you want to get your message out, then you have to understand the modern world of the media and what it is that drives it.

The business of media

The first fact is that media is a business, and a very big business. There is little ideology in it – what sells newspapers, wins viewers and listeners, gains market share, is the driving force. What's the point of being in the media business if no one watches, listens or reads the product? If there's one lesson above all others, it is that you never lose by underestimating the intelligence of the mass audience. It's not an original thought; it was first coined in America by the journalist and editor H. L. Mencken. Today that idea – like so many others – has been compressed into just two words. It's called 'dumbing down'. Marvin Kalb, a former CBS News correspondent, said, after the Clinton impeachment trial was over, that the Lewinsky story, with its tabloid details, and all the news, all the time-culture of cable and Internet, inspired a level of sensationalist coverage that has 'trumped old-fashioned mainstream journalism'. Sensationalist coverage,

Kalb says, 'years ago established a beachhead on what could be called the island of journalism, and gradually it has extended that beachhead'. As a result, says Kalb, America's other stories, serious stories, were receiving less coverage 'because there is not enough time and space on network news when there are so many pressures forcing editors and producers to come up with more Monica or more "news you can use".'[25]

Nothing these days dare be too elitist or too highbrow. You may hate the show hosted by Cilla Black called Blind Date. But we find ourselves watching it, if only to be appalled. TV companies live in dread of 'minority audiences'. They don't want to incur the wrath of the regulator who every now and then sounds off about the lowering of standards; yet nor do they want to incur the wrath of the shareholders who want decent dividends.

Imitation – the sincerest form of television

The crucial and most obvious fact about the media world is that it doesn't so much compete as feed upon itself. What works for one will soon be imitated by others. An American humorist, Fred Allen, once remarked that 'Imitation is the sincerest form of television.'[26] No story stays exclusive for long. All news-rooms watch what the opposition is doing, and they move at the speed of light and sound to stay up with the story that a rival got a few seconds ahead of them. That is why the most daunting moment for anyone wanting to manage the message is the crisis. That changes all the rules. The media seems to indulge in a feeding frenzy. (I'll deal with crisis management later). But the media doesn't just cover a story, it begins, willy nilly, to reinvent it. It doesn't mean to distort – it's just that the media is looking for better and more telling ways to make sure we read, listen or watch. It uses everyday language at its most effective.

Let me give you an example. Jocelyne (sic), the former wife of the art-dealing billionaire Alec Wildenstein, got into the news headlines when, during their bitter divorce action, she claimed she needed at least £120,000 a month living expenses because she did not even know how to make toast or boil water. The husband retaliated by accusing her of spending all her money on plastic surgery. The photographs that began to appear were, how can I put it diplomatically, surprising. Her face seemed, in the photographs at least, to have acquired very curious dimensions thanks to the cosmetic surgeon's knife. The headline was 'The Bride of Wildenstein'. That headline, the curious doings of the ultra-rich, went round the world. It wasn't news, just grist to the media's mill.

The power, if it is power that the media has acquired, is because of its ubiquity. There's no escaping from the media's reach. Television, radio and newspapers surround us. Every cab driver, in every country in the world, seems to have his radio tuned to the local news station. In most public places there will be a TV set to keep the passer-by or the passer-through up to date. You get news on the hour, every hour, whether you want it or not. There seems to be a radio or TV set tuned to news in every public space. 'News' is happening, news is now. Almost all conversations will include the phrase, 'Did you see that story about …' Our lives are shaped by it in ways we yet don't fully understand. John Naisbitt, who wrote a book called Megatrends, says, 'We now mass-produce information the way we used to mass produce cars.' He used the word 'information', but I read it to mean 'news'.

Broadcasters and newspaper people talk about the 'news business', as if there was something special called 'news'. But in fact the definition of what is news is changing all the time. The daily weather has become news. Events in countries we have not heard of, will never visit, and have no control over, now are 'news'. The definition is getting broader all the time too. News or information – there's little difference because in the end what the media tries to do is inform you – though many might argue that the information is biased, partial and distorted. I'll come to those criticisms and their validity in a moment.

The power of the small screen

The most powerful of the media is obviously television. Every second of every day, somewhere in the world, there are millions of people watching news, or something like it, on television. The most widely watched is CNN – Ted Turner's once ridiculed,[27] now respected global TV network. During the Gulf War the propaganda battle was fought out on CNN's broadcasts. This has led to a debate about whether TV shapes the event or events shape TV's coverage. As always, the truth lies somewhere in the middle. Saddam Hussein allowed a CNN team to remain in Baghdad and kept them on the air. President Bush kept up to date with what was happening and being said, via CNN in the Oval Office. The press briefings in Saudi Arabia for the Coalition concentrated on providing TV images of the Coalition's highly sophisticated weaponry in action. It was more like a computer game than the real thing. CNN itself turned the whole exercise into a 24-hour-a-day commercial for itself, as the world's news network, priding itself in showing the whole conflict wall to wall. Today some of the most dramatic scenes in that war are used in a fast-edited and breathlessly spoken commercial about itself as the world's news leader. And you can see the BBC and Sky aping the style in their own version, claiming you'll get all the news on the minute from the world's best correspondents.

The success of CNN has prompted other broadcasters to try to develop the same approach, not just in their commercials. Most notably the BBC is trying to build up the same kind of 24-hour-a-day news network; but it does not have the resources to do it, because it is a state-funded operation. Yet its reputation for honesty and for balanced reporting may help it, not least since CNN shot itself in the foot with a report, later discredited and then withdrawn, about the US government allegedly using nerve gas in Cambodia and killing US prisoners of war. The third competitor in the global TV marketplace is Rupert Murdoch's Sky News. Each of these seeks to dominate what the news organisations believe is the future growth market – news when you want it, and as it happens. Significantly, they all use the same advertising techniques to sell their product – and this is very much the feature of modern TV operations, they watch each other and imitate. But then imitation has always been the sincerest form of flattery. So for the person who wants to gain access to any channel, once you've studied what they want and how they operate, you'll find it works for all of them.

Greed-soaked hustlers

The public has become cynical, and this explosion of TV news, needless to say, has prompted some pretty nasty things to be said about the faces we see on the screens in our living rooms. An American writer, James Fallows, in his book Breaking the News: How the Media Undermine American Democracy, says that the American media have become 'arrogant, cynical, scandal minded and destructive'. He says they are 'greed-soaked hustlers'. Much the same is often said about British media personalities, though in less emotional terms. The perceived power of the TV 'face' obviously provokes strong emotions from those who consider themselves rendered powerless by the exponential growth in all media.

Watchdog and other media animals

Over the years I have been invited to many a business conference to talk about the media and business – and I find that the best way to start is to ask the audience what they think of the media. There is never a moment's hesitation. Hands shoot up – and out comes a litany of 'sins' committed by the media. Their favourite target is the Watchdog consumer programme on BBC, and its anchorperson, Anne Robinson. It has attracted a huge audience because it gives the individual consumer a voice and gets results in terms of compensation or full refunds. It's a particular bane of the travel industry. And the car makers haven't come off lightly either. In fact it became so popular that the Ford Motor Company and companies in other industries got together to persuade the programme, as they termed it, 'to give industry a fairer representation'. In my view that only confirmed the public's view that Watchdog was right, and industry scared of the truth. A much better tactic from industry's point of view was pointing out those errors of fact on Watchdog and seeking a correction via the Broadcasting Complaints procedure. Mind you it's a double-edged weapon: the more they make Watchdog ensure that its facts are watertight, the less industry will be able to claim that they exaggerate. Only the consumer wins.

Based on the occasional example of Watchdog, everyone in the business sector believes that the media quotes out of context; the editing process always distorts; reporters have their minds made up before they do the interview; reporters aren't interested in the truth, only in a good angle to the story; reporters don't let the facts get in the way of a startling conclusion; they are biased against business; they are all on an ego trip; you cannot believe anything you read in the newspapers; they only want sex scandals ... all this and more is what comes from the audience at these conferences. To a lesser degree the 'sins' shouted out by my audience apply as much to radio and newspapers as to television. This is the general perception and so we in the media must give it some credence.

I have to say that when I ask for specific examples of distortion, misquoting and so forth, the audiences tend not to have any to hand. That does not mean that they do not happen. Given the number of media these days, it is inevitable that they do happen. It's just that few people care enough to keep chapter and verse. Somewhere, I am sure, an academic is quietly doing a doctoral thesis on inaccuracy, untruth and distortion in the British media. The sooner such a seeker after truth publishes, the sooner the media will have to start on the hard business of putting its house in order, correcting some of the attitudes which lead to distortion. There have already been two news documentaries on Channel Four television in Britain where it was found that some of the scenes claimed to be true were in fact no more than actors taking the parts of the villains. Even as such evidence seeps out, the media still climbs on its high horse and talks about the 'public interest'. It ought to be worried that so many people believe these things to be true. If business is seen to have an 'image' problem, then so too has the media.

Although the public will criticise at every opportunity, it still stays tuned. It's like the person who condemns pornography, but has to watch it, so that he can criticise in an informed manner. But the growth in coverage is splitting audiences. Overall there are about as many people watching and listening, but the numbers for individual programmes are falling. This trend will become even more pronounced in the years ahead, as we move further into the digital age. There could be up to 200 TV channels on tap for those with the necessary equipment to receive the digital signals. And, come to that, just as many radio stations. This is where we get to the nub of the problem. Audiences have lost the excitement that media used to generate. The whole business is now taken for granted, and therefore valued less.

The media themselves realise this as they try, sometimes desperately, to find new shows or programme formulae that will attract and keep audiences. The programme makers come under increasing pressure to find subjects that will fascinate people. So you see suddenly a new genre appear. There was a time when so called 'fly on the wall' documentaries about ordinary people's lives were all the rage. But after hotels, travel reps abroad, or neighbours from hell, the genre began to pall and it was back to the drawing board. In the 1990s, the confessional programme was popular – mainly imported from the United States, they usually carry the host's name – Oprah, Gerry Springer and many others. Now British television is imitating the confessional format in the daytime slot. A lady named Vanessa Feltz changed channels – from Anglia TV to BBC TV – and was reputed to be paid £1m a year to talk to 'ordinary' people about their lives. The Daily Mirror ran a story that some of the guests on the show were not what they claimed to be – they were hoaxers. The BBC's Board of Governors immediately investigated – three staffers were sacked, one freelance contract was ended. The show was shortened by fifteen minutes. What this sordid tale illustrates is the pressure that producers are under to 'deliver' an audience for their shows. And the lengths to which, mercifully, only a very few will go.[28] The programme has subsequently been dropped.

Then the Sun decided to trap the BBC and sent an attractive female reporter to a documentary unit which was making a programme about sex and the single female. They made her sign a form saying she was telling the truth and then filmed her talking about her (imagined) sex life. The BBC pulled the programme, and then decided to sue the Sun for entrapment. The battle between print and TV is becoming increasingly vicious.

Television in the twenty-first century

There is a huge challenge facing programme makers as we move into the twenty-first century. The crudest language, the most explicit confession, fail to stir much debate except among the professional critics of the Box. Long gone are those days, just after the Second World War, when I recall going with my mother to a neighbour's house to watch the first television set in the street. That was the time when, on Saturday afternoons, I remember seeing crowds pressed against the windows of the main department store in town gazing intently at the BBC test card. In the early days of television people put the lights out, and sat in silence to watch as a family. Now the population take these incredible inventions for granted. I recall seeing some research that suggested that no one really pays that much attention to TV or radio any more, but are usually doing something else at the same time. And that something else ranges from sex on the sofa, to doing the ironing, having a row, or sleeping. So the programme makers have to find new ways to be seen and heard. But what new ways are there? We have reached saturation coverage.

Will newspapers vanish?

The newspaper industry is feeling the pinch too. Not because of TV's success, but again because there is so much more available and from so many different sources. As in the golden age of radio and TV, there used to be a time when readers called the daily newspaper the 'daily miracle' because they could not fathom how there could be so much 'news' to fill it day in and day out. Nowadays, the Sunday newspapers, with different sections and thousands and thousands of words and images, are often left unread. They are only bought as a comfort blanket so that you feel you are keeping up with the news – 'information anxiety' again. Indeed Richard Saul Wurman in his book presents some frightening statistics about newsprint. On 13 November 1987, The New York Times was 1612 pages long and contained about 2,030,000 lines of type and over twelve million words. It weighed a hefty twelve pounds. I'm sure that these figures have been exceeded many times since. In Britain, too, the Sunday newspapers are serving up the same stodgy diet, and we, the consumers, have millions of words and hundreds of pictures to look at, if we want to do the paper justice. Usually most readers skim, just as most viewers only half-watch, and most listeners to radio programmes are doing something else.

The growth of local and regional news

One has to factor in to this equation, what seems to be the growing appeal of the regional and local versions of the news media; the specialist programmes and journals; as well as the free sheets which are pushed through the front door on an almost daily basis. All very interesting, you might say, but what has this got to do with 'managing the message'? I think that this is the key. The explosive growth in all media has had the effect of spreading the journalistic talent and ability very, very thinly; even though today there are more students signing up for media and journalism courses – I know, I teach at some of them. The investors in the media business are looking at ways of controlling costs to maximise profit. Like any other business, the trend is to cut or control costs. This is being done – and here the BBC is a good example – by investing not so much in people as in technology. You let the computer do the work, you ask your correspondents, now that they have the technology available, to produce the same item for all outlets – that is TV, and radio, domestic and world service. The BBC has got rid of the separate newsrooms that serviced radio and television – and moved to a central newsroom. Any BBC correspondent in the field will tell you – though off the record – that they now work much harder than they did in making what are called 'packages' for the various programmes, radio or television, but they cover fewer stories.

The growing power of PR

I believe that this is why all broadcast organisations are more open to support from the PR fraternity than ever before. It has also helped to drive up the quality of people seeking to work in this field. In my young days it was the failed hack who went into PR. Nowadays young people see it as a fulfilling and exciting job. They no longer feel the poor relations. My son is of one of them – he never considered for a moment following in his father's footsteps – and I have to say that he has had some fascinating assignments to get his teeth into. From the journalist's point of view, by seeking more help and access from publicist or lobbyist, you have more time to produce the 'packages' that will then be broadcast. It partly explains the rise of the spin doctor – the specialist in briefing the media on what someone really means – in a positive light when it's their own, in a negative light when it's the opposition.

As always the media itself denies that the spin doctors have the power that others perceive them to have. Mark Damazer, a senior BBC news and current affairs executive, was quoted in one of the media trade papers as saying, 'Our job is to try to resist them when we feel it's appropriate. We should be aware that they do provide useful and accurate information sometimes.' The phrase 'try to resist' suggests that they can twist arms quite successfully – and the second point is that they have 'accurate and useful information'. Someone once said that the relationship between a spin doctor and a journalist is rather like that between a dog and a lamp post. Who is which is another question.

Radio and television production is an immensely complicated business: I'll be looking at production in the section on page 101. And it is also an immensely expensive business – so any help that has an impact on the bottom line will often make the difference in the final story. The 'facility' trip, involving transport and access to some foreign plant is gratefully received. The travel trade is a notable example of how the travel writer is fed most of the relevant information and flown around the world at someone else's expense. In the car industry, the motoring writer gets to 'test drive' cars. The discreet lunch at a fine restaurant has launched many a story too – there being no such thing as a free lunch. Since the days of big production budgets are long past, any useful shortcut which has a beneficial impact on the bottom line will obviously be acceptable. But tact and discretion are part and parcel of such an offer.

Newspapers, too, have been fighting the cost battle. The struggles to keep the independent newspapers going, for example, are well chronicled. While the writing process is still the same as it ever was, fewer journalists are writing more every day. Consequently, especially in trade magazines, the background press release, which explains some complicated process, often runs without a word changed. In many ways it is possible to argue that the original stories these days come more from the PR and press relations functions than from the reporters themselves. I'm not saying that the news editor doesn't keep his or her eyes open for puffery and false claims, but often the journalist doesn't have the luxury of checking and double-checking every fact. That's how the errors creep in; and those errors get repeated because the first move any reporter makes is to send for the cuttings from the library. Once it's in print, it's deemed to be true. And that's how some stories that once would not have been touched with a barge pole, make their way on to news pages and the airwaves. They then become an accepted part of the world in which we live.

All this puts a great deal of pressure on the individual writer and reporter. And the pressures are such these days that some journalists – if one can still call them by that title – have actually resorted to making up stories. Happily the cases are still rare. One notorious example was that of Stephen Glass, an American writer on New Republic. He was found to have fabricated at least one of his stories, concerning a teenage computer hacker. Glass had even devised a phoney voice mail recording for the fictional company he invented, along with a bogus corporate website on America Online, which included – a nice touch this, it has to be said – scathing criticism of his own article. Apparently fame was the spur.

People like Glass can make a lot of money and become famous with a Washington by-line. Charles Peters, editor of Washington Monthly, who hires and coaches promising young journalists, says sadly, 'Journalism didn't use to appeal to people who wanted to become famous.' The most notorious example of false reporting was the case of Janet Cooke back in 1981 who wrote a bogus story about an eight-year-old heroin addict – she went on to win the Pulitzer Prize for it. These are just two, still rare, examples that have come to light. By and large these young journalists were hired at relatively low rates of pay, and only by being famous could they make the big time.

Do you blame them or the industry? Whichever part of the media you look at, the same challenges exist – maximum audience for minimum budget. The answer, as always, is to shock. Audience participation, phone-in shows, and lots of sex and violence, with stories of outrageous behaviour by the rich and famous, and not so famous. In fact, anyone who is doing something outrageous. The public now view a world through the media's eyes – a world of simple solutions, with business in the enemy camp, the politicians not to be trusted.

This then is the dumbed-down world for the twenty-first century: the world of the new millennium. The media in its various guises champions the individual's rights, and the establishment's responsibilities. And your message – well you shouldn't try to dumb down. But you should make it simpler and easier to grasp. Don't be elitist. Most of all, make it relevant. By and large the media knows what it needs to survive, even if it doesn't always get it.

TEN KEY FACTS ABOUT DUMBING DOWN

1   Watch the Jerry Springer TV show to see how low the medium can get.
2   Consider the audience figures for consumer shows like Watchdog.
3   The emphasis these days in on the people's rights, not responsibilities.
4   Understand the mood of the times – this is the age of the victim.
5   Audiences want simple solutions to difficult problems.
6   Audiences believe business has unlimited funds.
7   The public believes business should pay handsomely for the smallest error.
8   Business should simplify its messages, not dumb down.
9   Business should take account of the popular mood.
10 And remember H. L. Mencken who said, 'Never pick a fight with someone who buys printer's ink by the barrel.'

What the news media demands

The media is a demanding beast. It has an ever increasing appetite for what it calls 'news'. And it demands that it gets that 'news' in the shape and form that allows it to get on air or into print as quickly as possible. So one of the key ingredients in managing the message, has to be making sure it finds its target. Marketing has been defined as getting the right product in the right place at the right time and at the right price. So it is with managing your message. The message is a product. The marketplace in this instance is the media in general. There are also clearly defined market segments where specialist interests are catered for – sport, women, health, books, films and so on. As in all good marketing, messages should know the market they are aimed at. In short, you need to know what your customers' needs and wants are – and appeal to them. So let's take the media as customer and see what it wants.

The media, in its own jargon, is looking for a 'story'. A story is something that will appeal to its own audience. Sometimes a story is called news. Many have tried to define both concepts. News is what the powerful don't want you to print or broadcast. News is something that will surprise and intrigue – dog bites man is not news, man bites dog is. The media won't thank me for telling you, but sometimes news is what you happen to have to hand as you go to press or go on air. On a better and busier day you would not have even bothered to read the stuff. But on a quiet Sunday in, say, the middle of August, news values change. That's why it's called 'the silly season'. No paper or programme can have any gaps. So the exasperated news editor or assignment editor will tell the duty reporter: 'See what you can do with this.' That usually means trying to find someone who will rubbish the whole idea, start a debate, get a reaction, or just laugh the whole thing into the ground. Many a journalistic career has been launched by making something of nothing.

Someone once defined the journalistic process as 'collection, selection and rejection'. The journalist collects everything, selects what seems interesting and bins the rest. So everything that comes into a newsroom is logged and divided into what may or not make the programme or the paper. The key to managing a news operation is keeping a diary of forthcoming events – events which may or may not be covered, but which are in the book, so that as the day approaches the editors can plan who does what and who goes where. It costs money to allocate resources – reporters, camera crews and photographers. Resources are scarce, so the news editor or assignment editor, as this person is sometimes called, wants to get value for money – a good 'story' that will attract an audience, enhance the reputation of the paper or programme.

There is surprising unanimity among journalists as to what constitutes 'news'. According to Richard Spencer, the news editor of the Daily Telegraph, it is simply 'what is happening today, that didn't happen yesterday'. In the opinion of Nick Pollard, head of Sky News, it is 'what intrigues or interests us, and which will do the same for our viewers'. John Kay, chief reporter for the Sun, suggests that 'it is something that is unusual enough to be noticed so that the reader will want to talk about it to his wife at home or in his local with his mates'.

The news-gathering process begins with the editorial meetings, where heads of department join the editor to review yesterday's news and plan the new day. So every day the news team will meet to review what the opposition have been up to, what they have in the diary, who they have available, match reporter to story, and begin the process of gathering all the possible stories into what, in broadcasting terms is called a running order, or in newsprint, the main stories that will leader the paper and the various sections, page by page.

Protecting their sources

The sources of stories are many and legion – from an anonymous tip-off, the humble press release, to a top secret briefing by a disgruntled minister. It is an article of the journalistic faith that you never reveal your source for a story, except to your editor. Even under threat of imprisonment, you keep quiet. Otherwise, the logic runs, how else would anyone give you a good lead in the future? All journalists, if they are worth their money, can spot a story and see the potential for an interesting item. Sometimes an injudicious remark in the pub can start them off. Each reporter is keenly aware of what his or her readers or audience want. Everything is done in the name of the audience. In many respects, journalism is an object lesson in getting the product right – even if they sometimes get the story wrong. But of course the best laid plans of any news operation can be knocked sideways when a 'big' story breaks – this could be a huge bomb going off in Belfast or a leading figure in Britain or abroad being assassinated. Suddenly those stories which would have got on air or in print are dropped – resources are concentrated on the main story. This is the most frustrating part for those who wish to manage the message – they've done everything right, they've sold the idea, got the event in the diary, provided the people to be interviewed and expect to make the front page when, wham bam, the call comes, and the reporter is off to Washington, the Kosovo border or Birmingham, because a 'big story' has just broken.

The myth of the exclusive

While every news operation in the media aims to be different in the way it tackles a story, and provides a service for its audience, it is also competing with everyone else. This has led to a herd mentality. Editors in all media have become obsessed with getting an exclusive story of their own, yet following up every other story so that their audience won't think they've missed something. Cabinet ministers and their advisers know that if they appear on the Today programme in the morning, the 'message' they gave to the interviewer will be used as a sound bite in the news bulletins, and quoted in the print media. Others will react, and the story builds. Exclusivity these days lasts only for minutes as the media pile in and start to 'cover' that story from as many different angles as possible.

Those who have little experience of dealing with the media are worried about the 'angle' that is taken; but it sounds worse than it is. The angle is the way in which a story is tailored to meet the perceived needs of the audience. For example, the Financial Times is more likely to be interested in a business or financial story than the Sun which is more interested in glamour and gossip.

Madonna in the news

Let's imagine a story about the pop singer Madonna, and how she spends the millions of dollars she has earned. That could appeal to both papers. For the Sun, there would be a sexy picture of the singer, and fewer words, but her millions would fascinate its readers. There might or might not be a picture of Madonna in the FT, but readers would be interested in what she was doing with her money, especially if she was doing something that other investors could benefit from. Yet that story has angles that many other papers could employ – the woman's page in the Guardian, for example, might picture her as a strong feminist icon; the home pages might feature her domestic expenses; the fashion page might focus on how much she spends on clothes and who are her chosen designers. All of it would build up the story of the pop singer and the fortune she has made.

There would also, no doubt, be paragraphs galore in the story for the gossip columns. And just to add spice, most reporters would check the newspaper cuttings library to see what has been written before on this subject, and whether she has now changed her views about money or what to do with it. There will almost certainly be at least one paper that will get one of its star authors to write 'Has Money Spoiled Madonna, the Material Girl?' Each paper and each programme would hope to approach the story in a different way so as to appeal directly to their audience. The treatment of that 'story' and how it would apply to different papers is the 'angle' that everyone talks about. When you begin the process of deciding on a message – think of the angles that may be used by the various media.

So you need to make sure that you understand what each section of the media is after, and what sort of stories it runs. Professional advice is always useful. Common sense is probably even more necessary. It is pointless trying to sell a story or a message to the wrong paper or programme; you are wasting your time and theirs. You need to look at what audiences take which papers, and why. There is plenty of research available on these topics, and the media, as a subject, is increasingly being covered as a 'story' in its own right. Then, too, there are the media trade papers which are stuffed with information about readerships, viewing and listening figures, and which media stars are working where at any given time.

Your own research, combined with some professional input, will soon help to establish where your message is most likely to find a receptive audience. Say you are putting out a statement on behalf of the Tory Party: if you send it to a paper or magazine with known leftish tendencies, they may well run the story, and mock it as well. Don't believe the old saw, 'All publicity is good publicity'. Most newspapers reinforce the prejudices of their readers; that is how they keep them, and that is why the readers continue buying. A Telegraph reader does not want the Guardian or vice versa.

Let's go on with our 'story'. I've linked it to Madonna, because media today nearly always prefers stories about individuals to groups or nations. All journalists are taught to start with a person, and broaden out the story. So does your message in any way involve an individual? Is there a named person or persons who could be interviewed later by the media?

Thus far we've looked at our 'story' in print terms. In radio terms it might make a 30-second item at the end of a news bulletin, but it would obviously get more air time if you could provide Madonna's voice; and you would get hours if she were prepared to go live, play all her records, plug her book and appeal for funds for cancer research at the same time. So let's go back to your message. Is there someone who is prepared to be interviewed by a radio station; and is that person known, talented or with anything interesting to say?

If we send our story to television, then obviously pictures are the main ingredient; but have we up-to-date pictures of Madonna, have we got her speaking about her millions? Better yet – and this would win her a one-hour special – would she come on live and talk about her millions? And yes, of course, she could sing her latest release.

So much for national media. Local and regional media might well take the story, but it would need a local or regional angle. Madonna in Bristol would get her on BBC West and HTV like a shot. The Bristol Evening Post would interview her, and take pictures of her in the city.

This example provides in only the broadest terms what the media wants, and how it treats a story. In later chapters I'll be going into more detail about managing the message. What the media want, above all, is a reaction to what they say and do. If a story appears which seems to put you or your organisation on the spot, you can't ignore it: it won't go away. You can't really say, 'No comment'; that's not an option. Nor do you have much time. While the print media have hours, the broadcast media are dealing in minutes and seconds – they want to hear from you now, not after the programme has gone off air. A crisis scenario, everyone seems to be after you, and special management techniques are required, of which more later. But the golden rule is that given the way the modern media operates, there is no hiding place. Information technology has given them, as well as you, the most powerful communications tools. They will find out if you have a mobile, and phone you, if need be, in Alaska.

You need to know not only what the media wants, but how it operates in what has become a 24-hour-a-day operation. Round-the-clock news needs round-the-clock vigilance. And round-the-clock management of the message. That comes next.

TEN KEY DEMANDS FROM THE MASS MEDIA

1   They want a story – your story.

2   They want the story that you don't want aired.

3   They want human interest.

4   They want scandal in high and low places.

5   They want exclusives.

6   They want to shock.

7   They want to keep the powerful in check.

8   They want to be noticed.

9   They want to be first.

10 They will settle for less as a deadline approaches.

AND FIVE THINGS THE MEDIA DON'T WANT

1   They don't want to get involved with your lawyers.

2   They don't want to be duped or tricked.

3   They don't want to be ridiculed if the story is false.

4   They don't want to be censored.

5   They don't want to be last.

News that shocks around the clock

Managing the message can never be a nine-to-five, five-day-a-week job. That's because the news business works round the clock. And at every moment it hopes that a story will emerge that will shock the world. Just as the financial markets work a 24-hour day because there is always a market open for business, so the news gatherers follow the sun, because news is happening somewhere. The money makers have long understood that the pursuit of profit demands eternal vigilance, and have set up their organisations to cope.

Information technology, which drives markets, also drives the news business; and in many ways they are interlinked. On every desk in every dealing room is a computer linked to a news provider, such as Reuters, that not only updates prices but also updates events which move markets. That's why instant news demands instant response, and the implication for business – and any organisation that wants a public profile – is that there should be someone in the organisation who can deal with news as it happens. More and more business news is market sensitive. It's no use trying to catch up in the office next morning.

There are other parallels between the financial markets and the news business. If enough investors become bullish, then markets rise, but as soon as there is a whiff of worry the markets can turn. Investors often watch other investors, and try to jump on the bandwagon. Correctly sensing the mood of the market is an important skill. The media business has a similar approach to its marketplace. You keep your eyes glued on the opposition so as not to miss something. The media feeds off everyone else in the business, for stories, for leads, for ideas, for names. It was best summed up Tom Lehrer, the Yale professor and part-time singer/song writer, who penned the following verse a few years ago:

Plagiarise, plagiarise,
Let no one else's work evade your eyes.
Don't shade your eyes
But always remember to call it
'Research'.

So always remember that when you talk to one part of the media, you are talking to them all. It may be the smallest local newspaper or free sheet, but someone may notice, or have their attention drawn to the paragraph innocently nestling between the picture of the winner of the largest vegetable competition and the times for church services. Suddenly the story could be taken up and made into something much bigger.

A typical news day

With that in mind, let's follow a typical day, starting with the midnight news bulletin on the BBC's main speech channel, Radio Four. It's an arbitrary choice; you could in fact start anywhere in the day. The midnight bulletin, though, sums up the preceding day's news, and at the same time looks ahead to the next day, highlighting what may be happening or is likely to happen. Those working the night shift in news organisations around Britain will have an ear cocked to the bulletin just in case there is something they have missed; likewise to reassure themselves that their news judgement is on the ball. It's a curious fact about the brave and wonderful world of journalism. Editors hate it to be too far out on a limb on any story. The fact that others are following it confirms its status. And one might add, cynically, that it also means if the lawyers are going to get involved, then it's going to cost the plaintiff a lot of money before they bring the case. It's almost as if the news hounds huddle together for comfort. They certainly hunt as a pack.

These night-shift workers are preparing either the final edition of the morning newspaper or the morning news shows on radio and television. The newspaper final edition surfaces around three o'clock in the morning, although the time can vary from paper to paper. This edition will carry the editor's considered view of the day, as expressed in the way the stories are run – from the front page lead to the big sports story at the back. Sometimes a really good story, especially an exclusive, will be run in this edition, so that the competition have little or no time to run what's called a 'spoiler' – the same story, with a slightly different angle, which makes the rival's 'exclusive' seem small beer.

The morning news

These final editions are then rushed to other news organisations, and to road, rail and air freight companies who make sure they arrive in time to be on the nation's breakfast table. The overnight team on, say, the Today programme may well decide that the Mail's lead story is worth following up. While they will not necessarily wake up the minister in question, they will call the duty press officer. By the time that the minister has got out of bed, he will have learned that the radio car will be arriving outside his home in the next 30 minutes. So this is how you can be reading the story when suddenly you hear the main character live on air, telling more.

Mind you, some people don't want to give an interview at that time – even to the Today programme. In one celebrated instance the late and great Brian Redhead teased a minister who had refused to make an appearance. Live on air he told him that if he changed his mind and looked out of his bedroom window he would see that the radio car was there, just in case. Brian got his knuckles severely rapped by the powers-that-be for what was seen as unacceptable arm-twisting – but only after the minister, in his pyjamas, had come down and been interviewed. And as Brian related to me much later, 'They told me off sharply, but with a smile.'

While the Today programme is still probably the most effective way (in Brian Redhead's phrase) 'to have a word in the ear of the nation', other programmes are making their mark. The BBC's morning show on Radio Five, for one, is beginning to attract a younger audience. And Talk Radio, under Kelvin McKenzie, who used to edit the Sun, is also building up a following. The so-called 'breakfast shows' on TV also provide a platform. They are quite distinct in the way they approach stories, and their audiences are very different – from the younger set for the Big Breakfast to refugees from Radio Four on the BBC's Breakfast News. But they all have a news section, and all of them spend quite some time reviewing the morning newspapers. You may think that they are providing it as a service. Far from it, it means they can mention some of the stories that they have missed. 'Research', remember.

Getting your message on these TV shows means that you appear in vision as well. If you are invited to be interviewed, the television video also provides the radio sound bite – so you straddle two media for the price of a trip to just one of them. Now that the BBC has moved its radio news operation under the same roof as television at White City, the chances of making a round of the studios grows. One taxi ride to West London, and you appear on any number of outlets.

Once again, in newspaper offices and press agencies, these programmes are being monitored, and so the Press Association and its competitors are putting out 'news copy', giving the quote that seems newsworthy. And in this competitive world, something else is happening to help spread your message. The image that news organisations like to claim is that they speak to the 'newsmakers'; so they are busy, too, drawing attention to newsworthy interviews, providing clips to other broadcasters or stills to the print media in exchange for a line which credits the original source. Like you, the news media have a message to manage, and they are very serious about it. Again to quote the BBC (but I did work there for many years), the biggest growth in the organisation has been in marketing. Indeed some marketing people are paid more than the journalists, which shows which of the two callings the BBC rates more highly. It's an inevitable trend because unless you market the news product effectively, you will lose market share. Journalists may jib, but it's now an integral part of the news business.

Getting ready for the lunchtime news

The day has hardly begun, and already there seems to be feverish activity. The best sound bites begin to appear on all the broadcast news summaries, both national and regional. The early morning conference, as the meeting is called when the editors meet to decide what's news and what's not, have a lot to discuss. Before nine o'clock they will be deciding which story to follow and who will follow it. Once the decisions are taken, the evening papers and the lunchtime programmes start calling the people who figure in the news that day. Their task, as they say, is to 'take the story on', which means adding another, preferably new, ingredient.

Let me give an example. William Hague says something about the way the Prime Minister's spin doctors are behaving. The programme or newspaper that can get either the spin doctor or, better still, the Prime Minister to comment has taken the story further. Once there is nothing new to be said, no new angle, no new interviewee – then a story dies. But while there is 'some mileage left', then news organisations will keep going. This kind of approach to reporting news has now become the norm.

It is worth bearing in mind when you frame a statement that someone some-where will be asked for a reaction. To manage the message from start to finish, you need sometimes to frame a quote that will get a reaction to which you your-self can react. Better still, have someone in mind when you make your state-ment. Leave nothing to chance but name that person, so that you can start a debate or draw a response. You must decide what best suits your cause. A stan-dard ploy by the single-interest pressure group is to accuse a company or an individual of some heinous crime. Of these tactics more later. Suffice it to say, the media are willing helpers in this approach, and politicians exploit it all the time. As I explained in the last chapter, the media aim to feature named individuals, not anonymous spokespersons. People matter in modern journalism. It's called 'human interest'.

We are up to lunchtime now, and the lunchtime bulletins are on the air. Once again newsrooms are monitoring who is speaking and who isn't. The first editions of the evening papers in London and the provinces are going on sale, adding yet a further dimension to the day's collective journalistic effort. They may also be running stories which emerged from morning press conferences or press briefings in Whitehall for the political and specialist correspondents. The morning press conference is one of the key ways in which to launch a campaign and capture the headlines. In this context the example of the political parties during an election campaign is the one to follow. They make sure that they don't clash and allow enough time for the journalists to make the rounds. They see to it that the stage set looks good on TV, and they deliver their statements in pre-prepared sound bites. Sometimes they make a blunder, but they are getting sharper at it all the time.

Outside the political world, which probably takes the 'oxygen of publicity' more seriously than any other section of the community, the rest of society is setting out its stall. Sometimes there are product launches, or industrial and financial press conferences, to accompany the annual report and accounts. There are photo calls, and press showings of the newest films. There are celebrity conferences when someone notable is in town. The list is growing every day as more people seek to manage the message.

This morning infusion of new material will of course begin to push some of the stories that were running earlier in the day down the page in the newspapers, or down the running order for the broadcasters. Some will disappear altogether. The lifespan of any story in this system depends on how much more can be added to the original story. Are there any more discoveries to be made, will more of the key players suddenly break cover; can media pressure flush out more information for its readers and audiences? Watch this space. Some stories are just a flash in the pan – fifteen minutes of fame for someone; others become what seems to be an almost permanent part of the current zeitgeist.

Some types of story follow an almost predictable pattern. A major accident, for example, can run for quite a long time and go through distinct phases. Depending on the time of the day, the first news would be the hard facts of the incident. As more become available, so the story will gather pace. As key individuals begin to talk to the press, reacting to one another and the various pressure groups that will have climbed aboard the story, so the story will begin almost to have a life of its own. There will be speculation about the cause, political reaction, pressure for change or for official inquiries to be set up. In the event of an inquiry, that, too, may be reported. If it is a judicial inquiry, then all falls silent, until the report is published. For really big events, the story is revisited on the anniversary – as with the Aberfan disaster in South Wales, when so many young lives were lost in a mud slide that buried a school. Another example was the sinking of the Channel ferry, Herald of Free Enterprise. Coverage of the latter will inevitably lead to calls from those in the shipping business as to whether all the safety regulations are in place or whether more are needed.

What is driving this process nowadays is the size, energy and, above all, professionalism of the public relations industry. Some would argue that the industry now makes the news, the media only report it. PR professionals help to set the agenda by the way in which they release information, marshal and train the interviewees, time the press release and select the media that they favour. Most journalists would disagree. Yet it is true that the most notable feature of the news business these days is the way groups and individuals see an opportunity to make a point, send a message or just get noticed – and exploit it to the full. Sometimes it's impossible to find the original source of a story, so well do they cover their tracks.

Get me a quote, get me an expert

This need for the someone to interview on any story has led to the profession of 'expert'.[29] It is a much abused word. At worst it means someone who might conceivably have something to say. But every type of story – medical, political, social, historical, comic, show business or sports – has its attendant coterie of 'experts' who are trotted out whenever the need arises. Many of them are academics, real or self proclaimed. Others happen to be writing a book, or thinking of writing a book. Yet they are nearly always billed as experts

The press often dismiss them as the 'rent-a-quote' crowd, but they use them all the same. Any story that involves single mothers or family problems will almost always mean that sooner or later we will get the views of Claire Rayner. I say this not to belittle Ms Rayner in any way, for what she says is always good common sense. But the fact that she is good for a quote, and all her contact numbers are known, means that a news desk under pressure to meet a deadline is likely to call on her, rather than anyone else. It also underlines the lack of imagination on the part of the researcher who hasn't bothered to find an alternative.

But I digress. Let's get on with the news of the day. By the early evening, most broadcast journalism may have changed quite a lot from the morning; new pictures and new sound bites guarantee that the stories start to appear more complete, and less partial, than when they first broke. Spin doctors, publicists, pressure groups, PR people, as well as politicians, trade union leaders, directors and academics will all have offered or been induced to say something. On the big set-piece news days like Budget Day, part of the pre-planning has been to make sure that such people are available for a quote.

The evening news

And so the day draws to a close – with the last formal national news programmes later in the evening, and the current affairs programmes such as Newsnight, which is almost all comment on the day's news. Then the system seems to wind down until we arrive back where we started at the midnight news bulletin on Radio Four, and the wheel starts turning all over again, some stories surviving for another day, some left on what reporters call 'the spike'. In the old days that was in fact a metal spike on which you stuck news copy that you did not use. It was a rough and ready filing system, because no news organisation likes to throw anything away. One day it might mean more than it does at the moment.

The canny spin doctor, managing his master's message, tends to follow events and choose his moment to intervene with as much precision as possible. For example, do you talk to the lunchtime news? It has relatively smaller audiences, so the canny spin doctor may well refuse to put his client on air, preferring to wait for the early evening bulletins, or better yet the main nightly news, which has audiences of between five and ten million depending on the stories and the time of year. And of course the later you leave it to respond, the more feverish the desire to get you to talk. You have control, not the media. I will be dealing with this in greater detail – when to speak and when to stay silent – later.

The future of news

All of the foregoing is about what you might call the traditional forms of media. These morning and evening papers still exist, and the regular news programmes still appear on our screens or emerge from our radios at set times. But this form of news is under threat, because in the past few years they have been joined by the 24-hour-a-day news operation. News addicts can get news as and when they want it, not when the editors are ready to deliver. This type of operation was once the preserve of the news agencies, who serviced the papers and the broadcasters. Nowadays TV and radio provide that service directly to the public. They are all modelled on CNN which, when it was first launched in the USA, was called the Chicken Noodle network. Now it is arguably the most important single outlet for anyone's message in the world. In Britain we have Sky News, part of Rupert Murdoch's News International operation, and latterly the BBC has chimed in with its News24. This is still the baby of them all, using largely unknown – and until they got the job, often untried – presenters. But more and more resources are being pushed its way, and more and more cash, as the BBC gears up for the digital age which it sees as the future. The operation draws on all the BBC's vast resources for its output, so the chances are that if you figure in a BBC news report, you'll make that channel as well. Not that many people will see you – its audience is still very small. There is also the BBC Online service, which uses the net to disseminate its product – the news that's gathered by its reporters and correspondents worldwide.

Sky has made great strides since it came on the air, and its audience is growing, on the back of its all-embracing sports coverage, which has brought in the subscribers. Around Europe you are more likely to see Sky than the BBC. You will always find CNN. There is a debate as to how far these networks really do work, or whether they only come into their own when there is a major news story. During the O. J. Simpson trial, for example, they broadcast the whole event from start to finish and audiences rose. Then the same thing happened during the Louise Woodward trial, with the added ingredient for the British audience that it was one of their own on trial for her life in a foreign country. Once again audiences increased. The spin-off from this is that such massive coverage gives the so-called terrestrial broadcasters and the newspapers more opportunity to comment. So it increases the need for punditry, the need for 'experts' and so on.

It's also worth remembering that the judge in the Woodward case actually delivered his verdict via the web.

News goes digital

Another category is the CEEFAX or equivalent operation which provides a digest of news. In addition, of course, there are the websites which you can launch yourself, or which are created in response to a major news story. More and more companies have their own website. The Guardian is but one newspaper which regularly reviews the websites that are worth watching, and gives the addresses. The Times has its own IT supplement every week. These websites are a constant source of news, information and surprise. On one of the many Monica Lewinsky sites, for example, you have every form of this genre – from the very serious, discussing the constitutional implications, to the downright scatological and what she did and how.

Newspapers, too, have gone electronic, with varying degrees of success; but all report that there is a growing audience out there surfing the web. My own modest initial experience was following the fifth and final Test between England and South Africa via the MCC website. It needed patience to log on – I was abroad – but none of the locals would have known what I was talking about, assuming I had been able to translate into the local language the phrase 'Has England Collapsed?', except to wonder whether the Queen had been overthrown and the government removed by some latter-day Cromwell. Now I have the hang of the Internet I can follow the game ball by ball.

When you work in this fast-moving media world, there's no denying the excitement of feeling part of the great events; even for those journalists who spend most of their time stuck in front of a VDU, whose job is to write, and edit the copy or the pictures for the paper or programme. Indeed 'journalist' is a courtesy title – they are really information processors. Virtually everything comes to them at their work station. The cameraman in the field can now link directly into the system, as can the photographer, and the reporter. No longer do you have to dash for the phone, like Jack Lemmon used to in that classic movie Frontpage – everything goes via the laptop. This is why the most visible symbol now, in modern media, is the 'anchor', or 'presenter' named columnist. In the broadcast world, more often than not, such people are chosen for their looks and audience appeal, rather than for their journalistic skill. In Britain their worth – in terms of attracting and holding big audiences – is beginning to be properly remunerated. We are into the six-figure salary, and moving fast towards the seven-figure pay cheque. In America it has long been the case that people such as NBC's Tom Brokaw or ABC's Peter Jennings will be paid millions of dollars a year.

There's no business like news business

Which leads neatly to my final point: not only is the news business really a business – about winning market share and therefore audience so as to maximise advertising revenue – it is increasingly a branch of show business. That celebrated sceptic I. F. Stone wrote in 1963: 'The important thing about the so-called communications industry is that it is basically concerned with merchandising. News is a kind of by-product, and if you want to sell things you don't want to offend anybody.' Nearly forty years later nothing has changed that perception, and very few would disagree. How the anchor looks, the set behind him or her, the music and the titles, the glitzy computer graphics – all add to the package. In broadcast journalism the programme is called 'the show'. Newspapers, not above building up their own stars – and getting them on the box if they can – now cover the media much as they cover football. But beware. Don't assume that all programmes and all journalists have sold out to fame and fortune. Some still see the job as it always was – trying to find out what the powerful are doing and what we, the public, should be aware of. In the next chapter I'll be looking at the corporate culture of the news business and how it sets the attitudes of its practitioners.

TEN KEY FACTS ABOUT ROUND-THE-CLOCK NEWS

1   News gathering never stops.
2   Every minute of every day, somewhere in the world, there is a news update.
3   Media watch one another like hawks.
4   They will follow one another's stories.
5   Their main task is to add something new – a new angle, a new fact, a new quote.
6   If you are quoted prominently in one medium – you'll soon be quoted in all.
7   Exclusivity, these days, can be measured in seconds.
8   Once the news is out – you are fair game.
9   There is no hiding place.
10 There's nothing so old as yesterday's news.

Who's who in the news business

When you manage the message, sooner or later you are going to meet the various figures who crowd the media landscape. In many cases their (often imagined) reputation precedes them. Strangers meet them with trepidation and view the whole encounter with some alarm. There are many common and often erroneous perceptions. They are, it is alleged, an egocentric, single-minded, cynical, unforgiving bunch who have only one wish in life and that is to dig the dirt and ruin your reputation, regardless of the facts. It is also believed that they would sell their mothers or their children, probably both, to get a story first. They care for nothing and no one. All they want is the story. They let no one stand in their way. That, as I say, is a common perception. Every time I ask an audience whether they trust the media, the overwhelming majority put their hands up to say 'no'.

Yet people in the media are not really that different from the rest of the community. The job makes them look at the world in a particular way, but most have mortgages and overdrafts just like everyone else. They have wives, husbands or partners who give them a hard time for the hours they spend at work. They are under pressure to deliver. It's an insecure business. Yet they are in many respects as average a cross-section of the population as any other group of people. Unlike the professions – law or accountancy – there are no really stiff entrance exams. Journalists and media people, by and large, are born to it; they do it because they want to or need to. Some are idealistic and want to change the world, some think the money's not bad, some just like the excitement, others enjoy the power they think they have. Individually, therefore, they should not be seen as alien creatures.

Having said that, there are times when they will seem like hostile beings. And that's when the media camps outside your house or office, because you are considered a key player in the middle of some crisis. (I'll be discussing how specifically to handle the crisis on page 141.) This is the time when you need a clear idea of what it is you want to say, and how to say it. In these circumstances the media won't be fobbed off with a 'no comment'. It's easy to say, I know, but you must not be bullied. There is little to be gained by trying to escape through a back door, or cowering in an unmarked car as you make your getaway. Such manoeuvres are nearly always taken as admissions of guilt or of something to hide. After the accountants Coopers & Lybrand were found guilty of short-comings in the way they had audited the late Robert Maxwell's businesses, the former managing partner refused to say anything, and appeared, judging from the press pictures, either to be trying to hide his face like a criminal or pulling a face as if in pain. The late Diana, Princess of Wales, was hounded in this way for no other reason than for who she was. Hers is the cruellest example of the media baying for blood.

Sometimes a simple gesture can change the whole mood of such a moment. One neat example was when Jeffrey Archer's 'fragrant' wife brought out a tray of cold drinks and cups of tea for the hacks who had assembled outside the Archers' country house when he was in the news. She said nothing except that she thought that they might be thirsty. The offer provided a neat picture oppor-tunity and lowered the tension. It also underscores the rule that in dealing with the media, doing or saying something is always better than doing or saying nothing. The TV news bulletins that evening ran the 30–40 seconds of video pictures of Lady Archer coming out of the house, offering the drinks. The reporter was able to say, with the confidence that suggested inside knowledge, that 'neither she nor her husband are saying anything until the time is right'. In other words, a non-story, made into a story with a picture for TV.

Significantly, what Lady Archer did not dispense that day was alcoholic beverage. She knew that drinking while working is not a good idea if you want to be first with the story. She also knew that it would have sent the wrong signal. Yet the notion has a long and persistent history. When I was a very young reporter I heard one old-style PR man (complete with red carnation) ask how much booze was on hand at the reception. 'They'll murder us, if there isn't enough.' Let me try, as all people defending themselves would say, to put the record straight. There are still those who work in the print media who may be able to enjoy a liquid lunch and still write good copy in the afternoon. But the pressures are growing all the time on the drinking culture, and alcohol usually features only when the reporter is buying lunch and wishes to get as close as possible to someone in the hope of getting a lead to a good story. I don't mean that drink is deliberately employed, but it helps. Drink loosens the tongue; it always has, and it always will. So beware the liquid lunch that seems to have no purpose.

Drink is the enemy of the broadcaster. The very earliest example was the reporter, whose name I have not been able to trace, who back in the very early days of radio was commentating on a review of the fleet by King George V. He had been royally entertained in the officers' mess, and then went on air. He is heard, somewhat excitedly exclaiming what a wonderful sight it is to see the ships of the line in Portsmouth harbour. 'There are lights everywhere. The ships are all lit up. We are all lit up ...' He was not heard of again. The late Reginald Bosanquet lost his job reading News At Ten because of drink. And there was the famous occasion when a certain newscaster was reading the BBC's nine o'clock news and was plainly having difficulty focusing on the autocue in front of him. He was finding it equally difficult to pronounce some of the words. Slowly the screen faded to black. It was later explained that he was on medication (prescribed by his doctor) which had unexpectedly affected his sight and speech. Jack di Manio in his later years managed to keep his job on Today, but some-times it was touch and go.

In this day and age broadcasters are among the most abstemious – at least before they go on air. There used to be a time when drink was freely available in the 'Green Room'.[30] Nowadays there is less of it on offer, partly because programme budgets are smaller, and partly because producers are worried about providing temptation to nervous programme guests. But if there is alcohol available, my advice is don't touch it. Let the adrenaline, which pumps as the pressure builds, do the job of giving you the boost. This natural drug is secreted whenever the human animal feels threatened. It heightens the senses and arms the defence mechanism. Alcohol will stop this effect. You get too relaxed, and that way, you make mistakes.

The danger with generalities, though, is that there are so many exceptions. Instead of wholesale condemnation of the media for what are perceived to be its sins, a much more constructive approach is to look at the job they do, and the context in which they work. News people fall into certain well-defined categories, and those categories depend on their job description. Let's take them one by one. First, in the realm of print.

The newspaper editor

This is the person whose decision, it is said, is final. He or she is the boss. Be it a daily national newspaper, a national TV or radio news programme, the editor is the individual responsible for the line the paper or programme takes. They are protected as far as possible from the public, and from PR people. Only the grandest can get them to lunch or dinner – the Royals, the government, very senior politicians in the opposition, and the important embassies. Some editors, like the late David English, become legends in their own lifetime, creating successful newspapers such as his Daily Mail that leave their rivals in the shade. Others come and go at the proprietor's whim, usually with a handsome pay-off, and return as columnists on other people's newspapers.

The columnist

The columnist's job is to write on a regular basis about whatever is in the news. Sometimes it is comment, sometimes opinion, sometimes it takes a different slant just to be provocative. Whatever the approach, it should be readable and spark reaction. These people are difficult to influence because they are driven by the news of the day or the week. Some are highly respected specialists, such as William Keegan, the economics editor of the Observer; others have a wonderful capacity to enrage and amuse at the same time – the best example is Richard Littlejohn. They are all worth reading if only to keep you in touch with opinion in the media as much as the news. They should not be confused with the next category.

The leader writer

This individual is usually anonymous and seeks to produce in the leader column the newspaper's collective view on the issues of the day. In the field of public affairs, the leader writer will give you a guide as to what a paper thinks on current issues, and which party or policy it supports or opposes. In the broadcast media this approach has been tried a number times – I recall the late Gerald Priestland being given a one to one-and-a-half minute spot after the main evening news. It wasn't his fault but it never really worked, any more than it did when tried in the United States, where, similarly, the newspaper leader column is far more effective.

The specialist correspondent

The key word is 'specialist', and the specialism is obvious from the job title: politics, economics, finance, legal, social affairs, business. They seem to be proliferating. Over the years specialist coverage has been demanded by the fashion industry, for women's issues, for sport (subdivided to include the most esoteric of pastimes) and, most recently, the media themselves: the press and broadcasters are as fascinated about their own business as everyone else's. These are the key people to target when you want to get your message out. These are the people you should make it your business to get to know, find out what they think, what they write, and keep them fully informed on what you are doing.

The feature writer

This is the person whose main skill is elegant writing on any subject, and taking what is called 'the human angle'. I remember when I was somewhat in the news after the Today programme had not renewed my contract. Rather gratifying, from my point of view, was that The Times was running a campaign to 'Save Hobday for the Nation'. The Daily Telegraph contributed a profile headed 'Collapse of One Stout Party'. Geoffrey Levy of the Daily Mail rang me at eight in the morning and talked to me about a phrase I had used when the Observer's media correspondent asked why the programme was letting me go. I had replied that I did not know: it could have been any one of three things – my age, my gender or my accent. Geoffrey latched on to the phrase, and in less than a 30-minute conversation managed to draw enough out of me to write a very friendly full-page article, taking my side against the then editor of the Today programme. A BBC executive rang me up the next day when the article appeared and complained that I was waging a vendetta against the corporation. Auntie had become so sensitive to criticism that one feature article taking the corporation gently to task was seen as a 'vendetta'.

The general reporter

The reporter is the workhorse of the paper. Reporters may be sent anywhere at any time to cover any story. Their job is to get the facts and get them back to base as quickly as possible. If at all possible they should get something 'exclusive' so as to make the other papers seem less than fully informed. They are sometimes called 'firemen' in that they rush to the scene like fire-fighters, not knowing what to expect until they get there, and are thus prepared for anything. They are usually very young and very ambitious, each expecting to be editor before very long. These are the people you will find outside your door, in your garden, behind the bushes and up trees. They don't very easily take 'no' for an answer. Time and again the Press Complaints Commission has tried to curb what are seen as their 'outrageous' activities in 'hounding innocent victims'. The very powerful sometimes manage to have them called to heel. But whether we like them or not, it is to what they find out and get into the paper that the readers always turn first. They are part and parcel of a free press.

The sub-editor

The sub is the final category – and is desk bound, writing the headlines, rewriting the reporter's copy, designing the pages and making the paper look attractive to the reader. The problem they can cause you is mainly one of interpretation. The headline they put on a story about you or your business may well get the readers to pause and read on. It may give wholly the wrong impression. The biggest problem is the question mark. Take an example from my own fifteen minutes of fame at the end of my time on Today. One headline read 'Hobday for the Chop?' The question mark covered the paper's back, but to the consumer it would have read as a fact not a query. It can lead to many a difficulty. Firm denials are called for when such headlines appear. If nothing is said, then they go into the cuttings file which every reporter gets out when sent on a story.

The danger in headline writing for those of you who may feature is that the art of devising a good headline – and few really excel at it – is to fit a certain number of words into the space available. The Sun's famous headline 'Gotcha' was a classic. The word, the size of type, perfectly fitted the mood the paper wanted to create. Six letters in bold black type, leaving no room for doubt. It is the headline which pulls in the audience, sums up the story, whets the reader's appetite. It does not pretend to be a perfect summary of what the story is about. It is like a naughty child shouting to be heard. That's why words like 'lash out', 'hit hard', 'beauty', 'angry', figure a lot in headlines. 'Angry PM lashes out at backbenchers.' No one really believes that the Prime Minister is physically hitting his backbench MPs – but the image makes the story demand to be read. There's also a trend towards the jokier headline – even the pun. The Lord Chancellor was in deep trouble over the way the public reacted to the redecoration of his apartments, and the cost involved: not least the £59,000 he spent on wallpaper. So he sacked his current PR person, and in the words of The Times headlines writer, 'Irvine Hires a Personal Renovator'. Rolls of wallpaper featured above and within nearly every story about Lord Irvine for months. The one word became a memory jogger for the whole story. The Times also gave us 'Queen picks £230,000 a Year Spin King'. Sometimes the joke headline can do more damage than the serious one.

Sometimes people in the news can be known solely by their first name or their initials: O. J. is all that is needed to bring to mind the controversial American athlete and film star who was found not guilty of murdering his wife and a friend. The British nanny who stood trial for murder in Boston accused of killing a small baby was soon 'Louise' and nothing else.

I'll have more to say about language and its uses and abuses later, but for the moment remember that it usually begins with the skills of a headline writer, or sub-editor trying to make a grabbing headline fit a space for ten letters on one line and, beneath it, another nine letters. The headline writer today has as great an impact on the British language as ever Chaucer or Shakespeare. Just one recent example. Food which contains genetically modified ingredients was dubbed 'Frankenstein Food' by one newspaper. Monsanto, which then was in the forefront of this research, had a tough time getting away from that two-word attack on its products. In the end it gave up the business.

The broadcast media

The broadcast media have the same aims as the print media: to break the big story, to make people sit up and notice, to set the agenda for public debate and political action. But there is one vital difference – the print journalist has much greater freedom and control in covering a story. As an extreme example, the print journalist can make a few phone calls and then write the story without moving from the news desk. And what has been written will find its way into the paper without a word being changed. Of course there will be some editing to make it fit, and the headline writers will add their own words at the top.

Television and radio demand that someone is actually on the spot to film the story, or in radio terms get what's called 'actuality'. In this way technology plays a much greater role. TV must have a picture, and radio must have the sound. Picture and sound add a dimension to a story that print lacks. And of course editing pictures and sound can change the way the story is perceived by the audience – because they tend to believe a picture they can see with their own eyes, or the voice of a minister heard with their own ears. There is always a vague tendency to discount the printed word. Radio and television, for their part, cannot really fudge their coverage of an event. While newspapers can use the line, 'It is being said …' or 'Sources are saying …', print journalists don't necessarily have to identify those sources. A newspaper reporter can say, 'The minister is letting it be known that …' But in broadcasting, the audience expects the minister in person to give that information.

There are ways in which TV, specifically, can convey the impression of inside knowledge. ITN's extremely well-informed Political Editor Michael Brunson usually stands in front of Number Ten Downing Street when he reports the big political story of the day. It looks as if he has just come out after a private briefing with someone in authority; and for Michael this is usually the case. It is known in the trade as the 'stand-up' or 'piece to camera' (PTC for short), or in some media the 'camera statement'. TV reporters choose the spot for a stand-up with care – the background is as important as the words. For most of the 70 or so days that NATO bombed Yugoslavia in 1999, TV reporters had a limited choice of where to stand before the camera, either at a border post or in a refugee camp. No wonder when the Yugoslavs released pictures of bomb damage inside the country – the pictures were used everywhere. Television needs new pictures all the time.

At the end of the day television, despite the limitations, gives the audience a closer look at an event. Pictures have a sense of truth about them, so that it's harder for the individual to claim that the quote was used out of context. The audience has seen the person utter the words. When a quote appears in a newspaper, what some spin doctors in America call 'plausible deniability' is much easier. Anyone with a message to manage these days needs to think about in which medium it will be used, and tailor the presentation accordingly. One story can be handled in three different ways.[31]

Print journalists measure everything in the number of words, or column inches. Broadcast news is measured in seconds. In print the headline is king, in television it is the image, the picture, that grabs us. Striking examples were of the young Chinese student with two plastic bags standing in front of a line of tanks in Tiananmen Square; or the East Germans bringing down the Berlin Wall.[32] It has to be said that sometimes image and word can coincide in print and TV. Mrs Thatcher's handbag is, in BBC jargon, a 'bi-media' image.

Let's meet the people who control the news in broadcast.

Editors

There are more people with the title 'editor' in the broadcast media than in print. Obviously there is the programme editor, who is in overall control. There is also the day editor, who is responsible for the programme that day. In the case of the morning shows, the day editor works until early evening, beginning to fashion the next morning's show, but it is the overnight editor who will actually take the final decisions of what goes into the programme. One of the most usual complaints on the Today programme in my time was that the day editor and team had left nothing for the night team; and the day team always complained that the night team had dropped everything they had set up. As in print, the editor's word is final.

Producers

Next in rank, producers are the managers of the individual items on the programme. They work with reporters to get the interviews and supervise the editing process of the audio or video tapes so that the final product comes to air in the best possible shape. Increasingly, the producers take editorial responsibility for the item, acting as mini-editors to the reporter who does the leg work and carries out the interview. Sometimes producers are on the road or in the field with the reporter, sometimes they stay back at base. These are among the people you need to talk to about an item. Their names can usually be obtained by a simple phone call to the radio or TV programme; and often producers' names are given at the end of a programme.

Researchers

These are the lowest of the low in the pecking order. They are the people who do the most work, checking facts and phone numbers, making the calls to find out if someone is available for an interview, researching the story and so on. They are very young, badly paid, on short-term contracts, and hope to make it in the media. Researchers ensure their future career by working harder than anyone else, by being more willing to stay later, get up earlier and fetch more coffee or bacon sandwiches than anyone else. In Ancient Greece they would have been called 'slaves'. They are usually the most idealistic members of an editorial team, although they have virtually no say in the final shape of an item. But treat researchers well. Many of them end up as very important people within a surprisingly short time.

Presenters

The presenter (or anchor) is the acceptable face of broadcast news – simply the fancy packaging on the product. The oldest joke in the media business is 'I see they've sent (insert the name of any famous anchor). It must be a big story.' Sometimes it can backfire, as in the now celebrated case of CNN which got one of its star war correspondents, Peter Arnett, to 'front' a special investigation into the US government's alleged use of nerve gas in Cambodia. The story was false and so the producers got the sack – but Arnett stayed on the payroll. It seems that his authority with the public was not diminished one jot – after all, it was reasoned, it was the producers who got the story wrong.

It used to be said of one famous British presenter that when the autocue went blank so did her mind. She was among a significant number of presenters who are, in the insulting phrase, nothing more than larynxes on legs. The trend is growing because the way the audience responds to presenters – how they perceive them rather what they really are – is important in terms of the viewing or listening figures that they help to deliver.

Many presenters are good journalists, who take their role seriously. But such can be the demand for their services, increasingly it is the back-room staff who write the scripts. Some presenters suddenly become flavour of the month, and crop up everywhere. As I said in the previous chapter, their salaries are growing as broadcasting organisations seek to capture bigger audiences. The sudden rise to fame of Kirsty Young on Channel Five News is a case in point. Everyone wants her. If you are interviewed by her, then it would seem you are guaranteed a bigger audience. All sorts of names come and go, and such stories may or may not be true, but they crop up all the time in the print media because of its obsession with celebrities. Apparently anyone who appears on television has become a celebrity. The very word, of course, undermines their status in the news business. Those lucky individuals who can escape the 'celebrity' tag are the so-called 'heavyweights'.

Although women presenters such as Kirsty Wark from Newsnight or my former colleague from Today, the magisterial Sue Macgregor, are beginning to be taken much more seriously, the big guns of broadcast journalism are still for the most part men – Paxman, Humphrys and Dimbleby. But male or female, at this level, they give no quarter and expect none. They work hard to brief themselves on the interview beforehand. They know what needs to be asked, and they try, within the time given for the interview, to make sure they get the answer. They are at the very top. An interview with them is the equivalent of playing in the final at Wimbledon.

It pains me to say, although it will be a relief to the would-be interviewee, that most other interviewers on local radio and television are not in that league. The gap between the best practitioners and the run-of-the-mill is very wide indeed. You need have few qualms that they have the knowledge, the forensic ability or the imagination to pin you down if you are wriggling out of answering a question. Too often they don't have the time to do the research, but rely on the producer to do their thinking for them. In fact, sometimes the producer insists on doing the thinking, and the interviewer simply asks the questions that are supplied. A really good interviewer will listen carefully to your answers and test them; a bad interviewer will go on to the next question on the list. As the business expands, more and more people find themselves being cast in the role of presenter – they have little experience, but they look the part. This is especially the case in those programmes aimed at the younger generation. The most alarming lack of talent seems to endear them to their audiences.

Even so, anyone who believes that they will have an easier ride with the less talented interviewer could be in danger. The more naïve the interviewer, the harder they are to cope with. First they ask very simple and direct questions which demand an answer. Often they may not understand the answer, which can mean that the interviewee is soon talking at cross-purposes. You can be lulled into a false sense of security when faced by such people in an interview. Indeed, you can become your own worst enemy by not paying attention to what you are saying.

Well, that's the background to the whole business of managing the message in the most effective way. For the rest of the book, I'll be looking in some detail at the 'message' itself, in all its forms.

TEN KEY PEOPLE IN THE MEDIA

1. Always go to the **editor** if you want something done, or some redress.
2. Make the **specialist correspondent** an ally, not an enemy.
3. Remember the name of the **staffer** you are dealing with.
4. Don't patronise the **researcher**; he or she could be tomorrow's editor.
5. Treat **reporters** with respect, no matter how difficult.
6. Famous **presenters** are an asset at the lunch table ...
7. ... but it's their **producer** who is in charge.
8. Do not ignore the **camera crew**.
9. If a **journalist** breaks his word, tell everyone.
10. As a last resort – when in difficulties, consult your **lawyer**.

Defining the message

The first step towards managing the message is knowing exactly what the message is. You need to define very clearly and precisely what your key messages are. It's like the preliminary first sketch that is made before you arrive at a full-scale portrait in oils. Precision of thought and, equally, precision of targeting are all part of the management process. They are the essential prerequisites to success in the public arena. Ignore them at your peril. First though let me tell you what a message is not.

Your message is not a mission statement. As far as I am concerned mission statements are a waste of time because they always express ideas that are obvious. Of course you want to be a market leader, set the standard, innovate, compete successfully and give customers total satisfaction. These are the givens of the modern business world, yet every company seems to set great store by them, and plasters them over annual reports and accounts, on notice boards, and anywhere else that they will catch the eye.

Mission statements are usually so bland that no one reads them. And if they read them, they don't really believe them and soon forget them. It's rather like the motto that British Airways has adopted under that rather grand coat-of-arms that you find in the aircraft. 'To fly, to serve'. Well what else would they do? Not fly? Not serve? Of course a motto is not a mission statement, but inevitably there are business academics who have made a study of the genre. The director of the Ashbridge Strategic Management centre in Hertfordshire says that mission statements define the purpose of an organisation, together with its values and strategies. 'They should be updated to reflect new challenges and opportunities, but not changed so often as to confuse staff and customers.' All very sound, I am sure, but somehow I don't see your customers ringing you up and saying, 'I see you've changed your mission statement then. I like your new values, but are you sure your strategy is right?' Nor can I see the staff sending messages to the management saying, 'Great new mission statement, please cut our pay so that we can contribute the extra money needed for investment in new plant and machinery.' Somehow the mission statement seems to have become a comfort blanket. Worse, I think it's fashion. Obviously that assertion will anger and offend many people who have gone through the laborious process of fashioning the statement, and then spent quite a lot of money on market research, consultants, and printing the results on the letter head and elsewhere. So I'll make some concessions, while not deviating from my main message. Yes, some mission statements do spell out to the wider public what an organisation seeks to do. Of course there are always exceptions to the rule. Amnesty International has a mission statement which says quite simply, 'Working for the worldwide release of prisoners of conscience, fair trials for political prisoners and an end to torture, extra-judicial executions, "disappearances" and the death penalty.' What I like about this is that it tells it straight – it doesn't seek 'excellence in freeing prisoners of conscience'; or to be a global player in reducing the number of political trials. It tells you what Amnesty is about. It leaves you in no doubt. It is factual yet graphic. Yet it is the exception, not the rule. In my opinion the rule should be that your messages say something. Above all, they should be memorable. Otherwise, why bother?

'Not waving, but drowning'

This chapter, however, is not really about mission statements. It's about what you say and how you say it in a whole range of circumstances. It's about surviving in the public arena when the war of words can get out of hand. There's a poem by Stevie Smith about someone seen from the shore who is 'not waving, but drowning'. It's the perfect metaphor for badly defining the message – if you get your signals crossed, then it could be the end. To make sure that you send the right signal, you need to send the right message. You need to define your message. So let's begin with the basic message that is put out in a press release.

This is something that you feel you want to tell the world about. Let me give you an example, chosen at random from the Internet. I pulled down the following press release from what's called the PR newswire:

BARRY NICHOLSON JOINS ELDER-BEERMAN
AS VICE PRESIDENT OF REAL ESTATE

Dayton, Ohio, Aug. 21 /PRNewswire/ – The Elder-Beerman Stores Corp. (Nasdaq: EBSC) today announced that Barry A. Nicholson has joined the company as Vice President – Real Estate. In this newly created position, Nicholson will manage Elder-Beerman's real estate portfolio and will direct the company's store location, property management and leasing functions. He reports to Frederick J. Mershad, Chairman and Chief Executive Officer.

A real estate attorney, Nicholson, 41, most recently served as Assistant Real Estate Manager for Mercantile Stores Company, Inc. where he developed and implemented the company's real estate expansion strategy and negotiated purchase, sale and lease agreements for stores and other real estate holdings. Nicholson previously served as real estate attorney and representative for J. C. Penney Co., Inc. and was an associate with the law firm of McCreight, Marriner and Crumrine where he specialized in real estate, defense litigation and business law. As a U.S. Army Captain, Nicholson served as a Judge Advocate assigned to the 18th Airborne Corps from 1982 through 1986.

'Barry brings Elder-Beerman over ten years of valuable experience in retail real estate management with a strategic focus on expansion and portfolio optimization,' said Frederick J. Mershad, Chairman and Chief Executive Officer. 'As Elder-Beerman continues to grow, the evaluation of market opportunities, direction and management of an increasingly complex portfolio of real estate assets and the negotiation of key agreements becomes more critical. Barry's technical expertise and his understanding of the strategic location factors involved in the retail industry make him the ideal candidate to direct our real estate operations.'

Elder-Beerman's Divisional Vice President of Real Estate will report to Nicholson.

Nicholson is a member of the Pennsylvania Bar Association. He graduated cum laude from Washington and Jefferson College in Pennsylvania with a Bachelor of Arts degree in economics and political science and earned his Juris Doctorate degree from Ohio Northern University's School of Law.

The Elder-Beerman Stores Corp. is a regional department store company headquartered in Dayton, Ohio. With 48 stores at the end of fiscal year 1997, the company reported total revenues of $607.9 million and net sales from store operations of $581.4 million. On July 28, Elder-Beerman completed the acquisition of 21 Stone & Thomas stores and plans to retain 10 of the locations. With this acquisition, Elder-Beerman will operate 58 department stores in Ohio, Indiana, Illinois, Michigan, Wisconsin, Kentucky and West Virginia. The company will also open its first store in Pennsylvania this summer. The company's Bee-Gee Shoe division operates 61 El-Bee and Shoebilee! shoe stores in seven states. Elder-Beerman also operates two furniture superstores.

So it's a fairly straightforward story and there's nothing really wrong with the press release, though maybe the quote from the chairman and CEO, which is in the third paragraph, should have been in the second paragraph straight after he is first named. The next thought that occurs is that in detailing Mr Nicholson's past career, an awful lot of other names – perhaps competitor's names – are mentioned. What could have been said is that 'Nicholson started with a law firm, and after a six-year tour with the airborne division, his subsequent career has been as a real-estate lawyer'. Put that way it is much shorter and snappier. The actual detail could be contained as a backgrounder on a separate sheet of paper. So could the details of the Elder-Beerman Group. This background information fills out the release, but is intimidating to the journalist who likes to keep everything simple. And if you tried to say all of this in a radio interview, the audience would be quickly bored. But perhaps the most surprising addition for an English reader of the press release was this disclaimer that is printed at the end of it:

Note: This press release contains forward-looking statements that are based on management's current beliefs, estimates and assumptions concerning the operations, future results and prospects of Elder-Beerman and the retail industry in general. All statements that address operating performance, events or developments that management anticipates will occur in the future, including statements related to future sales, profits, expenses, income and earnings per share, or statements expressing general optimism about future results, are forward-looking statements. In addition, words such as 'expects', 'anticipates', 'intends', 'plans', 'believes', 'hopes' and 'estimates,' and variations of such words and similar expressions, are intended to identify forward-looking statements.

The statements described in the preceding paragraph constitute 'forward-looking statements' within the meaning of Section 27A of the Securities Act of 1933 (the 'Securities Act'). Because these statements are based on a number of beliefs, estimates and assumptions that could cause actual results to differ materially from those in the forward-looking statements, there is no assurance that forward-looking statements will prove to be accurate.

Any number of factors could affect future operations and results, including the following: increasing price and product competition; fluctuations in consumer demand and confidence; the availability and mix of inventory; fluctuations in costs and expenses; the effectiveness of advertising, marketing and promotional programs; weather conditions that affect consumer traffic in stores; the continued availability and terms of financing; the outcome of pending and future litigation; consumer debt levels; and other general economic conditions, such as the rate of employment, inflation and interest rates and the performance of the capital markets. This list of factors is not exclusive.

> Forward-looking statements are subject to the safe harbors created in the Securities Act. Elder-Beerman undertakes no obligation to update publicly any forward-looking statements, whether as a result of new information, future events or otherwise.

This legally required disclaimer is a wonderful example of doing what you are told, but doing nothing that will avoid having to print the disclaimer. Why make 'forward looking statements' if you then have to print a long statement saying such statements are not to be believed, because of all the problems that can occur? After all, Mr Nicholson is a lawyer, and a real estate lawyer as well; surely he could have drafted a quote which did not contain statements that could not be used without saying that they are meaningless. And one last observation: there was a whole raft of names (I cut them out because the piece was already pretty wordy) who could be contacted for further information. Nowhere was a contact number given either for the chairman and CEO or Mr Nicholson so that the reporter could get his own quote. This was either – and here I am speculating – because neither gentleman wanted to speak to the media, or you had to go through the PR department who would then decide whether you would get an interview or not. That's a useful form of control and screening of media interest, and is best deployed when you are handling a crisis, but here, presumably, the company wanted as much coverage as it could get on a story which was just a new appointment.

As I said I chose a press release at random, taken from the Internet. I did not call them to ask them what their policy was, I just drew my conclusions from what I read. I was putting myself in the place of someone who had just received the press release and was casually glancing at it, before, I suspect, throwing it in the bin. In the end probably two lines appeared in various local newspapers and real estate magazines. It would have been written more or less as follows:

> Barry Nicholson joins Elder-Beerman as Vice President Real Estate. Nicholson, 41, is a lawyer by training, and has spent all his career in the real estate industry, working for a number of leading firms including J. C. Penney.

There might be a line about Elder-Beerman, but not much, say:

> Elder-Beerman is a regional department store group headquartered in Dayton, Ohio with 48 department stores and with total revenues of $609 million dollars. They recently completed the take-over of 21 Stone & Thomas Stores.

I have deliberately stopped the story there, because this might happen for reasons of space. The take-over of 21 stores is important, but more important is that they will keep ten locations, thus making the total number of stores they operate to 58. It may well be that the reporter wouldn't even bother with that line because it would lengthen the paragraph too much.

But the message could be managed better by linking the two stories in the opening line:

> Barry Nicholson has joined the expanding regional department stores group, Elder-Beerman, as Vice President in charge of real estate. With its acquisition of a number of Stone & Thomas stores last month (July) Elder-Beerman will add another ten stores to its existing 48 and will be trading across seven states.

This might then followed by a quote from the CEO and – this I think would be very useful – a quote from Mr Nicholson as to why he has joined the group. With proper planning the two quotes could further the story. Instead of the chairman and CEO saying what a wonderful guy Mr Nicholson is, he could say, 'This is what we want him to do', and Mr Nicholson could have a quote about 'This is how I hope to do it.'

I'm looking at this story as any reporter would. But that's how it should be seen, too, within the company. I get the impression that this press release was written more with an internal audience in mind, given its lines about who is reporting to whom, and the masses of detail about the company and the man who is joining it. So this rather detailed example is to show how the thinking should be right at the beginning when you want to manage the message.

In the Beerman example the story was that the company was making an important executive appointment; it was being made in the context of a company that was expanding; these are some figures to illustrate that expansion; and this is what the chairman and the new man had to say about the move.

That's for the print media. Now let's develop our story and imagine the press conference: obviously the two people quoted in the story will be present, and the media should be able to hear from both of them. But this is where the message management must go a step further: both men must be brief on what is perceived to be the 'real' story – key appointment in an expanding company. Therefore all statements should be aimed at reinforcing that message: more examples of the places where the company will now be trading ('across seven states'), and the range of products (with examples of the shoes from the shoe chain on display as well as other goods).

In effect what they are announcing is the take-over and expansion story rather than the individual appointment. Thus there is a two-way benefit. It's good for the company's image, while for the new appointee it is a chance to enjoy a high profile from day one. He can also make contacts with the media in his new role and at the same time begin to have his name associated with the company in a very positive way. As for the media, they have a better story, with more in it than just another 'Executive changes jobs'.

I must point out that all of the above is what I have built on the rather flimsy foundation of a single press release pulled at random from the Internet. It may well be that the company did all that I suggested, or didn't do it for very good reasons of which I have no knowledge. The point I'm making is the importance of setting any event you wish to announce into a context – of the business, of the industry, of the area in which you operate. If the rest of your industry is retracting and your are expanding, then that context should be taken into account. Identifying and defining a message means thinking beyond the immediate piece of information, and setting it in a framework that makes it more interesting.

In the instance quoted, there is little more that Mr Nicholson could have said in that early press release other than he was happy to be given a challenging job. Perhaps that's why in the end we didn't hear from him: he had nothing to say. Explaining the business, the context and his role would be something to say – to his and your benefit. But don't stop with the press release: these days it's about as useful as putting a message in a bottle and throwing it out to sea. It will certainly wash up somewhere, almost certainly someone will open it to see what's written inside – and then throw it away because it has absolutely no relevance to them, or has arrived too late to be of any possible use.

Finding the target

If these messages are made more interesting, more attention-grabbing, then not only will the print media be interested, but the broadcast media as well. But remember, the same messages then have to be carried over into any broadcast interviews that are done. Once again we take the same message about joining an expanding firm, and use the examples given at the press conference in any radio or TV interview. Based still on the Beerman example, if the TV interview or radio interview is done in any of the individual states, then specific and local references should be included that tally with the message. In Ohio, for example, talk about Ohio issues, stores and plans – and so on for each state. Managing the message involves not just getting it right on the day, but staying with the message and adapting it for different media and different locations.

The last management detail in such a scenario is that everyone knows the message, so that even those who may not be directly involved (someone, say, in a regional office), should be able to answer any local media while sticking to that message.

The local angle

I was once asked to give some advice to an American executive who was about to go on a 25-city tour to promote a management manual he had written. TV and radio spots had been lined up by the publishers, who arranged for the book to be on display in each city or town's leading bookstore on the day. This man was a senior executive with the Dale Carnegie Institute, and it seemed to me that this fact, plus the book itself, could be used to mutual benefit. I suggested that he check the institute's presence in each place, and we found that it was there in every one. Then we got each local office to send us the issues that they dealt with on a day-to-day basis – the business concerns of the individual and the local businesses. We then checked how long they had been in business in that place, how many people had been through the system, and when the author had last visited the place. We also checked the names of the local main industries and businesses, the names of the mayor and of other prominent citizens. With this background we began to devise a message about what help the book could bring to … and at this point we begin to fill in the local details. I also suggested a call the night before he arrived in case there had been any development that would help or hinder the promotion of the book – if, for example, the leading employer had just laid off 20,000 people. (Luckily it was a time of boom and in fact most were hiring.)

By modifying his messages in the course of his national tour, he was able to bring a local touch to each TV interview he gave. He was a national figure, yet he could talk familiarly and knowledgeably to local news people and audiences. Such people think their town is very important. It is. And it's important to you as well, so find out more about it, if you are going there.

No message should be carved in stone

A few last points. Sometimes the message might need to be changed because of changing circumstances – yet another take-over, a dispute at one of the new acquisitions. Don't run away, but sit down and build it into the message as before. Don't answer on the hoof – think before you speak. And finally remember that there is a danger of just speaking the words parrot-fashion – or as one Labour MP said of his colleagues, 'like daleks'.[33] In the chapters on inter-views (pages 189 and 205) and body language (page 179) I look at the need for some acting skills and public speaking expertise. Any quote given to the media should sound as if it is being made up on the spot and being used for the first time. Don't just intone it, suggesting you've said it so many times before.

Let me give you a final example of that sort of control. A few years back I was waiting in line for my turn to interview the then Conservative Chancellor of the Exchequer, Geoffrey Howe. This is quite usual with government announcements – each programme wants its own interviewer talking to the minister. So the minister can go through half a dozen interviews in turn before he or she is free to get back to work. All ministers are briefed beforehand on what to say, the key points of the message, and examples where necessary. Some are better than others in absorbing such a brief: Geoffrey Howe was good at it. I don't remember what the subject of the interview was, but I recall that Lord Howe, as he now is, had a quick joke he wanted to tell – and I watched as he told this two-line joke to every interviewer. I thought I would try to avoid it, but I got told it as well. We ran the interview – with joke – and so did all the others.

All broadcasters are keen to find out if they have missed anything, so they keep an eagle eye on what other programmes are doing, and how a particular interview has gone. Geoffrey Howe had given a masterly performance – none of us got a word that was different, the joke was told, and in reality we could have intercut the interviewers from any of the programmes and used just one set of answers, they were so similar. Not much fun for the broadcasters, but what a way to manage the message. To cap it all, each interview looked as fresh – if that's the word to apply to a usually rather soporific speaker – as any of the others. No member of the audience, watching but one channel, would have thought this was an interview that had been repeated at least half a dozen times.

Hollywood, of course, spares its stars the necessity of masses of interviews, and quite happily sends out ready-shot answers, to which interviewers from the various programmes around the world supply their own questions. It's a crude form of managing the message, but it works because in a sense a new film is not going to shake the world. And the smaller radio and TV stations could not afford to send a team to interview the star in Hollywood. What's more, they can use the footage they get for free, and it looks as if they can get the stars to appear on their station just like the big and rich networks.

The Central Office of Information provides a similar facility with some of the programming that it distributes free to broadcasters around the world; and the

United States Information Service carries out a similar role. There have also been attempts in the business community to send out pre-recorded interviews. So far, however, most broadcasters, in Britain at least, tend to insist on the real thing – their own interviewer face-to-face with the subject.

On the other hand, when I spent a couple of years editing a business programme for a European satellite channel,[34] I asked for and received permission from most of Europe's leading companies to use footage from their corporate videos – for free. At least it allowed me to illustrate stories with good pictures, while the companies such as Shell or Nissan knew that the pictures I was showing on screen had all been cleared for use in public. Again, it's another example of managing the message – in this case, the visual message.

If you've done your homework, defined your message, and can deliver it in a convincing manner, then what is there to be worried about? The problem is whether your message is tamper-proof; can the editing process still leave you at a disadvantage? What questions will the reporter ask, and could they stump you?

TEN KEY POINTS ON DEFINING THE MESSAGE

1   Establish exactly what the story is.
2   Decide what you must say – main facts of the story.
3   Get quotes from the people involved in the story.
4   Determine the context in which it is taking place.
5   Put it together so a reader gets to the nub ('message') quickly.
6   Give the story a local slant when on the road.
7   Adapt the story, but don't change it, for broadcast media.
8   Make sure everyone is signed up to the message.
9   Check before you begin to change the message.
10 If you are giving the message, make it sound natural – don't speak like a talking clock. Make an impression.

■

The five questions every reporter asks

Any reporter will tell you that the 'five Ws' are the key questions every trainee is taught to ask. Put more grandly, they are the basic research tools in journalism. The questions are Who? What? Where? When? and Why? In the course of any interview – be it with the print or broadcast media – all of them will be asked, in no particular order, to get at the facts. Once these basic facts are established, the process begins all over again; and in testing the initial answers, the interviewer will resort again to the five Ws. Now all this would seem to be obvious, yet interviewers will tell you that some people still appear surprised to be asked basic questions such as 'Why did you do this?', and immediately suspect some kind of trap. Caught on the hop, they seem to find it hard to give straight and unambiguous answers. As a result they may confuse the interviewer as to the real facts, and so create the wrong impression.

There's half a column in my Shorter Oxford English Dictionary explaining and defining 'impression'. I like number 6: 'The effect produced by external force or influences on the senses or the mind; a sensation; an effect produced on the intellect, conscience or feelings.' So if you want to manage the message, you need equally to manage the impression that you make when that message is tested by the five Ws in an interview. Is the interviewee confident, evasive, shifty, hesitant, too ready with glib answers, riddled with doubt or too keen to impress? The way the five Ws are answered adds up to the impression you make.

You can improve or destroy that impression with the language you use in the answers you give. It's also the way you marshal the argument and keep to the point that will convince a sceptical interviewer of the justice of your case. Persuasion through unanswerable logic is the aim.

It all adds up to one of those algebraic formulae that maths teachers used to plague us with at school. If the five Ws get five good answers (5A), then $5W+5A$ = a good impression. If the answers are not straight As, but are marked down to the level of B or even C, then the impression is less good.

So let's take the five Ws one by one and look at what constitutes a good answer.

Question one: Who?

Who are you? This is one of the most leading questions any reporter can ask. Your answer establishes not only your identity, but your relevance to the story that the reporter is covering. If you have any kind of public profile, who you are is defined as much by your job title, or position in the company or organisation, as your reputation. The reporter is not looking for your full CV so much as the relevant facts. It never ceases to amaze me at the amount of useless personal information an individual will give a reporter – about the committees they serve on, whether they are chairman, treasurer or secretary, how many clubs they belong to. The very grandest will airily hand you a photocopy of their entry in Who's Who.

It is far better that you, rather than the reporter, should decide what you think is relevant. From your obviously glittering and lengthy CV choose the few – very few or better still no more than two – facts that seem to be most germane to the interview in hand. The object of the exercise is to make sure that you are seen as the right person to be talking about this issue. Beware of job titles on their own. I once met someone who revelled in the grand title 'Head of European Relations'. It meant everything and nothing. Actually the person in question was a liaison officer between the European Commission and the trade body that he served. So it may be that your visiting card should be looked at – does it give you a title that means something? If you have various titles or job descriptions, should you have a visiting card for each function? And while talking of visiting cards, is the name you use how you want to be referred to? If you are 'Robert', but known everywhere as 'Bob', does your visiting card call you 'Bob'?

Having decided who you are, or who you want to be for the purposes of an interview, the same applies if you are answering questions about other people. Do their job descriptions fit with the points you are making? Are they the right people – and again how do they want to be referred to? Does your mate 'Pete' hate that diminutive being used in public. Does he insist on being called 'Peter'?

The 'who' question is in some ways equally applicable to the business or organisation. Don't assume that everyone has heard of it. Do you have a one-line description that says everything the casual inquirer needs to know? Does that description contain any jargon – scientific, professional or corporate, that needs to be explained in simple English? Sometimes, of course, well-known firms have well-known slogans – slogans that have cost millions of pounds to establish. They may be used in your advertising and sales literature. Don't be afraid to use them too – why not? If they are that well known, then everyone will quickly understand. If you are brand manager for Opal Fruits – why not add, 'The sweets made to make your mouth water'.

Question two: Where?

The 'where' question is, obviously, about place and location. Try as far as possible to confine a location to a specific and identifiable place. Don't just say 'Great Britain', when it would be better to say 'England' or 'Scotland'. Don't just say 'England' if you can say 'Worcestershire'. And why say 'Worcestershire' when you can say 'Malvern'? A good answer to 'where' would be 'In Malvern, a small country town in the English Midlands'. It takes three seconds, but says so much more.

Question three: What?

The 'what', as in 'What happened?' demands attention to detail in the same way. Once again, time is of the essence, especially in a broadcast interview, where most answers should take no more than 30 seconds. In fact you should apply your own five Ws to supplying the answer – but don't stray from the point of 'what happened', otherwise you open up a new line of questioning.

The 'what' question is the broadest of them all and is quite often used as part of what some reporters call 'a fishing trip'. They cast a line and hope to catch something. Try to avoid ever being asked, 'What do you mean?' That would suggest that you haven't paid enough attention to the content and the way you express it. Keep the language simple and direct, avoiding jargon. The form also crops up in what is becoming one of the most asked questions in the modern media world: 'What is your reaction to ...' or 'What is your message for the Prime Minister (or whoever ...). This is the best opportunity for anyone with a message to get that message across. Because of the fast pace of the news business these days, much journalistic time is spent getting reactions to what was said or what happened earlier in the day. This is the moment for the carefully crafted sound bite.

Question four: When?

The 'when' question is about time, obviously. Time is the driving force in the modern world of communications. 'When' should be as current as possible. The closer you are to the event the better it is from the media's point of view. Immediacy is the aim of all good journalism. So if the 'when' question is put, make sure that it happened at least in the same week, better the same day, better yet, that morning or afternoon; and if you really want to get the broadcaster drooling, say 'In the past few minutes ...'

Question five: Why?

The 'why' question is potentially the most dangerous. Sometimes it is obvious why you are announcing something – the time is right; it is to beat the opposition. But when phrased 'Why do you think it happened' or 'Why do you think they said that?' you are being asked to venture an opinion. Opinions can lead to problems. You might be on the money in explaining someone's motives – but can you prove it? Will it steer the debate into rather more dangerous paths? Why did you say what you said? That would be the most likely retort. A golden rule here would seem to be: speculate about others as you would have them speculate about you. In short, don't.

Naturally, the five Ws come in all sorts of guises, wrapped in sentences that can have so many sub-clauses you've forgotten the point. But at least one of the famous five will be in there somewhere waiting to spring out at you.

I've deliberately kept this quite simple. I think that is the best advice I can give you. I have seen briefs for questions that are likely to be asked by journalists at a press conference or in an interview. They are, of course, framed by people with inside knowledge of the company or organisation. They are based on a level of knowledge that few journalists could lay claim to – and if they could, they would be hired to help run the business. People get into the most terrible state of nerves thinking that they are going to be found out. If they have done something wrong, or illegal, then one day justice will probably catch up with them.

The vast majority of press interviews are fairly straightforward. The journalist is there to find out everything possible about an issue, an announcement or whatever. You have agreed to the interview because you have a message or two you want to make public. I sometimes wonder how much the PR people in some companies like to keep their colleagues on the hop and quietly afraid so that they can exercise some control of them so as to further their own careers, or keep their jobs. By bad-mouthing the media all the time, the PR function can make a case for its own existence. Remember, you are, or should be, your best PR person. After all, you are the one in the spotlight, you are the person answering the questions – you are the one with the message.

Testing the message

Let me construct an example of how it might work out in practice. Say you are the head of a recently privatised public utility. There is a public row about the amount of money people like you are being paid. 'Greed' and 'Sleaze' are the words being bandied about. One or two MPs have thrown in 'snouts in the trough' for good measure. It's the time of your AGM when you and your fellow directors will be telling the shareholders about the year in review. The media want to cover the event, and you are the person they all want to talk to.

I have always believed that keeping silent in such circumstances does not work to one's best advantage. It's no use hoping that by keeping your head down no one will notice you, the press will drift away, and soon they'll forget. Because you are a public company, all the details of pay, bonuses and dividends are in the public arena. Your own career and background will be at Companies House. Much of what you have said will be in the cuttings library at any rate. The Internet has made the search for information that much easier and quicker for the journalist.

So the event is going to be reported anyway. And they – that is those who do not wish you well – will speculate and talk of your 'shame' and 'greed'. I would argue that it's time to show leadership. Presumably you know why you are being paid what you are being paid. The decisions weren't just taken without any thought of the best interests of the company and its shareholders. The amounts of money involved weren't picked out of a hat. Presumably you will have justified the decisions in the past – at shareholders' meetings or before the regulator. Knowing what you've said and why; knowing when you said it and who you said it to; not forgetting where you said or did these things – all this should stand you in good stead. If you said it all before, why not say it again?

But choose your time and the ground when and where you will make your stand. Remember you must stay in control. Perhaps you opt for just one full-scale interview. The choice is broad – either TV, radio or press. A large spread in the Financial Times or The Times would be noticed. Perhaps you choose to talk to the Today programme on the morning of your AGM: the quotes will run for the rest of the day. Or maybe you try to interest a television news programme such as Newsnight. If you go for a late-night show like this you can see what's been happening to the story during the day, and this gives you the chance to adjust the news agenda in your favour for the next day.

This is where your PR people should be putting their efforts in seeking to get you invited on to specific programmes or interviewed in specific media. If the PR person can say that it will be 'exclusive' (always an attractive proposition to a reporter or editor) you'd be surprised at how often the media will take the bait.

And in this fictional case, you are news. After all, you're one of the Greedy Executives with their Noses in the Trough. Don't avoid the description even if you hate it; it's that insulting definition that gives you news value and will get you listened to. It's not easy because you are up against prejudice – but it will provide an opportunity to put the record straight.

Learn from the Tory politician Ann Widdecombe. She takes the cruel jibes and insults, and turns them to her advantage. The PR function can give you advice and support. It can do the necessary research, tell you who's who in the media, and who you will be talking to. But the PR function can only go so far. Like football managers, they do their work off the field. It's the players in the actual game who have to play. So think for yourself, be ready with the answers. Most of all, do your own homework. Look at what you've said in the past; what others are saying. Who are your critics? If you were going into a court of law you would discuss this with your lawyers. You would be prepared to give all the time possible to making sure you had a watertight case. Apply the rules of evidence to everything you say; can it be challenged, and if so, how?

By choosing the person or media you will talk to, at least you have not ducked out of public view. The broadcasters may even accept that you dictate some of the terms on how the interview is handled. Not the questions. Never suggest what questions you want. If you've done your homework, you will know very well what they will want to ask. Journalists feel that this is an infringement of their editorial independence. But you can say where the interview will be given, and at what time. Obviously if you have agreed to 'go live' on a radio or television programme, this limits the options as to time and place; but all the rest holds true.

Whatever your choice, unless you have some deep dark secret, some crime you have committed, some private vice you want to keep private – what harm can come to you? Who knows, you might be able to do what Jonathan Aitken couldn't do – 'use the simple sword of truth and the trusty shield of British fair play'.

TEN KEY POINTS ABOUT TESTING THE MESSAGE

1 Apply the five Ws to everything you say or do.

2 Deal with facts, nothing but the facts.

3 A fact is safer than an opinion.

4 Have answers ready when they ask: Who, What, Where, When or Why?

5 Beware the reporter on a fishing trip.

6 The most difficult question of all is 'Why?'

7 Concentrate on the issues at hand, keep to the point.

8 Answer the question as put, don't volunteer information.

9 Don't let the PR function frighten you.

10 Always do your own homework.

12

Controlling the message

The key to managing the message is staying in control. By control I mean antic-ipating as far as possible events which will threaten to blow you off-course and undermine the message. In everyday life we all need some element of control. Total control is impossible. We must be prepared for the unexpected; but we can try to minimise the threat the unexpected might pose. For example, one unwise phrase, and you could have a full-blown crisis on your hands, as Glenn Hoddle, the English football manager, found after he mused about karma in previous lives, reincarnation, and a possible explanation as to why some people have disabilities.

There are five ways that you stay in control:

1   Choose your agenda with care.
2   Be flexible but say nothing to contradict or undermine a previous message
3   Learn the technique of 'rapid rebuttal'.[35]
4   Get your retaliation in first.
5   Make sure the competition is discussing your message, not advancing its own.

Let me take them one by one. Choose your agenda with care – in other words, what are the issues you wish to discuss? What are the key issues that affect your business, and what is your considered view? But stay flexible. Rigidity can break you. Just as trees bend in high winds, so you must learn to be flexible and maybe give a little. Rugby players are taught that they should get their retaliation in first. In the public arena, you must not let the other side in the debate settle into their game. You must try to make all the running. You do this by ensuring that your initial announcement has all the right ingredients to explain the story, start a debate, defend your position, counter the criticism, or take the fight to the opposition. It must be direct and to the point. There should be no ambiguity; no need for people to call and ask 'What do you mean?'

It was an American, James Carville, who developed the technique of 'rapid rebuttal'. He does not have a very high opinion of the media, which he has dubbed 'the beast'. Carville is sometimes called the 'king of spin', and he set up what was called the 'war room' for the Clintons in the 1992 presidential campaign. His business interests now stretch to Britain where he is involved in a political consultancy. During a recent flying visit to Britain he fired off some missiles in defence of the job of the spin doctors. Talking to Patrick Wintour in the Observer, Carville said he believed that all briefings should be on the record. He asserted that a spin doctor does not lie ('That would be stupid. You cannot do your job afterwards'.) But his main advice was to stay on the attack, not go on the defensive. 'You just handle the incomings. You've got to get out there and be an advocate. If you just try to handle the incomings, the beast will eat you.'

As a warning he cites the health care reform debacle in the early years of the Clinton White House. 'We did not do the proper explanation and get the proper amount of support, and the other side did it better. That's what happens in democracies. You have to do it better.' So attack, respond, but don't stay silent.

The power of passion

Obviously the next point follows on from that. If you are a lively advocate, passionately pushing your message at every opportunity, and countering any response with good robust argument, then you will be listened to. Even if it is an odd message, this strategy works. Take the case of Mohamed Al Fayed, the boss of Harrods. He believes that there was a plot by the Establishment to kill his son Dodi and Diana, Princess of Wales, because the Establishment could not accept the idea that the former wife of the heir to the throne would marry an Egyptian. At every opportunity he advances this theory. Some opinion polls suggest that he has a measure of support. Britain's secret service was prompted to publish a report on its activities, stressing that it had never used assassination as a weapon to further Britain's interests. And there it was left. Al Fayed still goes on making his claims; even on the day of the first anniversary of the tragic couple's death, when unveiling a memorial fountain in the front window of his store, he stayed 'on message'. He has said it in France at the magistrate's inquiry into the accident; he's said it on British television, he's advanced the theory in speeches and in off-the-cuff remarks; he's said it in the Hamilton libel trial at the Old Bailey. It's more than likely untrue that there was a plot; but Al Fayed will not let it drop. He has already got a response from the security services – what next? Will he succeed in his obsessive drive to blame someone for the tragedy? Time and again people who have encountered tragedy keep the story going by their persistence. A detective whose daughter was murdered in Kenya; a doctor whose daughter died on the PanAm flight that was blown up by terrorists over Lockerbie – these are just two of the examples. We have seen relatives of men and women wrongly imprisoned carry on their battle for years, seeking what they see as justice.

Keep your head above the parapet

These are the extreme cases of making sure your message is heard at every opportunity. The other lesson is that all these people – rightly or wrongly – are ready to speak to the media whenever they are given the chance. When new evidence emerges, or new facts, they re-assess the message, but it rarely changes. The most persistent and dedicated was the man who gave up everything to ride a bicycle around Britain, seeking the complete banning of smoking and the manufacture of cigarettes. I used to see him at every party conference and the Trades' Union Congress year in and year out. Sooner or later some desperate reporter, needing some colour to brighten up a dull conference piece, would seek his views.

Such people are obsessive; and there seem to be more and more of them ready to give up almost everything to pursue an idea or an ideal. The more they are ignored, the worse they may become. What are single-interest pressure groups, but obsessive people with access to a fax and telephone? And now of course they can wage their struggle for recognition via the Internet. If business wants to make its messages heard, then sometimes it, too, needs to be a little more obsessive in its pursuit of what it wants to say – via the various media. A single press conference, a single speech, does not a campaign make. As James Carville said, 'You have to work at it.'

Listen to Des Wilson

I suppose the most famous and the most successful public campaigner in Britain is Des Wilson, who made his name as the first director of Shelter, the campaign for the homeless. He masterminded the campaign for lead-free petrol throughout Europe. He has been chairman of Citizen Action and of Parents against Tobacco. He has written a very useful book for all campaigners – an A to Z of Public Advocacy.[36]

Des sets out the ten principles that he has applied to his campaigns:

1   Tell the truth.
2   If you don't like hard work don't get involved.
3   Maintain a sense of perspective.
4   Abhor violence.
5   Be positive.
6   Remember who the enemy is.
7   Be professional.
8   Confront perceptions.
9   Remember the bigger the audience, the simpler the message.
10 Have faith.

The words of the master – and if you are on the receiving end of one of his campaigns, then you will have a pretty tough time of it. The increasing professionalism of the people in public advocacy campaigns means that no business can afford to keep quiet, hope they'll get bored and then slowly drift away. Among campaigning groups everyone is involved. Too often the business sector hires a PR specialist and thinks it's done the job. There has to be interest and involvement from the very top of an organisation. There must be the necessary resources, and the willingness to speak out whenever the need arises. It's no use just leaving it to the PR department to handle it. Ultimately control must come from the top – the very top.

If your PR policies are right, and work effectively on a day-to-day basis, then they should be able to withstand the very special and exceptional pressures when the company is hit by some crisis. In the next chapter I deal with those exceptional pressures.

TEN KEY STEPS TO CONTROLLING THE MESSAGE

1   Tell the truth – or as much as you can.
2   Be pro-active, not reactive
3   Always respond – remember rapid rebuttal.
4   Never stay silent.
5   The watchword should be flexibility but consistency.
6   Be persistent.
7   Don't send confusing signals.
8   Saying something once is not enough. Repeat, repeat, repeat ...
9   Keep a beady eye on the opposition.
10 Control must come from the top.

13

Messages in a time of crisis

The end of 1978 saw the beginning of what has gone down in the political history books as Britain's 'winter of discontent'. An object lesson in how one ill-judged remark can backfire. The country seemed to be in the grip of industrial anarchy with disputes in almost every sector of the economy. One of the most notable was a strike by gravediggers which had left the dead unburied; another was a strike by refuse collectors which left city streets piled high with rubbish. The unions seemed to have the Labour government on the ropes. Away on the sunny tropical island of Guadaloupe, Prime Minister James Callaghan was attending to affairs of state at a G Seven Summit. As he sought to manage world affairs, it seemed he could not manage his own. He did not take very kindly to newspaper headlines suggesting that Britain was on the brink of collapse.

Callaghan arrived back at Heathrow while the transport drivers were on strike and lectured the waiting press corps: 'Please don't run your country down by talking of mounting chaos.' The headline in the Sun the next day was 'Crisis, what crisis?' With a general election due in May, Labour, which had been ahead in the polls, began to trail badly, and Callaghan never seemed to recover the initiative. He went down to defeat against a woman called Margaret Thatcher. The cruellest cut of all is that everyone now thinks he actually said 'Crisis, what crisis?' So, first rule in life, never underestimate a crisis. In fact a crisis should not be a crisis, but something you have planned to deal with when it happens.

Crises come in a variety of guises – from the explosive and unmistakable, to a tiny nagging problem that won't go away. Crises can mean different things for different businesses. In the travel industry there always seem to be crises waiting to happen. The kidnapping of Britons in Yemen suddenly put paid to what had been a specialised but growing tourist business for one small travel agency. The travel trade, by and large, knows the drill. There are enough actual cases for them to study: the Channel ferry, Herald of Free Enterprise, which rolled over and sank because the bow doors weren't shut properly; the people who were killed by Islamic fundamentalists in Egypt while visiting the Valley of the Kings; and then the mix-up over the bodies with a German victim buried in a British churchyard while a British family was buried abroad. And there have been murders in places like Miami, and a child's disappearance on a Greek island. The list grows every year. The travel industry, I know, rehearses for such situations, knows who will form the crisis management team, and who will speak to the media.

In heavy industry, a massive explosion at a nuclear plant must be the nightmare vision. It happened at Chernobyl, but lesser leaks and worries have plagued the Nuclear Reprocessing Plant at Sellafield. By any standards a huge industrial accident provokes a crisis – for the plant and business, and for the surrounding neighbourhood. The Exxon Valdez oil spill in Alaska and the Torrey Canyon in the English Channel are just two examples. I have been involved with the oil industry in running simulation courses to cope with a fire at the well-head or on the rig. Once again the possibility of a crisis concentrates the minds of management and everyone knows their role when the siren sounds.

All such potential crises are identifiable and can be planned for, while all the time work goes on to avoid them. Indeed the safety measures followed, and the standards of good practice set and implemented, become part of the story that the media will get. And since they are so public, there is usually an inquiry afterwards which will apportion blame, if blame attaches, and produce recommendations that can sometimes be turned into law. The aftermath of the Hillsborough disaster meant that football clubs had to spend a lot of money on making their stands at grounds much safer. And consider public reaction to the Paddington rail disaster in late 1999.

So, a word of warning. While you are looking ahead to a potential problem, look back and see just how good your record is. Have you put in place all the right safety measures, or have you skimped and saved? When it comes to managing the message in a crisis, it's not just the moment that is under intense scrutiny, but your past as well. And if there is anything in your past, it might mean that no matter how well you handle the immediate crisis, there may not be a future. Woe betide the football club which had failed to follow those post-Hillsborough recommendations, should another disaster cause crowd panic. No matter how you handled such a crisis, the fact that you had not even taken the legally required precautions would ensure that no amount of spin could save you from the consequences.

'Don't turn a crisis into a drama'

One of the most persuasive advertising campaigns in the insurance industry told people that the company would not 'turn a crisis into a drama'. The message was a simple one. By taking out the proper insurance, a crisis can be dealt with in a straightforward manner. Crisis planning is an insurance policy and it will pay off handsomely when something happens. The key to handling a crisis successfully is to identify a worst-case scenario, and have a plan to deal with it. So the first rule must be to expect a crisis one day. The second point to take on board is that the way the media covers your crisis is not, as some people would claim, a personal vendetta. When the news breaks, the media go into a set routine. They cover it as a story – if you like, just another everyday crisis. They will be asking you the same questions and seeking the same answers that they would ask any business in a similar situation.

There are five things the media looks for in any crisis:

1   The media wants the facts – when, where, what and, most of all, why. Facts also include information about your firm, your people, your reputation, and whether there are any skeletons in your cupboard.
2   The media needs people it can talk to – a spokesman it can quote, someone with authority. The media will also be talking to the police, fire and ambulance services, so make sure that your story tallies with theirs.
3   The media needs everything **now** – the bigger the story, the bigger the team to cover it.
4   The media needs communications facilities. They have deadlines.

5   The media will listen to anyone who might be able to give them some detail, or theory that might help explain what's happened – pressure groups, disgruntled ex-employees, the local MP, the police, the trade unions.

Now set those five key drivers in the context of an intensely competitive news business that operates around the clock; you will appreciate why you might need more than a secretary answering the phone, and saying that her boss hasn't arrived yet. You will be besieged. There will be cameras filming all arrivals and departures and anyone who sticks their head above the parapet. There will be radio reporters recording interviews with anyone they can find, while the print media will be watching, discussing and filing updates. Your switchboard will not be able to cope. And it will go on 24 hours a day. Every radio station, every all-news TV station will be running hourly updates.

Don't hinder, help

You can help, or hinder. The choice is yours. I would opt to help the media in their job as far as possible. This doesn't mean being at their beck and call at all hours, or just slavishly trying to answer the questions. But deciding not to help does not mean that they will go away. If you won't talk, someone else will. 'No comment', in my experience, equals 'no hope' of putting your side of the story. In fact, refusing to help, and being downright obstructive, brings out the very worst in the media – they become even more determined to 'get the true story'. I don't admire or condone what happens in these circumstances – but they believe that the public has a right to know, and that it is your responsibility to explain.

By helping, at least you gain some measure of control. Let me explain. In a crisis you are the news. You are the principal source of good, accurate information. Your words must carry more weight than the army of experts the talk show producers will invite on to their programmes and who will speculate endlessly. They are in it for the fame and the money. So the more you can give, the better it must be for you.

Be straight with the media – tell them when you have nothing new to say, tell them when you will next be able to make an announcement. Above all, tell the truth. If you don't know the answer, say so. Stay calm despite the pressure. And if you can, give interviews when asked even if you have nothing new to say. An interview has a strangely mollifying effect on the reporter anxious to get his or her news editor off their back. When I say, 'Give interviews', what I mean, strictly speaking, is be prepared to say something for the camera or the microphone. The various media will be almost certain to use it. After all, you are one of the main characters in the story. One of the best recent examples was the daily performance by NATO's spokesman Jamie Shea during the Kosovo crisis. He was always at the daily briefing, but he also gave one-on-one interviews. He never wavered in giving the NATO line.

Are you the hero or the villain?

You must choose the role you want to play, not have the role thrust upon you. It's a simple choice – hero or villain. Just as actors need lines to say, so interviews need to be properly prepared in your mind. I'm not suggesting you learn your dialogue by heart from a prepared script. That will lock you into an inflexible position. But you must clearly identify what you want to say, and what you must not say. You must be sure of your facts; you must not be prompted into any speculation that you might later regret. If other people's comments are given to you and you are asked for a reaction – try not to react at once. You'll be talking again soon, so take time to think about it. 'I can't comment on that idea, until I have the full facts' is a useful delaying tactic. If you have built up the right rapport with the media covering the story, they will trust you to keep your word.

The right relationship is vital. One that is based on trust will serve you better in the long run than one that is based on evasion, half truth or just temporising. In fact, the more you think about such interviews in any rehearsal, the more it will be obvious that you can avoid most of the tricky questions that might get you or the business into trouble. Compensation, for example, is now the norm. You cannot offer it, nor can you say there will be none. A useful answer – and a true one – is 'That's for the lawyers when all this is over. Our main concern now is to help the people trapped in that building.' Keep in mind the time sequence to a story – what happened before, what is happening now, and what might happen in the future. Concentrate on the present: 'Our concern now ...' But don't forget the past. Avoid looking into the future: 'We have to solve today's problem first – we can discuss that when we come to it.'

No comment, no hope

If no one from your side of the crisis will talk, the basic assumption made by the media is that you have some problem that your are ashamed of, or cannot cope with. Or worse, that you are hiding some guilty secret. This may be nonsense – but in the absence of a witness for the 'defence', the prosecution can make its case that much more easily and convincingly. The more you talk, the more you can control the situation.

There are random factors, of course, over which you cannot have much control. The media will talk to anyone, and there always seems to be someone with an axe to grind in these moments. What is said may actually be totally untrue, and whereas the media will try to check it out, such is the pressure to get on to air or into print, these views are quoted directly. If you are given the chance to put the record straight – take it. But don't get into a debate. Take the option of raising the issue at the next news briefing you give. Know exactly what you need to say to make sure the wild rumour is scotched.

More difficult to handle, of course, is the so-called 'expert' on some talk show, speculating as to the cause of an accident. Such people are invariably around when there is a plane crash. A useful case-study in speculation was the Egypt Air crash off the north-east coast of America. They may well be people who have a fine reputation and are indeed experts. But speculation blurs fact – and again you may need to take a decision as to whether you raise the issue and deal with it at the regular briefing.

To brief or not to brief

Regular briefing is one of the best ways of controlling the media coverage in a crisis situation. It's media jargon for discussing what's going on. The Whitehall press officer spends a lot of the time 'briefing' or 'giving guidance', as it is called. Quite a lot of it is off the record, and therefore the source is never known. The off-the-record briefing is one of the politician's favourite ways of sticking the knife into someone or some policy and then disclaiming all knowledge of it. Briefing in a crisis should all be 'on the record'. Even when you are talking on a one-to-one basis, always say what you want to have reported. Don't confuse a reporter by suddenly saying, 'Oh this bit is off the record.' There is no guarantee that it will be; not because the reporter cannot be trusted, but because he will have been confused as to what was on or off the record. Indeed you might even have said that something was off the record when it was already in the public domain – you had said it before in other circumstances. If everything is on the record, then everyone knows where they stand. I must stress, as I did in the last chapter, that you must have a clear idea of what you want to say, and what you don't want to say. And it must be your message. Don't leave it to others.

There are any number of case studies in the management text books about how to manage a crisis in PR terms. Equally there are any number about how not to do it. The classic case of handling a crisis with the product is the Perrier mineral water case. It's well worth reading the whole story, but suffice it to say, they met the problem full on: the water was contaminated, they withdrew the product, reassured the public in all their markets – and then came back even more strongly. There are many other instances.

Let me give you an example of what not to do. I was once talking to a supermarket chain about handling an imagined crisis of someone claiming that they had injected poison into some bars of a particular chocolate in three of their stores. I asked them what they would do, and they said they would immediately call the crisis team together – its members were clearly identified. Next they would call in the police and take their advice as to what to do. I asked whether they would clear the shelves of the allegedly lethal product. 'Only if the police tell us to.' Would they make any public announcement. 'Again that depends on police advice.' I suggested that the crisis management team was not actually managing anything – the people in charge were the police. I believe that while the police play an essential role in these kinds of crisis, you will need to take some decisions. After we had gone through what they had said, they saw for themselves that they had built a system based on other people's responsibility, not their own. They went back to the drawing board and got it right.

The biggest issue here is whether to clear the shelves. Is it the only thing to do? Should you wait? Sometimes you may not have a choice. It might be that if the news leaks out you will need to talk to the media and media pressure may force you to clear the shelves just to reassure public opinion.[37] The golden rule must be that you remain in control of your own crisis. Otherwise at those regular briefings I'm suggesting, you will be parroting someone else's views.

Such briefings provide the perfect opportunity to put your point of view; and they give you control. You know who will be speaking; and you will be able to choose the location – either in a conference room, or on location near the scene. Personally I would suggest that anything that puts you at the location helps establish that you are, figuratively speaking, on top of the job. The pictures will be that much stronger. A bare conference room with the company logo tacked up on a wall behind you makes it seem remote. You are not only beginning to manage your verbal message, but the visual impact as well. If you hold these briefings on an hourly basis, then you can control the way the story develops, you can take some of the issues that others are raising and deal with them. No reporter on the spot will want or dare to miss your briefings, which enables them to raise the new angles as they arise. For your part, you get a better sense of what's being said elsewhere.

While you should have someone to monitor the media during a crisis, you need all the help you can get. Maybe one reporter has been talking exclusively to someone and doesn't want to run the story yet – but needs to check facts with you – this way he still keeps his exclusive, but you are part of it and able to help shape the resulting piece. These days it's not unusual for the 24-hour news channels to run press briefings as they happen. This gives you a moment in the spotlight which allows you to talk directly to the audience, above the head of the media.

The ego has landed

There can be, of course, political problems in choosing who is going to deal with the media in these circumstances. If it is a major crisis, naturally, the spokesman will become quite famous – at least for the duration: rather like some of the generals who briefed the journalists during the Gulf War or the Kosovo crisis.[38] This can prompt jealousy, and even plotting to 'take the spokesman down a peg or two'. If you are the chairman or chief executive you may or may not be the right person to speak on behalf of the company. Are you sure you have the right skills? Sometimes the chairman or chief executive will feel that they are the right people in these circumstances simply because of the job title. Sometimes they are the wrong people because they have an attitude problem vis-à-vis the media,[39] or are not very good public speakers. These difficult decisions must be faced. Some chief executives, on the other hand, will be managing the crisis itself, and are, therefore, fully stretched and have little time to make public pronouncements. The make-up of the crisis management team, if it is properly selected and trained, should help to solve any personality problems. The pressures will be enormous, and soon the strain will begin to tell. Stress can help, but it can also hinder. You really need a roster of people to brief, and they should be established quickly in the media's eyes as the people who will speak.

I remember once watching a breaking story on local TV in New York. One of the power companies had had a blow-out – streets were closed, traffic was diverted, apartments were evacuated. 'With me is the duty press officer …' said the reporter live into the channel. Later I caught the evening news and there was another 'duty press officer on site …' talking to the same reporter. The first was a man, the second was a woman – both wore the safety helmet with the company logo prominently displayed. At one stage the woman press officer said, 'As Bob told you earlier, our equipment …'

The appeal of 'the breaking story'

A crisis is a 'breaking story', as the media likes to call it. The media likes breaking news because it gets the adrenaline pumping – as much, it hopes, with the audience as with the reporters. It is also what the news business is all about – being there, and telling the world. Those helicopter tracking shots of O. J. Simpson pursued by the Los Angeles police along the city's freeways made for gripping television. I suppose you would call this a personal crisis. But it had everything the media likes in a crisis – a clearly identifiable main character – was he a hero or a villain? It was live, it was real, and it was unlike anything ever seen before on TV screens. People stopped what they were doing and just went to the nearest set. Better yet, as the Americans would say, at the time no one knew how the story would end. Would he live or would he die? At the time the public were on the side of the man they called 'The Juice'. And remember, this was a local story, in Los Angeles, yet the images went round the world. It was a local crisis that had international appeal. The perfect media event. It gained audiences, and it earned money through the sale of foreign rights. We've seen other examples, of shoot-outs with fugitives, and football supporters rioting on the streets of Marseilles during the 1998 World Cup. In the 1999 Cricket World Cup, when India met Pakistan in a qualifying match, the media hoped for a clash between the fans. It didn't happen – much, one feels to the chagrin of the networks who had to report the 'good' news.

Some critical situations seem tailor-made for TV, and the pictures say it all. But of course there are other types of crisis – quieter, less visual, more drawn-out. The take-over battle, for example. This can go on for months – and as far as television is concerned there is a terrible lack of pictures. There are also rules and regulations about the coverage of a take-over battle. Both sides should be given equal weight and both must speak to the media. A lot of the detail of the battle would be lost on the average punter – the challenge here is how you reduce some of the verbiage to manageable proportions. I once made a short film for a business programme on Channel Four. The two companies involved were Dixons and Woolworths – it was Woolworths who wanted Dixons. I had marvellous co-operation from both companies – with access to shops and stores around the country, permission to speak to staff and customers – and proper interviews with key players at board level. This ready access enabled me to make a film full of pictures, packed with detail and, I hope, brief the audience on the issues at stake.

150

After the crisis is over – plan for the next

We have covered just some of the ways in which your messages can be better managed in a time of crisis. But simply because you've had one crisis, that doesn't mean something else won't crop up and the midnight call from the duty manager will get you out of bed and back into another crisis. So you must have a proper debriefing after any encounter with the media; could you do it better, what went wrong, what went right, who performed well under pressure, who was believable in from of cameras and microphones. If necessary get in some consultants to do it for you – they will be much more objective and helpful and less prone to be a victim to any internal politics. And don't just analyse your own crisis, but assess how the competition handled theirs. Often when one part of an industry has a problem, it could well become your problem too. In the food industry, for example, some information is shared with the trade association and is available to all members.

I have talked a lot in this and the last chapter about defining the message and managing the message in a time of crisis. I've discussed giving interviews, the power of the picture and the power of language. In the following chapters I want to concentrate on language – its traps and its possibilities. Because it's only half the battle to define your message – deciding on the content, the ideas, the issues or policies you want to talk about. Now it's time to decide how you are going to say it.

TEN KEY POINTS ABOUT CRISIS MANAGEMENT

1. A crisis can happen to anyone – be prepared.
2. Select the best person or persons to deal with media inquiries.
3. If there are human victims, put yourself in the place of the bereaved.
4. The media's coverage of your crisis is not personal; it's just another story.
5. Make sure you understand how the media is reporting the crisis.
6. Keep everyone who needs to know fully briefed on developments.
7. Watch for those who seek to exploit your crisis for their advantage.
8. Always respond to questions – even if there's no new information.
9. Silence denotes confusion; inability to cope, or worse, guilt.
10. When it's all over – make sure any lessons are learned.

14

Watch your language

Every time I hear an interview with a business executive, I find the use of language gets more extraordinary. They indulge in 'business speak', which has had precise meaning squeezed from it. It is made up of phrases that don't really give offence – verbal placebos with no real value. When an interviewer asks, 'Why are you sacking 300 people?', the audience has the right to expect a straight answer. But the executive will talk about downsizing, right-sizing, restructuring, de-layering or flattening. Barclaycard said recently that because it wanted to 'deliver significant improvements to customer services, 1100 jobs would fall away'. As one reporter on The Times pointed out: at least they didn't use that increasingly popular word from America – 'de-emphasised'. Yet when it's good news, firms talk simply of 'taking on more people', or 'creating new jobs'.

Richard Hoggart has some compelling views on the desecration of language in modern society in his book The Way We Live Now:[40]

> More and more this (business) language sounds as though it has fallen off the back of a computer: tranche, revise downwards, trialled, strategies, function, analysis, spectrum of views, structured, targeted, flow charts, matrix management. A higher profile, continuing dialogue, focal, pivotal, interactive, flexible, mainstreaming, sensitised. Many of these words and phrases have justifiable professional uses. They are more often used loosely and inaccurately as modish signs.

Perhaps the tidal wave of such verbiage has peaked. Some of the younger generation see these words for what they are and are beginning to poke fun. While I was working on this book, my daughter, a city lawyer, sent me a copy of an e-mail going the rounds of the Square Mile, which started off:

You know you've been in the corporate world too long when ...

1   You ask the waiter what the restaurant's core competencies are.
2   You talk to the waiter about process flow when the dinner arrives late.
3   You refer to dating as test marketing.
4   You write executive summaries of your love letters.
5   You celebrate your wedding anniversary with a performance review.
6   You decide to reorganise your family into a team-based organisation.
7   You explain to your bank manager that you prefer to think of yourself as 'highly leveraged' not 'overdrawn'.
8   You never have any problems in life, just issues and improvement opportunities.
9   You can use the term 'value added' without falling down laughing.
10 You give constructive feedback to your dog.

Now these are just ten of thirty or more examples of corporate jargon. People may see it for what it is, so why do they go on using such language? They use it because they don't want to be different. They are scared that people will think they don't know the right words. But if you are saying things in exactly the same way as everyone else, no one will notice, let alone remember your message.

Humpty Dumpty

This is why I think industry spokesmen, in the main, have become Humpty Dumpties. 'When I use a word,' Humpty Dumpty said in a rather scornful tone, 'it means just what I want it to mean – neither more nor less.' A lot of people fall into the trap of using words in such a haphazard fashion that you can't always tell what they mean, and they may not mean what they seem to say.

The effectiveness of any message depends primarily on the words. The ancient Greeks and the Romans knew the power of words. One of the greatest of the Roman orators was Marcus Tullius Cicero. In 55BC he wrote a useful little handbook[41] for people contemplating a career in public life. Rhetoric was a recognised skill. This is what he urged his contemporaries:

> To begin with, a knowledge of very many matters must be grasped, without which oratory is but an empty and ridiculous swirl of verbiage; and a distinctive style has to be formed, not only by choice of words but also by arrangement of the same; and all the mental emotions, with which nature has endowed the human race, are to be intimately understood because it is in calming or kindling the feelings of the audience that the full power and science of oratory can be brought into play.

The modern world has developed sophisticated means of communication that would astonish Cicero, but what he has to say about 'the science of oratory' is as true now as it was two millennia ago. And because more of us now need to speak in public, oratorical skills are at a premium. As Cicero went on to point out, to the science of oratory must be added 'a certain humour, flashes of wit, the culture befitting a gentleman and a readiness and a terseness alike in repelling and delivering the attack, the whole being combined with a delicate charm and urbanity'.

Today millions can see, hear and read your message. It can go round the globe in a nanosecond. So ponder well which words you use – don't allow your vocabulary to let you down. We may know what the message is we want to communicate; we've defined it, and tested it, but does it really say what we mean, and do we really mean what we say?

'Peace in our time,' said Neville Chamberlain, waving a scrap of paper he happened to have in his hand at the time he got off the plane from Germany and his fateful meeting with Adolf Hitler. He hoped it was true, but in the end it was a lie and his reputation has been haunted by it ever since. Winston Churchill understood the use of language better than almost any politician in the modern world. He had the knack for the right phrase at the right time, and gave expression to a whole nation's feelings. 'Never in the field of human conflict was so much owed by so many to so few.' Or again, 'Give us the tools and we will finish the job.' And perhaps Tony Blair came close when he talked about 'the People's Princess' on the day that Diana died.[42]

Yet nowadays it's not enough just to come up with a good phrase, although it certainly helps a lot. There's a growing trend in the media to analyse what people say and how they say it. Among press people these days, much time is spent on what's called 'textual analysis'. Which words did you use; what did they mean? Most of all, why did you do it? Anne MacElvoy in a piece in the Telegraph, found a neat historic example in the death of Talleyrand. 'When the news was broken to the great statesman and intriguer Metternich, he was pensive. "I wonder what he meant by that," he said.'

Much the same was asked, of course, on the day that the arch-fraudster Robert Maxwell was reported drowned in the Med. Did he fall, or was he pushed? Did he know he was about to be found out and couldn't stand the disgrace? Actions, they say, 'speak louder than words'. More and more, these days, it's not only the words but the motives that are analysed, so you can't be too careful. And as if that were not enough, it's not only what you say but what you wear that becomes part of the equation. (I'll be tackling body language, clothes and general appearance in the next chapter.) But first, as broadcasters are wont to say: language – its uses and abuses.

Will they believe you?

The poet W. H. Auden wrote, 'Beware of words, for with words we lie.' As we have seen,[43] there is a growing sense of disbelief among the general public about what the people in authority say and mean. It is as if audiences tend to suspend belief in the official statement. What's more, they suspend judgement too – and therefore express very little surprise when the truth comes out, and that truth is at odds with what was said in the first place. In President Clinton's TV confessional about his relationship with Monica Lewinsky, most surprisingly, there was almost no reaction when he stated, 'I did not volunteer information.' Prior to the announcement, almost everyone had guessed that he would say he had lied to protect his family. They were wrong. In the event Clinton said only that 'while his answers were legally accurate' he did not 'volunteer information'. To use another famous quote by a British civil servant when under pressure: he had been 'economical with the truth'.

An example from nearer home, in Britain, was how newspaperman James Bartholomew, in the Daily Mail, covered Tony Blair's first cabinet re-shuffle. He wrote a column entitled 'What they said and what they really meant'. Alastair Darling, the new Social Security Secretary, said, 'The time for talking and discussing is coming to an end. We now actually need to implement our programmes. I am determined to ensure that the whole process of welfare reform moves from being a series of ideas into a firm plan that we can implement and work.' According to Bartholomew, what Darling was actually saying was: 'I haven't a clue what to do about welfare reform.' Of course, as Bartholomew pointed out, some people really mean what they say. Well, more or less. He quoted Diane Abbott, an MP and a member of Labour's National Executive as saying jokingly, 'I don't think Peter Mandelson is that friendly to any form of human life.' Bartholomew repeated it word for word but added, 'It wasn't a joke.' Denial is the easiest way to get off the hook of public interest. Phrases like 'We are just good friends', 'This marriage will never end', 'I'm staying with the club; there is no truth that I want a transfer', or even Mrs Thatcher's 'My wonderful chancellor', before she forced him out, are part of the modern malaise of 'Deny everything, explain later'.

In economics Gresham's Law states that bad money drives out good. If you clip the coinage, then people no longer value it as much. It's what's happening to the verbal currency of the day. The words these days may sound the same, but what do they really mean? John Profumo was the last man to resign from Parliament because he lied. He paid for that sin for the rest of his professional life by doing good works among the down-and-outs in the East End. Nobody nowadays would resign because of a lie. Worse, few would expect them to. 'Your mission', as they intone at the beginning of that TV series Mission Impossible, 'is to find language that the public will believe and trust.'

Say what you mean?

The first move must be to avoid ambiguity and keep the language simple and direct. You must not confuse. Let me give you one simple example. I once interviewed a senior executive at the Post Office about the changes that had been made in the 'business', as it was now called. 'The biggest innovation,' he said, 'is that we now have dedicated managers in our three main businesses – mail, parcels and counters.' I came back and asked, 'You mean the managers were not dedicated to the job before?' 'No,' he answered, 'no one was dedicated in any way. Then you did whatever job was to hand. Now we are dedicated to one particular business.' Slowly I began to see what he was talking about. What he meant by dedication was not the same as I had understood him to mean. He didn't mean 'dedication' as in 'love for the job, the determination to do your best'. He meant it as being 'assigned' to a specific business. Afterwards we chatted and he said he couldn't see how I had misunderstood the word. He used it all the time. I discovered that he and the other members of the change team had spent six months on the project – the key element of which was to bring about a system of 'dedicated' management. They had lived with that word and that concept every day. It had become a shortcut to a whole manual on the change in the business. No one ever questioned it, or saw it in any other way. In that interview, I had heard the word for the first time in months – possibly last heard in another context. My mind heard the word one way – he used it in another.

With a language such as English, which is changing all the while, the chances of getting it wrong when you create your message are huge. The BBC's News Guide for its reporters has some basic rules that are worth following. It tells its journalists:

> BBC news wants a style that is crisp, economical, direct and colloquial, but not slangy or slapdash, relaxed yet precise. It prefers the short word to the long one; the simple sentence to the complex; the concrete to the abstract; the active voice to the passive; the direct statement to the inverted sentence. We do not write for pedants. But we shun journalese.

The problem is that there is no such thing as Standard English, and many modern pundits seem to make it up as they go along – often with hilarious results.[44] Precision of meaning is not always easy to achieve – which is why the lawyers make so much money settling disputes caused by the careless drafting of important documents. What follows are some of the problem areas – and some of the grotesque new words that have popped into everyday use.

Mad cows and Englishmen

In today's psychobabble, when you don't want to know about something, you are 'in denial'. So is business in 'denial' at times when a popular word becomes the stick with which the media beat them. Thus when business comes up against a word or phrase from the real world which they find difficult to handle, they try to wish it away by using another word in its place. Let me give you an example of a phrase which the National Farmers' Union wishes had never been coined. That phrase is 'mad cow disease'. For a long time their officials always used the letters BSE or Bovine Spongiform Encephalopathy. They insisted that 'mad cow disease' gave the wrong impression of the true problem – in their view it was a scientific issue that would be cured by science. They were angry that the media insisted in provoking public concern with such an emotive phrase.

To make matters worse, television news programmes had come across some footage of a cow slipping and sliding. It looked 'mad'. The image and the phrase began to circulate quite freely, summoning up the image of that cow. I think the NFU spent a great deal of time trying to fight the way the subject was debated, and questioning the language, seeing the use of the phrase as an attack on British farmers. rather than grappling with the issue itself. They were convinced that Brussels duly became involved because of the British media and its wild talk of mad cows. The NFU also showed the typical reaction of a group that is suddenly under pressure – everyone else was wrong, only it was right. This allowed pressure groups for a whole variety of issues to get involved: the vegetarian lobby; consumer interests, animal rights and so forth. Such groups quickly caught on to the phrase and soon discovered that they just had to use the three words 'mad cow disease' to get attention and be quoted in the media.

Because the farmers and their representatives at the NFU felt beleaguered they came to believe that nobody was on their side. Every question by a reporter was seen as another attack. 'They', the media, had decided what the problem was, and 'we', the farmers, were not listened to. The head of public affairs tried to turn the tide – a daunting job in itself. Part of the problem was to get the farmers to accept that they had to do something. Yet even then there were some amazing moments when, for example, one farmers' spokesman told me, 'There were only 50,000 cases of BSE in the past twelve months.' I pointed out that this worked out at around 1000 a week, over 150 a day. What he hadn't said, I discovered later, was that he was talking about 50,000 cases down from many many times that in a herd of millions.

The curious fact was that the farming industry had had recent experience of a sudden outbreak of public mistrust. Edwina Currie's 'salmonella in eggs' remark had sent egg sales plummeting almost overnight. Egg producers went out of business. When it comes to food and health, the public is extra cautious. People prefer to avoid something over which there is a question mark, rather than risk their lives. Despite this experience, and the problems it had caused, the industry, like the Bourbons, seemed incapable of learning, and unable to forget. When supermarkets started to buy cheaper meat and eggs abroad, given the strength of the pound, the farmers tried to get public opinion on their side. The public may have been sympathetic, but no one boycotted the cheaper food in the supermarket.

The jibes that stick

Once a word or phrase becomes current, you can't refashion the language. My advice is that if you can't beat them, join them. Accept the word or phrase, and try to turn it to your advantage. The single-word or single-phrase reference coined by a sub-editor can be well-nigh impossible to shake off. Ask David Mellor, once a cabinet minister and Tory high flyer. Now justly famed for his own media career, he would, I know, much prefer to be back in full-time politics. But he found it difficult, if not impossible, to live down the notion that he wore a Chelsea football shirt while having his toes sucked by his mistress – a former actress, who, it was alleged had once appeared in a porno movie. Even with his media savvy, he then compounded the whole problem by getting his family and his father-in-law to pose uneasily at the garden gate while they played happy families. Soon afterwards divorce proceedings were started.

That was an extreme case of media inspired chickens coming home to roost. Politics is the cruellest of worlds, and a word or phrase uttered in debate can stick like cling-film. Geoffrey Howe was once famously likened to a 'dead sheep' by Denis Healey. In fact, the full phrase was even more hurtful. Healey claimed that he had been 'savaged by a dead sheep'. And it was another politician, Norman Lamont, who accused John Major's government of being 'in office but not in power'. Those remarks were meant to hurt. Sometimes, however, a word spoken in an unguarded moment at what you believe to be a private affair is suddenly blazoned over the front pages. The former Prime Minister, John Major, usually a mild-mannered man, was heard fulminating about the 'bastards' in his cabinet. These were the people who were working to stop Britain's entry into a single currency and in so doing were wrecking his own carefully constructed but very fragile semblance of unity. These words become part of the general currency of the moment: some have a longer life than others.

Politicians seem to thrive in this atmosphere – even though quite a few have their careers blighted by it. If you are a politician, you make sure that you know all such references in case an interviewer suddenly asks, 'Are you one of the bastards in Mr Major's cabinet?' Under Labour life goes on as before. The party brought over 100 women into the House of Commons, a massive achievement for feminism – yet in a misjudged photo-call they were dubbed 'Blair's babes' and haven't really survived that nickname.

They used to say that 'sticks and stones may break my bones but words will never hurt me'. Now the most hurtful thing you could say to someone is to ridicule their looks, and question their attractiveness. I suggested earlier that sometimes it is best not to fight it, but accept it and turn it to your advantage. The most unlikely heroine of the media, as I write, is Ann Widdecombe. She coined the famous phrase about Michael Howard, her boss at the Home Office, when she was in power, that 'he had something of the night about him'. He will never shake it off. Her own enemies cruelly called her Doris Karloff. Yet far from retreating bruised and depressed, Ms Widdecombe revels in the nickname. I'm told her answerphone replies 'Karloff here'. It's prophylactic self-disparage-ment, deflecting the arrows of criticism and turning a potentially hurtful and insulting attack into a triumphant assertion of independence. In her case, words do not hurt. She's a rare example, but worth studying for her ability to adopt unpopular views and yet be respected because people accept that she really believes in what she says.

Personal vendettas

Business is not quite as bad as politics in terms of personal vendettas. The top business executive seems to be more circumspect about showing his true feel-ings for a rival. Mind you, the running battle between Mohamed Al Fayed, the owner of Harrods, and the late Tiny Rowland of Lonrho, would take some beating in any walk of life. Rowland was not above using the Observer, a news-paper he owned for a time, in that battle. He published pamphlets and would brief any journalist prepared to listen on what he saw as Al Fayed's 'crimes and lies'. Al Fayed, however, is a man obsessed by his reputation and Nixon-like, is said to tape every conversation, and even bug telephone calls made by his staff. So in the business world, too, a battle can still get nasty and very personal.

Peter Tatchell's pressure group 'Outrage' has, of course, made a name for itself by 'outing' those bishops it sees as hypocritical about gays and the Church. Some, he claims, are in fact gay in private, yet maintain an almost monastic vow of silence in the debate as to whether homosexuals should be fully included in the life of the Church. Worse, some even take the Establishment line that gays cannot be included fully because of what the Bible says.

The danger is when verbal abuse turns to physical abuse. It's a sign that the argument may have been lost – so here direct action is the answer, since nobody will listen. That's the logic. Extreme Animal Rights groups have attacked various research establishments, and injured people, in pursuance of their aims. And every now and then there's the case of a product which has been interfered with, perhaps injected with poison, because of either blackmail or a vendetta. The Unibomber in America attacked technology-based targets. At the fringe there can be real personal danger; but in the mainstream, it is words that are the weapons. So if you are going to get involved in public debate, then be aware of who's saying what in general – and about you, your business or your industry in particular.

Paying for other people's sins

Increasingly the executive finds that the interview is as much about what others are doing in the industry, as in the executive's own firm. Let me cite a specific example. If you run a recently privatised public utility, you don't need me to tell you that the debate over pay rises for directors and huge bonuses has given rise to the 'greed' in the boardroom in general, and the 'fat cats' in the utilities in particular. You may be on a very modest income. You may have waived your bonuses. You may give any pay rise to charity, but as far as the media and the public are concerned you are one of the 'fat cats', the incarnation of 'corporate greed'. It's no use hoping that the charge won't be made in an interview. You had better have a good answer well prepared. To stay silent is an admission of guilt.

Another example might concern anyone in charge of one of the newly privatised railway companies. The relentless amount of data on trains running late, or not running at all, means that even the most successful company finds it difficult to be seen as apart from the dismal herd. And when excuses are made about 'leaves on the line' or the 'wrong kind of snow' holding up trains – then you had better be able to explain exactly what the wrong kind of snow is, or why leaves, so delicate and pretty as they fall in autumn, can halt a huge diesel train pulling half a dozen carriages with a few hundred people on board. The rule has to be awareness of the public agenda, and of the public's mood. For even the worst interviewer, there is some benefit to be won in raising such issues during an on-air exchange.

Political correctness

This is a huge subject, and I can't possibly do it justice here. But be warned that this can be the most difficult area of all in the management of the message. There are many pressure groups just waiting to pounce if you slip up here.

Sexism and Racism are the two great offences that you must avoid at all costs. In America, for example, you would not say 'Black People' but 'African Americans'. I was interviewing someone on the Today programme early one Saturday morning – at 7.22 to be precise – when the individual, talking about the amount of paperwork emanating from Brussels said, 'We've been working like blacks to fill in all the forms in time.' Almost before he had completed the sentence, the phone was ringing in the production office. Formal complaints were made, against him for uttering the statement, and against me for not stopping him and making him apologise. I remember once that a female boxer on the programme telephoned in to complain that Sue MacGregor had called her a woman boxer, whereas she was a 'lady boxer'. At times people seem to get their languages into quite a mix-up; for example, the gay community finds it acceptable to say 'homophobic', but not 'homosexual'. And you can find some members of the community who prefer the word 'queer'.

'He' is a simple word that these days can be fraught with danger. We must remember that 'she' is just as likely to be doing the job. So sometimes we say 'they', which seems to cover both eventualities. However, we start to get our grammar in a twist when we try to use the plural form of the verb when really we are talking about one person. If you know the gender of the person involved, state it clearly. Personally I don't like words like 'chair' for chairman or chairwoman. I hate 'chairperson' even more, just as I dislike 'foreperson', and I've even heard 'waitperson' instead of waitress or waiter. And another description in the catering trade is 'barperson'.[45] Whatever your personal views about the sense or nonsense of such verbal formulations, keep them to yourself to avoid trouble.

Avoid patronising words like 'girls' unless it's a girls' school. In fact, men of a certain age can find themselves in some difficulties as to what words may give offence. Check with your daughter if you have one. I do.

Suffix-gate

Beware words where the suffix 'gate' has been added. This has become the cliché to end all clichés. The Tory government's great sleaze scandal even became known as 'Sleazegate'. And under Labour I've seen the word 'Croney-gate'. The oddest fact about 'gate' is that I've seen it used in French and Italian added to some word or other, a truly international suffix. In the United States, where they are very adept at coining neologisms, it is worth remembering that the first use of the word was actually to do with a huge hotel complex in Washington DC which was called The Watergate. Some supporters of President Nixon were caught there breaking into the Democratic headquarters. It led inexorably to the fall of the President and the whole affair became known as Watergate.

By some curious leap of imagination, commentators thought it too good a piece of shorthand to lose when another scandal broke. Under President Clinton there have been a few – all with the word 'gate' added. His most persistent problem, it was said, was his 'zipper' – referring tactfully to his seemingly insatiable appetite for sexual activity with women. Very quickly it became known as 'Zippergate'. Will this spell the end for the ubiquitous suffix? If 'gate' is attached to anything that you are doing – you could have a problem. But I think you should not use it yourself except in very rare and obvious circumstances.

New words, old ideas

The English language is the richest in the world, with new words being fashioned almost every day; and these new words flood in from all over the world where English is spoken. Curiously, though, only some of these words reach the surface, and then become used relentlessly until they die of speech fatigue. But it's useful to be aware of the current 'buzz words' or fashionable phrases. Some are quite amusing – for a time. Some people, when they are sacked, say they've been iced. It's an acronym for 'involuntary career event'. There also seems to be a penchant for using prefixes and suffixes. Like the word 'gate' we were just discussing, one word or phrase can sometimes speak volumes. For example, there was a time, not so many years ago, when you either had 'charisma' or you didn't. Where did that word go? The media suddenly got hooked on the idea that diplomats or envoys 'brokered' deals. Nowadays you can find that everyone is 'downsizing'. And of course the media, if not the public, were obsessed with 'spin' and 'spin doctors'. A relatively recent newcomer is 'retro', which means something from the past, or something done later to, say, an existing building or piece of machinery. It's also very big in the fashion world, in the sense of today's clothes quoting from the past. Sometimes you can see such fashionable words paraded in a single sentence, which seems to say everything and nothing. I wouldn't be surprised to read a story with the headline: 'Spin doctor brokers downsizing deal.'

But such words, no matter how fashionable, will not always help if you want to make your meaning known to your audience. We all seem to be 'addressing issues' instead of 'dealing with the problem'. In fact, 'issue' covers a multitude of sins. It's a word that allows the speaker to slide off the hook. The interviewer alleges people are sick in your plant because there's a poisonous gas escaping from some decrepit machinery; and the answer is the comfortable 'That is one of the issues we know we have to address.' Furthermore, they'll probably set up a 'help line' and 'call in counsellors' to address the issue.

Another very widely used phrase is 'dumbing down'. The BBC has been on the receiving end of endless charges of 'dumbing down' its output. The phrase arrived in Britain from the United States; as always, American phrases tend to be more quickly accepted here than home-grown words. 'Dumbing down' is a handy lump of mud to sling at anyone or anything that tries to be more popular, and appeal to a wider audience. It smacks a little of the class system in Britain, where an elite minority don't want the masses to gain access to their own interests or art forms. For example, any attempt to render opera more accessible to people who don't think they will understand it is immediately condemned as 'dumbing down'. When the British Civil Service decided to do away with Latin expressions or words a few years back, obviously it was 'dumbing down'; the fact that very few schools still teach Latin (alas) did not enter into the debate.

Verbal imports

The English language is rich because it is so widely spoken, and therefore millions of people contribute to the vocabulary. Many of the world's other major languages complain that they are being swamped by English imports. We Brits are also on the receiving end of foreign imports. Some are useful, some are not.

There was a brief vogue for the German word 'Schadenfreude' – taking delight in a friend's difficulties. It was widely used when, surprise, surprise, Germany began to experience some of the symptoms of the English disease. But beware foreign words in case you get them wrong. Remember the case of John F. Kennedy who, meaning to say to the cheering people of Berlin on his visit to their then divided city, 'I am a Berliner', announced, 'I am a sugar coated cookie.' Or the time that President Carter, on a visit to Warsaw in 1978, meaning to proclaim 'I love the Poles', came out with 'I desire the Poles carnally.' No one had bothered to check the translation from the original American text.

Of course some imported words don't make it big in the verbal charts. Take 'SNAFU', for example. This is an abbreviation which stands for 'situation normal, all fucked up', and it was first used by the American military. Not everyone in a British audience will understand these imports. Equally, when talking to an American audience, avoid using British words. There are any number of British-American dictionaries available, and it's worth making sure that you are using a word like 'gabfest' properly.

There have been 'Plain English' campaigns galore, but to no avail. The insurance industry is notorious not only for the minuscule type size of its printed matter, but also for the cumbersome way in which its various restrictions or additions are expressed. Yet in the business world, increasingly, we worry about the 'bottom line' and talk about the CEO (chief executive officer) when we really mean 'managing director'. So pick your words with care, especially if they are imports. Faute de mieux, always plump for an English word.

Danger, wordsmith at work

The danger nowadays for the would-be communicator is that language is changing so fast that you can often be left behind. It would seem oddly old-fashioned if you announced that a 'deal you had just brokered' was 'a wizard prang', a phrase from a 1940s air force barrack room where the 'chaps' were waiting to 'scramble'. Sometimes the Prince of Wales's obsession with the Goon Show is a sure sign of someone caught in a time-warp. For younger readers I should explain that it was a cult radio show through the 1950s starring the late

Michael Bentine and Peter Sellers, and the still-living Sir Harry Secombe and Spike Milligan. They fashioned popular phrases galore – but they have faded as has the memory.

How to be original

Although it may be comforting to be familiar with the fashionable words that everyone else uses, it pays to be as original as possible. Some phrases become so over-used that they mock the person who can find no alternatives. The most famous clichés tend to come from the world of sport. 'Sick as a parrot' and 'over the moon' can only be used in a self-mocking way. 'A game of two halves' is another phrase which has had its day, but won't go away. Again, there are some phrases from sport which stick around for a long time. 'They think it's all over … It is now!' That was the sports commentator Kenneth Wolstenholme's immortal coinage when England scored the final goal to win the 1966 World Cup. On the other hand, cricketing expressions such as 'keeping a straight bat' and 'playing on a sticky wicket' seem to be useful for all occasions. But again they should be used with caution; not everyone likes or even understands cricket. I suppose the advice would be to use it in the season and not outside it.

There are no easy rules on how to acquire a good current vocabulary which you can deploy as and when the need arises. In my own business, words are the currency and means of exchange. You develop almost a sixth sense that registers a new or potentially useful word. Because I work in the media, maybe I am more receptive to the words that swirl around my head. Even when I am watching TV or listening to the radio, I'm researching what the other people are up to – what is said and how. For the business executive, developing this research skill is just as important as acquiring the rather limited business vocabulary that he or she is forced to use in the office or at work in general.

Business speak

Business speak is a dreadful concoction. I firmly believe it is the enemy of good communication. Its aim seems to be to make the meaning of what you say so vague that no one can be offended, and if your view is called into question, you can repeat the innocuous phrases and get away with the charge. What does a phrase like 'We are comfortable with that' actually mean? Or 'We can live with that'? And when companies say they will be 'aggressive' in building market share, are they, to use another phrase used by a politician, 'going to put tanks on your lawn'? And talking of lawns, what manure do you use to 'grow' a company? 'Let's talk schedules' so that we 'can do lunch one day'. Maybe the worst word of the lot is the ubiquitous 'meeting'. I actually heard two people who had bumped into each other unexpectedly say, 'We need to meet.'

People no longer give a view about something; they 'share a vision' or a 'concept'. Something that is easy is often dismissed as 'It's not rocket science.' Some of the older phrases seem to hang around forever. People still talk about 'blue sky thinking', and 'running it up the flagpole to see who salutes it'. Executives seem to want to hide behind the business cliché and no longer say what they really mean. Using such vacuous claptrap is no way to talk to the public at large. There are over 300,000 words and phrases in the latest Oxford Dictionary – business seems to use less than 100 of them.

The history of a word

In the business world, phrases and sayings seem to change very little. In the real world, words suddenly become current, and get lodged in the mind of the public. 'Sleaze' was a word that came to haunt the Tories. 'Cronyism' is a term that has been haunting New Labour since it came to office. Such key words only need to be said or written for the whole story suddenly to appear on the screens of our minds as the words on a computer screen will suddenly appear when you press 'go sleaze' or 'go cronyism'. It's not often that anyone bothers to trace the origin of a new word that suddenly makes it big, but James Landale did that in The Times one Saturday. I hope he'll forgive me if I use some of his research now:

It was the Tory historian Lord Blake who was the first to coin the sound bite 'Tony Crony' when he wrote about the appointment of the Queen's

> spin doctor Simon Lewis ... In a newspaper column on June 24 he pointed out that Mr Lewis counted both Peter Mandelson and Sarah Macauley, Gordon Brown's girlfriend, among his close friends. Mr Lewis's wife, he said, was a close friend of Cherie Blair and their children went to the same school in Islington. In short Mr Lewis might reasonably be called a Tony Crony ...

According to Landale, two weeks later William Hague spoke about the 'culture of cronyism' in an attack on the government's controversial links with lobbyists. And then comes a fascinating bit of research:

> In the four weeks since Mr Hague used the word it has appeared some 132 times in national newspapers. Over the previous three years it had been used on only 200 occasions, most frequently in describing American or third world politicians.

Further investigation by the seemingly indefatigable Landale also showed how Hague had so liked the phrase that he had systematically continued to use it. But first he did a little research of his own. He tried it out in a controlled environment – in a speech to party workers in Buxton. The speech was disseminated by Central Office, and Tory MPs then started to use the term at every opportunity. By the time it cropped up in Prime Minister's Questions, Hague had honed it and refashioned it into a number of phrases. Repetition, with variations, is a classic debating technique. And alliteration – as in 'culture of cronyism' always helps to jog future memory. The Prime Minister, opined the Leader of the Opposition, should 'tackle the culture of cronyism', not 'protect his cronies' who are 'feather-bedding, pocket-lining, money-grabbing cronies'. Great stuff, and then he rounded it off by saying that the government had 'too many cronies, not enough principles'. From then on every appointment had to undergo the 'crony test'.

Yet 'crony' is by no means a new word. Landale says it first appeared in print in Samuel Pepys's diary in 1665. The Oxford English Dictionary describes cronyism as 'the appointment of friends to government jobs without proper regard to the qualifications'. On the day that Landale's piece was printed, Gus Macdonald had been made an industry minister in Scotland – he was not even in the Lords, though a title would soon be his. The date was 8 August. It's not often than one can so easily pinpoint the emergence of a new piece of verbal shorthand, and trace its trajectory. Hague, in this instance at least, in terms of managing a message had done everything right.

How long 'crony' will stay the course is anyone's guess. It also depends on how Labour's spin doctors manage to get out from under it. So far they have come up with denial, and the accusation that it's a desperate ploy by a disheartened opposition to be noticed. It is always a sign of panic when people on the receiving end of a campaign in which there is some truth start trying to dismiss it as just 'play-acting'. The only answer is to make sure that no new appointment can fall into the crony category which would allow the opposition to make political capital.

Like a new star in the heavens, these are the words and phrases to try to spot and then use to brighten up your speech. It demonstrates that you are up-to-date, even in the know. And of course it helps get your message across in a more effective way. This shorthand way of speaking ensures that audiences who see or hear you in the broadcast media, or read what you have said in their newspaper, will more quickly and surely get your point and, better still, absorb it. But don't ignore the richness of the language, or the wonderful words at our disposal. I shared an office with John Tusa when we were presenters in the early days of Newsnight. John always like to include at least one word in his script that would send the audience rushing to look it up in the dictionary; not to see what it meant, which was obvious from the script, but rather how to spell it. My favourite word is floccinaucinihilipilification. It's the longest word in the English language. In plain English, it means 'without value'.

TEN KEY POINTS ABOUT LANGUAGE

1   There are 300,000 words and phrases in the English language – use more of them.
2   Make sure that everyone can understand the words that you use.
3   Don't be too technical; avoid jargon and boring business speak.
4   Keep up-to-date with language – the current buzz words which everyone is using.
5   Remember that words used in one context can come back to haunt you in another situation.
6   Make your phrases memorable, like Ann Widdecombe who said there was 'something of the night' about Michael Howard.
7   Don't go into denial when someone uses a word or phrase you don't like – fight back with it.
8   Listen to what others are saying about you, your business and your industry – in the public's mind you represent all of them, not just yourself.
9   It's not what you say but how you say it.
10 Words alone are not always enough.

15

Tricks for the memory

The place was the Today programme studio, the time around 7.20 a.m. I knew that the interviewee was going to have trouble from the moment he sat down at the microphone opposite me. He had immediately surrounded himself with a mass of papers set out on the desk in semicircular fashion. There were blue markers and red markers highlighting various lines. At a guess he had about ten pages of notes. Just to make matters worse, he had lines going from one phrase to another further down the page. Up the side and round the bottom were pencil-written additions. And all that was before we even got to the interview. He began, 'I've five points I want to make ...' He got to number three before he forgot what the fourth was, let alone the fifth. He tried to sift through his papers, he couldn't find his list, and his voice trailed away.

The interviewer at a moment like this nearly always comes to the rescue and fills the dead air with another question. 'Let's take the first of those points,' I said. 'When do you think that will happen?' Almost without thinking, 'There are three reasons.' You've already guessed, I'm sure, that he only managed two of them. The interview meandered on for about another minute, but his heart was not in it; he was desperately sifting the papers when the merciful release came. Via my ear-piece which links a broadcaster to the control desk, the programme editor told me that the next interviewee would be in the studio within seconds. 'Wrap, when you can, Peter.' I made a longish summary of what I had been told the interviewee's message to the nation was that morning. He said it was more or less what the situation was. And we moved to the next person, now safely seated alongside him, without a single piece of paper in sight.

I have told this story at some length because it is not a rare event in the radio or television studio. A good interviewer will not needlessly embarrass his interviewee, quickly filling any lacunae with another question, or less than challenging remark. Years ago when I was presenting the Money Programme I introduced a leading foreign exchange manager from one of the High Street banks. We were to discuss why the pound had fallen out of bed. There was one of those longish introductions much beloved by TV programme makers, in which they set out the background and recent events. It went on for about three minutes. When it was over I turned to the expert and asked him, 'Why ...?' There was absolute silence. Nerves had obviously cut his vocal chords. I offered to rephrase the question. Perhaps I didn't put it in the right way. Slowly the vein in his cheek stopped throbbing and he started to talk. After that I had trouble stopping him when the allotted time was up.

When I got home after the show, my wife said, 'I thought your foreign exchange man was interesting, but you really should keep your questions shorter and to the point.' Well, that's sound advice in any circumstances to an inter- viewer, but she had not noticed the interviewee's discomfort. A job well done.

You should never underestimate the pressures that build when you take your message out into the world and deliver it. You may have taken all the steps that I have been suggesting, but it won't necessarily prepare you for the real thing. It's rather like learning to parachute – until the moment you are standing at the open door a few thousand feet above England's green and pleasant land. Nerves are part of the process. In humans, as in animals, they set the adrenaline pumping: it's nature's way of making you more alert to danger, and more aware of what you have to do. So don't take any drug that will counteract the nerves or the adrenaline. Don't drink – even one can dull the senses. Worse, if anyone smells drink on your breath, the word goes out that maybe you have a drink problem and you'll never be asked back again.

When the mind goes blank

There is always, just before you go on air or up to the podium, a moment when your mind goes blank. Even after fourteen years on the Today show I still felt the pressure when the clock was ticking round to the start time, then suddenly the green light would go on, and you were off and running, 'And a very good morning to you, this is Today with ...' The very act of speaking seems to relieve the tension. It's almost on to autopilot now, though you can still flick to hands on if an emergency arises. So don't worry about the nerves.

When your mind goes blank, you haven't lost the message. It is still in the brain. The question is where is the message that you've put in the brain?

The man who couldn't remember his lists was suffering not just from information overload, but information confusion. As you refine your message, simplicity must be the watchword. Simplify, don't complicate. If lists are easier for you to remember, try to keep them to three rather than five – too many anyway for a three-minute interview, taking up so much time that you won't leave room for anything else. In fact, the preparation for a particular interview should involve concentrating on the interview in hand – you may only need one, at most two points. As I keep stressing, at every opportunity, stick to the point, make it simple and straightforward. If you yourself have difficulty in delivering the message, there is no way that that your audience, listening to it pass their ears at the speed of sound, will remember anything of it.

When Bill Cockburn was in charge of the Post Office, one of his press officers told me that he used to work on his preparation for an interview by writing the key points on a small index card. He could jot down any number of them in the time before he went on air, over and over again, sharpening, refining, lightening, adapting, improving, restructuring, until he had done it so many times that he would put the card in his pocket when he went into the studio, knowing exactly what he wanted to say and how.

That was his way. Some people, I know, try to learn their answers by heart. This is not a good idea for a variety of reasons. First of all the brain will stop if it thinks it's not quite right. Learning it by heart constricts you; and there is the danger that you will repeat it parrot-fashion. What you need, first of all, is a clear sense of what you want to say. But since all interviews on the day are slightly different, you may need to tweak the message ever so slightly. Don't lock yourself into just one way of saying something – as long as the sense is maintained, the English language is a wonderfully flexible tool. You should never be stuck for the right words. Make an effort to find them.

Too many interviews are used as an opportunity to make claims: 'We are one of the leading firms in the industry ...', 'We are the foremost providers of ...', 'No one comes anywhere near our level of customer service ...' What these proud interviewees forget to give is a fact or two to prove the claim. 'We have a customer care policy that is second to none ...' Where have we heard that before? Find a story that illustrates the point. It must be true, it must be current, and it must be brief. If you can't find a true story to back up the claim, then don't make it. Examples are more telling than too many individual facts and figures.

And while I'm on this subject, remember that figures don't help but hinder the message for the listener. 'We've had a 30 per cent increase in sales since last year.' A 30 per cent increase from what to what? 'We export 14.73 per cent of the production of our biggest selling line (which itself accounts for £3 million a year) to over 17 different countries.' You would have to be a mathematical genius, hearing that flung at you from a radio or TV set, to grasp the point. You would have to be 'Brain of Britain' to be able to remember it absolutely perfectly. And at the end of the day, does it actually mean anything? Or did the export sales director just give it you off the top of his head when you asked, 'How are we doing with exports?'

Examples, examples, examples

Throughout this book, I've tried to give examples to illustrate the point I was making. Nearly all of them are drawn from my own experience, so I know they happened. The example is a pertinent little story that you tell with conviction; and the interviewer cannot really interrupt while you are telling it. You should always tell these stories as if you have just remembered them. This way they are much more persuasive and seem very much more to the point. They will, of course, have been worked out beforehand; and because they are yours, you will find them easier to remember.

Let's look at an imaginary example. You are asked, 'What's your export record like?' Now rather than give facts and figures, great boring lists, the best tactic would be to take an actual product. So you answer, 'We concentrate on hair care products and our latest product is a new hair-dryer called

"Soft Breeze".' You've explained in a sentence what you do, and have managed to mention your latest product. You have identified one product, which narrows the focus of the story and makes it easier for the listener to follow. And since it is a single product, it's easier for you to remember the details that you want to give. So you can go on, 'We have sold over four and a half million of them since the world launch six months ago. Our biggest market is the Indian sub-continent where the main competition is so worried it tried to get the "Soft Breeze" hair-dryer banned. We took our case to court and won hands down. In fact, the publicity helped us enormously and we've letters galore from satisfied customers. Here's one that arrived this week. It's from Mrs Gupta, a housewife in Delhi: "You have changed not only my hair, but my life."'

You should always have a few example like this up your sleeve – because you may need them at any time, for the sales trip, the presentation, the interview or the annual report. By keeping them up-to-date, they will say more than you can convey with lists, bald facts and figures, or just boastful claims. Examples show the reality of the world in which you operate.

The best advice, however, is not to clutter your memory with too many facts in the first place. The object of the exercise is to be able to communicate your message as effectively as possible in public – the less you put into your mind, the less you need to remember, the less you forget, and the more you stick to the point.

TEN STEPS TO REMEMBERING THE MESSAGE

1 Simplify, don't complicate, the message.

2 Write the key facts as bullet-points on a small card.

3 Keep lists short – never more than three points to a list.

4 Keep refining them, until they are firmly imprinted on your mind.

5 Use real examples to prove a point.

6 Keep examples and facts up-to-date.

7 Nothing should be more than a week old.

8 Make it your own language, not that of someone else.

9 Avoid difficult or unpronounceable words or phrases.

10 The less you put into your memory, the more you will remember.

16

Ourselves as others see us

These days, increasingly, words alone are not enough. No matter how well you've defined your message, and no matter how well and carefully you've chosen your words — more is still needed. There is an equally important tool in the communication of any message. On a public platform and, most specifically, on television there's another language we use (or abuse) — body language.

The day after President Clinton's video-taped evidence was shown on world-wide television, newspapers dug around for experts in body language. In the Daily Mail, for example, Dr Raj Persaud, a consultant psychologist, wrote a column headlined 'Charmer betrayed by body language'. Let me quote just one small paragraph to give you the flavour. 'He waves his hands in a defensive gesture often used by people desperate to convince an unbelieving audience.' Or, 'He shifts uncomfortably in his seat, swallows a lot, and clears his throat prominently.' Some might argue that having to talk about what he had to talk about would make anyone shift uncomfortably, or swallow a lot — after all he gave four hours of testimony. The average broadcast interview is barely four minutes. Yet it is a fact that our bodies do a lot of speaking for us, even before we open our mouths. And what's becoming more common in the media these days, increasingly, is that this aspect of a TV performance is discussed and analysed just as much as the words that are uttered.

Another vivid example was obviously the interview that Princess Diana gave to the BBC's Panorama programme. How she sat, how she fluttered her heavily made-up eyes, her hand movements, her whole body posture — all came under the spotlight of media attention. It was judged a masterly performance and added to the power of such phrases as 'There were three people in the marriage. It was rather crowded.' That phrase, on its own, was dramatic enough, but when uttered by a seemingly fragile, hurt but still beautiful princess opening her heart to the nation – it was devastating.

The lessons were not lost on another young woman who felt that she had been wronged. Nine months or so later, Louise Woodward, the nanny found guilty of killing baby Eapen, gave her first TV interview. And who else did she choose but Martin Bashir, the man who had interviewed Diana? Louise faced the same searching analysis of her 'performance' by the media. She was not so much a convicted murderer trying to prove her innocence, it was as if she were a new actress portraying St Joan in a West End theatre for the first time. Grace Bradbury, writing in The Times, noticed what she wore as much as what she said: 'From the look of it she had received more coaching than Alan Shearer, but will it do her any good? ... Her hands rested on her lap, her suit was dark and her hair was highlighted ... if you are trying to establish your innocence, you would hardly go for blood-red lips and nails.' The Sun, as ever, got to the nub: 'Woodward Does a Di on Panorama'.

None of this should be surprising in an age where the visual dominates, with the verbal coming but second. Yet many people forget this part of managing the message. It's becoming increasingly important to realise that how you present yourself is an integral part of how you present your message. It's not a new thing – look back in history. The skills of the painter were harnessed by the powerful to present persuasive images of themselves as figures of authority. Early examples in Britain are the portraits of Henry VIII and Elizabeth I. The rich and famous in Renaissance Florence and Rome used paintings and sculpture, not to mention life-style, to impress the world. The Renaissance prince made sure he had the most talented musicians, painters and sculptors, as well as the best builders, writers and thinkers at his court. It was all designed to impress. What's different in our age is that the image is moving, superficially accurate and has the sound of our voice to go with it. Imagine Lucrezia Borgia on TV explaining why her husbands kept dying. We are told by historians that this beautiful woman was an expert in poisons. Today, would we believe the weeping widow, dressed in black? Or are we now so cynical that we wouldn't believe her even if she were telling the truth?

These days some people seem to have created for themselves an almost totally public persona. Everything they do appears to be done in the full glare of publicity. The American businessman Donald Trump is a good example. Trump names everything after himself, and unashamedly uses the media to further his ambitions. Somehow his excessive attention to his image rather undermines it, as do some of his business failures. He may get it wrong, but he is consistent in the way he keeps going and keeps talking. Perhaps his larger-than-life image even helps him survive where others would have sunk without trace. I remember the first time I met him was in an elevator at a Republican convention in New Orleans. He ignored me. Why not, he didn't not know me from Adam? But I saw him look at my badge – which said 'MEDIA' in big letters, and underneath 'BBC CORRESPONDENT'. Smoothly he turned and said, 'You having a good time here at the convention? I'm Donald Trump. Call me if you need anything. The BBC does a fine job.' It was all rather false, but was an example of not missing an opportunity for media attention.

Robert Maxwell was another entrepreneur who loved being in the public eye, and was a larger-than-life figure. He was a deeply offensive person in many ways. He reduced a press officer – a young man – to tears in my presence just to make a point. And when I interviewed him on the day he launched The European, he insisted that it was in view, and that I film him reading it. He almost directed the shots himself. I would have done it anyway, but he made sure of it, just in case I was not good at my job. After his death we realised that part of his behaviour pattern was to stop people inquiring too deeply into his affairs.

Another man who built his business empire on a media image was Armand Hammer, of Occidental. I made a film about him when I was on Newsnight and spent a week with him in Los Angeles. On a huge table behind his desk in his downtown office were pictures of him with the rich and famous. The first time I went there were photographs of him with the Royal Family, Prince Charles and Diana, and Mrs Thatcher. The American President was there, plus the Russian leader. I went back to his office later to get some TV shots, and his secretary let me in. He had just been meeting some Middle Eastern potentate. Charles, Diana and Margaret Thatcher had all been pushed to the back, and it was Arab leaders who were in the foreground. It was a subtle way of presenting himself to his visitor – know me by the people I know, was the message. His reputation did not stand much scrutiny after his death. But the point is a useful one – attention to detail in how you present yourself never goes amiss. These larger-than-life examples of men obsessed with their image are as much warnings as anything else. In the end the image can be your undoing. You must be true to yourself, and not try to be something you are not.

The image these days is not static; that is the extra challenge. The fast-cutting of the TV commercials, where a shot is on screen for a few seconds at a time, is increasing our visual vocabulary all the time. Subtly and sometimes not so subtly, we have our views changed and our tastes altered. There's a huge debate about the targeting of children in advertising. The pressures now put on parents to provide an expensive wardrobe of designer items for pre-teens, suggest that future generations will be even more open to such influences and will be driven to conform. The dress sense of the young is now almost wholly derived from advertising reinforced by peer-group pressure. Not only is our dress sense informed in this way, the manner in which we use our bodies to communicate is changing too. Certain gestures, like punching the air in triumph, are now so universal that we no longer really notice them. The 'high five' of winners slapping each other's hands in triumph originated in the African-American community but is now a fixture in our own culture, thanks to the power of the picture.

Ironically, while the impact of the moving image is increasing, the power of the still picture has not diminished. But it's harder to get the really dramatic still shot – unless it is taken by a long lens and invades someone's private space. Press photographers looking for the telling shot – one picture being worth a thousand words – try as far as possible to get the action as it happens. In sport or in war this is easier because the action is all around the photographer and with the modern camera it's possible to shoot off very many pictures, one of which is bound to be well worth the effort. In everyday life, however, there is less action, so more posing. The official opening of the factory with the managing director standing next to the local MP grinning inanely while the MP cuts the tape; the winner of an award holding the plaque or cup towards the camera while shaking the hand of the official presenting it. These are a boring inevitability, and don't do much when they appear in the local paper, or even the national press, except make the people in the picture very happy, and make the reader move on. So don't just think you've been rather modern when you ensure there is a photographer on hand. Choose one with care, and choose the most imaginative. Again, beware the cliché. Celebrities can be a double-edged weapon – did the Spice Girls need Nelson Mandela more for their image than Nelson Mandella needed the Spice Girls? Charles definitely needed the Spice Girls as he tried to tell the world, 'Hey, I'm just an ordinary bloke.' Mandela in his colourful shirt looked at ease. Charles in his double-breasted suit did not.

Some companies, of course, like to sponsor sporting events or personalities in the hope that it will add to their street cred. And it allows their executives, in their dark business suits, to give the impression that they are on first-name terms with the rich and famous. The footballer 'Gazza' Gascoigne was much sought after and well paid; at first it worked, then as the drink and the wife beating got into the headlines, his image changed, and the people who were desperate for a picture of themselves with the man, probably wished they had chosen someone else. There is always this risk with the celebrities around today.

For photographers, getting their subjects into an acceptable pose is part and parcel of the job. They do it every day of their lives, so no wonder they very rarely bother to create new images; as a result, we know what to expect with pictures of the grieving family, our wedding day, a christening and the other rites of passage in our daily lives. Photographic clichés they may be, but it's part of the way a message is managed. Yet there are pitfalls galore. And what is surprising is that many people in the business community will care passionately about how the product is marketed, the image in the TV commercials and the rest, and yet pay much less attention to how they market their own personal image and the messages that they want to impart.

Many will go some way down the line and then leave it to someone else to interpret their image. It's rather like getting Hello magazine to cover your wedding. Most of the people in its pages look like prize prats, grinning inanely in uncomfortable poses. If you don't know what image you wish to project, then others will be in control of it and get the wrong end of the stick. More often than not, what you see in some heavily posed and controlled images may be at variance with the truth. The body speaks in a way that does not match what you are saying. Just study the body language of Princess Diana and Prince Charles as their marriage begins to break up. On one state visit to Korea they were both looking in opposite directions. Although on the same stage, they could have been in different countries. Whereas the pose by Princess Diana at the Taj Mahal – alone and pensive – may have been manipulative, as some suggest, but it also told a 'truth'; she was alone, and was likely to remain so, despite being married to the heir to the throne. I quote Diana because she seemed to have an instinct for what was right in front of the camera, even though at times its presence drove her to distraction. The night that her husband opened up his heart to the nation, prompted by a solicitous Jonathan Dimbleby, she went out on the town in the very dramatic black dress she had worn in her own 'confessional' Panorama interview. Knowing that the photographers would be out in force, she chose absolutely the right image to remind TV viewers and newspaper readers the next morning about what she had said. Charles might have an extensive wardrobe of kilts, suits and walking sticks, but they were nothing compared to the power of that black dress.

In the United States, where the power of television and Hollywood combined to make Americans the most visually aware culture, the way you looked and dressed was quickly recognised as being important – and a skill that anyone could acquire regardless of their background. It was from America that 'power dressing' as a concept first came to the fore. And nowhere is the way you dress in America more studied than in the legal system. In the travails of President Clinton, the case of Paula Jones is a good example. When she first appeared in public after charging him with sexually molesting her, her way of dressing led his supporters to claim she was 'trailer trash'. This is an example both of how your way of dressing can let you down, and the way language, used with the precision of a scalpel, can sometimes win out over the image. When Ms Jones changed her clothes and went for a much more sober middle-class look, her detractors acknowledged the make-over and dismissed it by saying that she might be 'class' on the outside, but she remained 'trailer trash' underneath. The unanswered question is whether Ms Jones would have exerted a greater impact had she paid more attention to her appearance before she went public.

Again, in the United States there is widespread coaching of trial witnesses. This extends from what they say to how they say it and, just as important, what they wear. And as TV covers more and more trials, the impact a witness makes is no longer on the dozen or so jurors, but on the media covering the trial, and therefore on the public, whose own views then feed back into the media and sometimes, apparently, into the courtroom. This was made very clear in the compelling coverage of the O. J. Simpson trial where a fashion consultant and a jury consultant were at times, it seemed, on hand to describe the tactics, both in dress and delivery, being employed. Moreover, in the coverage of the Louise Woodward case in Boston, it was public pressure that helped her get treated in a way that no American nanny could have expected in similar circumstances.

This recognition of what is happening means, of course, that you now have to be much more subtle in what you do. What amazes me, though, about body language is how little you need to change. In the TV interview there are quite a number of clues to indicate that a person is uncomfortable. Be aware of them, and avoid them, is the simple rule. The most obvious signs of an individual lying in everyday life are when they put up a hand to cover their mouth as they are speaking or won't look you directly in the eye. Folding the arms is an indication of nerves, while tugging at the ear or scratching the nose are further signs that you are not in your element. Crossing the legs, leaning back, even sprawling, all signify that you wish the interviewer would go away. You can do something about all of this.

I am concentrating on television in this chapter, but it is worth pointing out that although sometimes you can get it right on TV, your voice may let you down on radio. The classic case of what you see is not always what you don't buy is the now celebrated example of the Nixon–Kennedy debates when they were fighting for the presidency. Nixon did not want to wear make-up. He had a dark beard line, and he looked nervous. Kennedy was young, fit and sun-tanned. He seemed to exude patrician ease and control. Not surprisingly, when the public were polled on how they reacted to the debate, Kennedy won hands down. But there was still a sizeable radio audience at the time, following the same debate. For them it was voice that counted – nothing else. Nixon was well ahead. His deep voice suggested maturity to middle America; Kennedy's slightly nasal, Boston Irish accent did not appeal in the same way.

To manage your message properly in a visually aware world means that you have to pay attention to how you appear. Yes, it's the dreaded word 'image'. John Major never really got away from being a 'grey' man, with his dark suits, stiff way of standing and talking, and awkward gestures at the podium. Margaret Thatcher needed to fix her teeth, do something with her hair, and dress with a little more style – but I think she would have triumphed whatever she wore. Ann Widdecombe breaks every rule in the book, and yet she has great appeal to the masses.

Beware the 'make-over', or at least seeing it as the answer to everything. There are any number of people in the marketplace who will – for a fat fee – make you over. They would argue that what they do is proven, tried and tested. One of the leading practitioners is Mary Spillane. Much of what she says in her Makeover Manual is common sense. The trouble with that approach, in my view, is that it's like having a professional decorator do your house. It will look splendid, but is it really your home any more? Look at all those women MPs on the Labour backbenches – all wearing their power suits, single items of jewellery on the left or right lapel of their sensible jackets. They are not individuals, but clones. The question you need to ask yourself is, 'Is it really what I want to be?' All too often the suggestions are too radical or too conformist. Yet, with discretion and good sense, it will sometimes work small miracles.

Cherie Blair, the Prime Minister's wife, is certainly looking more elegant these days, just as Norma Major before her benefited from fashion advisers. Yet some people never seem to know when to stop changing their look; Kylie Minogue, the Australian soap actress turned singer, went from girl-next-door to vamp to sex symbol in a matter of months. Madonna, another pop star, also went for radical changes in image. But these women, like so many others in show business, can become fashion victims slavishly following the dictates of the great designers. Don't be a fashion victim; and remember, if you want to get your message across, that the clothes you wear should work in the background, not clutter up the screen screaming to be noticed. The former news-reader, Jan Leeming, became famous as much for the dangling ear-rings she wore as for the gravitas she brought to a news bulletin. On the other hand, certain colours don't work well on television. Bright reds almost dazzle the viewer; and very very dark or sombre tones tend to make the person look dull or boring. I'm not criticising everyday wear, but rather what is seen through the lens of a TV camera.

Be sure to remember the following points:

1   Your body speaks a language too.
2   Your body can say things that contradict what you are saying.
3   Get someone you trust to tell you about your clothes sense.
4   Don't be a fashion victim.
5   Mirrors are the most objective observers of how you look.

If you've got a home video camera, get a family member to tape you in action, and then play back the speech you gave. If you appear on television, get a video of the actual programme, and be as hard on yourself as you can be – self analysis is a vital element in getting it right. But most of all, try to get an objective assessment of your public performances. Remember, your critic can be your best friend.

TEN KEY POINTS YOU NEED TO KNOW ABOUT BODY LANGUAGE

Body posture

1   In the TV studio, sit up straight, leaning forward rather than back, looking the interviewer straight in the eye.

2   Don't clasp your hands together in your lap. They will try to prise each other apart, and become a distraction to the viewer.

3   Keep your hands loose, use natural gestures when you speak, to emphasise a point, but try not to scratch your nose, pull your ear lobe or constantly push your specs back up your nose.

4   Either cross your legs or not, but don't try the move in the middle of an interview.

5   Don't be sombre, no matter how serious the subject; a smile works wonders.

Clothes

6   Avoid bright colours, especially red. Black absorbs a lot of light, and with white is too sharp a contrast. Muted tones are best – pastel shades and solid colours.

7   Men should avoid dark suits, and very striped shirts. Go for bold ties. Lighter shades of grey or blue give a less sombre look and prevent you being seen as a boring 'executive suit'. Shirtsleeve interviews are OK and to be encouraged.

8   Women should avoid bright jewellery.

9   Men should shave before an interview – the dark beard line always makes you look suspect. Bald men should have someone lightly powder the pate, so that it won't shine too much.

10 Women's hair can be a problem; the longer it is, the more likely you are to try to flick it back into place or push it away from your face. This is distracting – get a good hair lacquer that is light but firm.

In the eye of the camera

The most effective way of attracting notice these days is to get yourself and your message on to television or radio. These two media are most people's main source of information, television being the dominant partner. A couple of minutes on national TV or radio will alert the public to the story, if nothing more. People turn to their daily newspaper more for background and explanation. It's not that difficult to get on television. Given the ravenous appetite of the broadcast media, the chances of being asked for an interview are increasing all the time. This chapter looks at the way to handle the radio and television interview and make it work to your advantage. In short, how to be a victor, not a victim.

A few words of warning

Not so long ago a doctor from Scotland arrived in the Today studio to explain a scheme he had launched in his practice and which the government had decided should be tested nation-wide. I will spare his blushes by not giving his name. His idea was a good one. He had drawn up a questionnaire for patients on his panel asking them whether they had certain symptoms. The answers were screened, and in this way he had detected the early signs of a range of maladies – from the most minor to the potentially life-threatening. Those patients who needed to be seen were contacted. The results had been dramatic – helping potential victims reduce the risk to health. It also cut the cost of health care. Preventive treatment is usually much less costly than treating a serious condition: in short, prevention is better than cure. An old idea, but one that appealed to a cash-strapped Health Service.

This, roughly, was in the brief that the overnight producers had prepared for the presenters – a bare outline leaving us to ask the obvious questions – the five Ws. 'Live' interviews are divided between the presenters in no special order, and that morning it was the turn of Brian Redhead. The good doctor arrived well in advance, and wanted to know not what we were going to ask him, but whether we had his title right, and the fact that he had chaired several specialist and professional committees.

A few minutes before the interview was due to take place, he was ushered into the studio and seated opposite Brian. Brian began with a short resumé of the story and then, having named the doctor and just one of the many committees he had no doubt served with distinction, asked him how well the scheme was working. The answer was short and to the point. 'Very well.' 'Did you find many patients with worrying symptoms?' 'Yes we did', was the answer. 'A lot of patients?' prompted Brian. 'No', was the monosyllabic answer. 'What sort of symptoms are we talking about?' The reply was 'The usual range.' 'Cancer?' prompted Brian. 'Yes, that as well.' The interview meandered on for another minute or so, while the production team got the next interviewee in place. And the doctor left the studio after a 'thank you' from Brian. Later we were told that he remarked, before he left the office to get into his cab for his next meeting, 'I think that went very well.'

There are many other examples I could give, but just one more will do. Again, I do not give the names so as not to cause embarrassment. This case involved a company giving a press conference in Manchester later that morning about a new product. The press office said that the chief executive would be happy to talk to us. Up he came on the line from Manchester, and this time it fell to John Timpson to get the short straw. 'Tell me about your new product,' said John cheerily. 'I can't,' came the reply. 'The news is embargoed until ten o'clock this morning when we are holding a press conference. You're welcome to come.' Nothing could shift him from his stance – even though he had the chance to tell a couple of million potential customers about it over their cornflakes. Again, it was another very short interview.

Worried interviewees

After all my years serving before the radio and television mast, I have to say that there is something about the 'live' interview that brings out the most surprising reactions in people. Their first reaction is usually fear. And that fear is based on the notion that every interview is conducted at a ferocious pace with an interviewer who interrupts all the time and won't let you get a word out. The second belief is that the interviewer has some trick question up his or her sleeve which will reveal some awful truth about you. And the third fear – though this is always related to interviews that are pre-recorded, not broadcast live – is that the media will edit them in such a way as to distort the message that they are trying to give.

Let me take each in turn and tell you what it is really like. First of all, there are very few combative interviews. Those that make the headlines usually involve politicians who have some difficulty defending a position or a policy. In political interviews little quarter is given and usually none asked for. The interviewer takes the view that the politician has sought public office and is, therefore, answerable to the public who, after all vote them into or out of office. And I would suggest that the vigour with which some political interviews are conducted are mild compared with the venom we hear day in and day out in the House of Commons.

Politicians, of course, do their best to wriggle off any uncomfortable hook by blaming the interviewer. Redhead, in his day, Humphrys and Paxman now, are feared because they go for the jugular and won't let go. So afterwards the oppressed politico makes great play of the unfairness of it all. Months after the New Labour government of Tony Blair was in power, Alastair Campbell was complaining that the BBC was being unfair. He also decided that it would be better to encourage ministers to do 'soft interviews' with show business celebrities like Des O'Connor. The BBC fought back claiming that he was 'dumbing down' (that phrase again) the political debate. The Tory opposition backed the BBC to the hilt. Only months previously, the Tories in office had also accused the BBC of left-wing bias, claiming to be so concerned about it that they had also threatened not to appear on certain programmes or in front of certain interviewers. This, I have to say, is the stuff of political journalism in the broadcast arena – the politicians trying every which way to get their message across and blot out any dissenting voices. Survey after survey, done by the broadcasters, suggest that the audiences like the interviewers to take a tough stand: the public does not trust politicians.

The run-of-the-mill interview, which is what most non-political figures will get, is usually far from confrontational. The word that Americans sometimes use is 'informational'. The first time I heard that word was just after we had launched Financial World Tonight on Radio Four. Broadcasting financial news in those days was very much in its infancy, and few in the City had ever been interviewed. But the American banks in the Square Mile were very quick to seize the opportunity and we were soon inundated with invitations to meet various experts who would talk about currency, exchange rates, interest rates, markets, commodities and so on. All they requested, in what they called these 'informational' interviews, was that we mention the name of the bank or financial institution which had supplied the 'expert'. What's more, they gave us the direct line numbers of 'experts' in the States and in any other office or market around the world. It all helped us justify the rather grand title adopted for this programme. Nowadays, of course, the 'expert' pops up every-where, peddling some point of view which no doubt suits their business plan. I doubt if you'll hear any shouting or interrupting in these interviews.

Then there are the even less confrontational interviews in chat shows or sports programmes, where the opportunity to plug a book or a play or anything else seems to be part of the deal. On these programmes the interviewer is usually as big a celebrity as the interviewee. In sport, of course, Des Lynam, with his laid-back approach is the best at the job. And I don't think I've ever seen any kind of dust-up with his studio guests.

The broadcast interview call

When the call comes seeking a broadcast interview, you need to establish:

1 Which programme is inviting you?
2 What do they want to talk about?
3 Is it live or pre-recorded?
4 Will you be alone or with other people?
5 Who is the interviewer?

Once you have received the answers, you then know what to expect. Of the five action points above, by far the most important is to establish the line of questioning. But beware, broadcasters can be very vague. They don't do this deliberately, but rather because they themselves don't have a really clear idea of what is in store. If we follow the life of a broadcast interview for a moment, you can see why. It all begins at the first editorial meeting to establish the stories the programme will cover that day. The idea will have emerged from either a newspaper item or a press release, a comment during a speech, or a statement concerning you or your business. After some discussion you are identified as the best person to interview. At this early stage they want to make sure that you will be available, so the call is a precautionary one. You have to face the fact that a better story might yet break, and you will not be called. But since all broadcasters like to keep their options open, the call to 'stand you down', as they say, usually comes at the last minute.

Let's assume, though, that the story 'stands up'. All sorts of things can happen between that first call to check your willingness and availability. Someone else might have joined the debate – and they may have been invited to join in the discussion. You will be told later. A reporter may have been asked to produce a short report, setting out the facts before the interview or discussion. News is a fast-moving business, and, as I outlined in the chapter on what the media wants the news team is after a 'story' that will interest, intrigue, amuse, delight, inform or alarm the audience. The main objective is to cover every angle and then, nearer the time they go on air, decide exactly how they want to 'play' the story.

All of this could mean that you are at a permanent disadvantage vis-à-vis the broadcasters; they are deciding who talks, in what format and with whom; you are left waiting for them to decide. From your point of view, however, if you did nothing but wait for their call, then you would be a lamb going quietly to slaughter. But you are in the middle of the story. They want you, so you have certain rights. They can't talk to you unless you agree. You don't have to make that long trek into the studio. If they are really keen they'll send a radio car, do it on the phone. My first advice is always go for the 'live' option with an interview. The story is developing all the time – so if you do it 'live' in real time, then you too are up to the minute. The worst option is to record an early interview, only for it to be overtaken somewhat by events, so that what you say fails to do you or your message justice.

The nature of the message

If you say 'yes' to the invitation, and can assume the interview will take place, you need to establish what your message or messages will be. Now you know what the media is after, you have to decide exactly what it is you want to say. Then you need to be equally clear as to what it is you don't want to say. And during this soul-searching stage of preparing for the interview, consider whether there is anything else that you might like to say if you have time. A bonus quote, you might say.

Establishing what you want to say, of course, is easier said than done. The message will depend largely on what kind of 'story' the media are going for. For example, it could be a take-over battle; it could be that the competition are trying to dispute some product claims or market share statistics; it could be that the media want you to respond to a government announcement concerning your industry; it could be an Office of Fair Trading Report that is to be published. Some of these will be quite straightforward: but you need to establish quite clearly what the programme makers want so that you can frame your response. Obviously a crisis situation is very different and I deal with that on page 141. Let's assume, though, that this is a fairly run-of-the-mill story as far as the media are concerned. An MP has made a speech in which he criticises safety standards. It may be some pressure group which has targeted your industry; it may be the Consumers Association. Whatever the source, suffice it to say that something critical has been said about your organisation.

The first step must be to get the full text of what was said.[46] Once you have the text – and I don't mean just the one-line quote that is being used in the head-lines, but the full context – find out whether anyone else is saying the same thing; whether any of your competitors have already taken issue with the claim, and what they have said or done about it. Next, find out more about the person or organisation uttering the offending quote. Have they said this before? Do they have a reputation for criticising your business or industry? Are they well known and are the views being expressed this time new in any way, shape or form? Finally, find out whether anything else is happening that could be allied to this situation. Has the offending remark been made in anticipation of some other news event, for example, prior to a government or official report, or before some other announcement. Lawyers call it 'due diligence', but I would urge you to discover as much as you can concerning the statement on which you are being asked to comment. Remember, 'forewarned is forearmed'.

Doing your homework as thoroughly as possible means that you can avoid being caught on the hop in the studio by an interviewer. The researcher on the story will have been doing all that you should have been doing; they should not be able to find out any more than you have.

After discovering exactly what is being said, announced or decided, and when, then identifying clearly who is saying it, there comes the need to establish why. The why of the story is the key to answering it. You want to manage your message, but you can only do that effectively by understanding why someone else is doing likewise. Imagine that you are back in the school debating team; you know what the motion is and how you plan to answer those who oppose it. It's time to marshal the arguments.

The challenge here is to say what you want to say in as brief a time-span as the modern media demands. We are moving into sound bite territory now (see page 216 for more detail). But let me give you some of the basic figures. We all speak at roughly three words a second; that works out at about 180 words a minute. Allowing for drawing breath, pausing for emphasis or speaking slowly to make sure people follow the argument, in fact, it's probably nearer 150 words a minute or 75 per half-minute.

Don't ask me why, but this is the average length of answer that works best on radio and to more or less the same degree on television. If you can encapsulate your main argument into 75 words or so in your initial answer, then you are on your way to winning. It seems, as much by trial and error, as by hard scientific evidence, that the listener or viewer can cope with ideas expressed in these short bursts. Any longer, and the attention wavers. Once they start to think about something else, they are no longer listening, and your message is being ignored. Worse, it's not even registering in the subconscious. As Harvey Thomas, the former adviser to Mrs Thatcher and other prime ministers and world leaders, put it in the title to a useful little book on communications: 'If they haven't heard it, you haven't said it.'

Addressing the audience

Remember to speak to the audience, not to your colleagues back in the office. That really is one of the golden rules, as far as I am concerned. All too often, I find people are worried as to what their colleagues might think of their performance. But colleagues are not a normal audience. First, they know as much about the situation as you do, sometimes more, so their judgement will be much more subjective. You can use all the jargon you like, but they will understand. You don't need to spell out the tricky bits of technology or science, they understand. Second, they will rarely be honest with you. Your subordinates will praise, your equals will commiserate, and your boss will store up his views until it's time for promotion or a pay rise. In the media training sessions I am asked to do, I always try to insist that at least two, better four, at most six colleagues come from the same part of the organisation. They must all undergo the process of understanding the media, all of them share the pain and the pleasure of failing and succeeding. That way the individual has allies in the workplace, when called upon to go and speak to the media.

Speaking plain English

So how do you put all this information into these 30-second or so gobbets of information, and win? Put the audience first and remember that they can be or are distracted most of the time they are hearing or watching you. Why should they want to listen to you – just another boring business executive speaking some impenetrable jargon about 'focusing on relevant issues', while being 'a global player in a niche market' whose mission is to provide 'cutting edge' or 'state of the art' products that will guarantee 'customer delight'? Why should they listen to such guff over breakfast, in their cars, between the latest hits, or while watching TV after a long day in their own offices and factories, probably hearing the same jargon in meeting after meeting?

Let's assume you've done your homework as outlined in the previous pages. One trick is to try to write your opening answer in no more than, say, 79 words. It forces you to think clearly, and it means you have to cut out the wasted words, and only use those that say something. I remember that one of the first editors I ever worked for in radio had a simple way of establishing whether a story was good enough to broadcast or not. When you told him what you wanted to do, he asked you to write a 30-word outline that could be used in the Radio Times to get people to listen. His argument was that unless you could say it in a couple of sentences, then you had not thought about it and did not have a clear idea of what you wanted to do; thus the listener would end up with a report that was fuzzy and confused rather than informative.

There is something else, though, which needs to go in that first 79 words – an example to illustrate the point you want to make. It's my experience that most people, when faced with the challenge of writing their sound bite, start by making claims and making lists. At some of the public seminars I give on media interviews, I have great fun doing what my trade calls 'vox pops' with the audience. My long-term cameraman colleague Keith Bradshaw and I dive into the audience, pretending to be a news crew. Keith turns on the spotlight and I shove the microphone into someone's startled face. 'Tell me about your business,' I say, in the best reporter-like style I can muster. The answers are almost always a list of products and a list of dates:

My company was founded in 1863 as a steel-making company, but since then we've diversified. In 1903 we bought a small pen-making company, and then in 1942, during the war, we expanded into knives and forks. But since then we've sold the steel side, and now concentrate on plastics for the military. I'm the human resources manager, and I've been there for ten years now; before that I was with the AA – Alcoholics Anonymous not the Automobile Association.

The only success in that answer is that it is the perfect length for a sound bite – just under 80 words. But it hasn't told us the name of the business, nor what it does except that it now concentrates on plastics for the military. This is not an actual answer – although anyone who has been to the seminars will recognise that it is an almost perfect replica of the hundreds I've heard over the years.

They should begin with the name of the company and concentrate on what they mean by plastics for the military. Forget the history, and forget your own job unless it's relevant. If you are head of research and you have made a safe but effective plastic bullet, then maybe you should claim the credit, unless the introduction has already made that point. Next an example:

> Our new plastic bullets were used last week in that riot in eastern Paris. The French police fired 21 rounds, the rioters dispersed, none of them were injured save for a few light bruises, even when the bullet was fired directly at them from a short distance. The plastic is a special formula that melts on contact with a harder object, even the human body. There is nothing else like it in the world, and we claim that this is the only gentle way to keep the peace even in the most frightening riot.

I made that up, of course, but it has to be more interesting than giving a list of dates, or some meaningless description of the product.

Such an answer, albeit fanciful, is up-to-the-minute: 'Our bullets were used last week successfully ...' so this is more newsy, there are facts about why it is so good and even an advertising claim that 'this is the gentle way to keep the peace in the most frightening riot'. Here is what one has to strive for in answers: immediacy, coupled with plain understandable English. I did not need to give the name of this new magic plastic, only what it did. The science was reduced to a minimum by describing what it did rather than how it did it. It could well be that the interviewer might well ask, 'Tell me more about this plastic; what's it called, is it British and is it a world beater? Where else has it been used?' All these are possible questions and that leads on to another point about control of an interview and the agenda.

Controlling the interview

I keep saying 'avoid jargon' and then I talk of 'agenda', a word much used by the media. The Today programme on BBC Radio Four likes to claim that it 'sets the agenda'. What it means is that the stories it runs in the morning are those we all talk about for the rest of the day; they are the stories that prompt reaction from interested parties, especially the politicians, and keep the world turning. It's a big claim when these days the news 'agenda' is going round the clock, and Today is only carrying on where the previous programmes have left off. But in the interview you can set the agenda.

This is how you do it. We go back to that research you have to do when the calls arrive seeking your presence on a particular programme. You've decided what your message is. You've worked out your sound bite. But remember, that first answer is only the beginning. There will be a follow-up question. You have a twofold task. A well-constructed first answer does double duty:

1   It stands alone and can be used as a sound bite in news bulletins
    (it is your response to the news, your comment, or whatever).
2   It is nevertheless framed in such a way that you prompt the next question
    – a question you want asked to help develop the story you want to tell.

Let's go back to our plastic bullet. You have made it sound so interesting that the interviewer and the audience will want more. You've said just enough to tickle the appetite. And you've reached the point about its magic properties at the end of your answer. It demands – I don't think that that is too strong a word – that the interviewer follow up with another question. More than that, though, you've only talked about that bullet. There is nothing else for the interviewer to discuss. You have, in a phrase that is bandied about a lot these days, 'narrowed the focus'. By concentrating on a key product, or a single subject, it's hard for the interviewer suddenly at this early stage to try to change the subject. Every time you give a list of points, it is almost inevitable that the interviewer, more by luck than judgement, will choose the one you least want to discuss. As Winston Churchill is reported to have said, 'Tell them what you are going to say, say it, then tell them what you have said.'

One other stratagem – and it's one that politicians use a lot – is to say, at the end of the first answer: 'And that is why I think it is absolutely crucial that people know the answer to this question.' That's the idea, it can take many forms, but essentially it is a device which prompts the interviewer. The very best interviewers will have their own agenda, and may not fall into the traps that you set. They may reply, 'You may think it's a crucial question, but surely the question is rather ...' They are very adept at sticking to their own line of questioning, and you should be aware of that. But that does not mean to say that you immediately give in and follow them. Remember all that research, and the message that you want to get out. So keep your eye on the message and use every opportunity to get back to it.

A word about editing

Everyone I have spoken to about broadcast journalism is convinced that with the wonders of modern information technology the broadcasters can take any image and any set of words and turn them into a complete travesty of the truth, yet which looks so compelling on the screen that nobody will believe you when you protest, 'But that's not what I said.' I'll let you into a little secret. All of us who have ever done any interviews are amazed at the things people will say, without prompting, that will condemn them out of hand. This is why in the United States they have a very useful device known as the Fifth Amendment. You 'plead the Fifth' because you don't want to say anything that might incriminate you. But when you want to be heard, you are willing to talk; so pleading the 'Fifth' would rather destroy the object of the exercise. Before I give you a few pointers on how to make your messages tamper-proof, let me explain what editing is all about.

It is most definitely not about trying to twist a person's words. For professional broadcasters not only would that be completely unacceptable, and morally indefensible, it would be foolish and dangerous. They build their reputation, as far as they can, on fair dealing and honesty. Once they lose that, they lose everything. Since they believe in the truth, how could they serve it by lying themselves?[47] More often than not, what happens on the screen, when the interviewee sees the final product, is that they suddenly see it as others see it and realise that they may not have made themselves as clear as they would have liked. Or worse, others who see the piece talk about it in a way that proves they got the wrong end of the stick. The interviewees realise that they may have got the message all wrong; they realise that they did not mean that. Yet there they are, large as life, in living colour, with a friendly smile on their face, saying the offending words. How can you deny the wrong impression except by blaming the media?

Usually what has happened is that instead of keeping strictly to their message or messages, they've allowed themselves some latitude. They may have given longer answers than were strictly necessary. The programme maker has got a gallon to fit into a pint pot. So he will cut those sentences which seem to him less to the point than others. This pruning process is fraught with danger on both sides. The programme maker may well have misunderstood the thrust of what you are saying, and begins to build up his programme on the basis of quotes which fit his understanding. During the editing process we all run the tape over and over again, to see where we can cut to save time. The more you view it, the more you begin to see other meanings that that did not seem to be there before. They seem more important – the body language is more positive, the words more upbeat, a finger jabbed as a point is made. These look like strong images, yet imperceptibly the editor's understanding is changing. The problem is that you – the subject – did say those things; yet you did not realise you were saying them. By saying too much in an interview you give too much to the reporter who is only looking for maybe a minute's worth of air time from you.

Interviewees will argue that if the broadcasters were to let them vet the film before it was broadcast, all the grief would be avoided. Broadcasters instinctively reject this because they can't just show you the quotes you have given, but everyone else's as well. If they give you such an opportunity, then they must do the same for others who have contributed to the programme. In the end the changes and further changes would have to be shown to everyone, and in the end the programme would never get made. The media's defence is that you know how the system works – it's up to you to make it work to your benefit. If there are any serious lapses, you can call in the lawyers.

Another argument is this: if the broadcaster only wanted thirty seconds from me, why did they record fifteen minutes? Again I have no comfort – you allowed them to record fifteen. Perhaps you can see why I suggested that going out 'live' is the safest option – you do it in real time, and they can't change what you've said, because that is all they've got. With the pre-recorded interview you need to establish exactly what they want to ask you. Get them to give you every question; then ask how much they are going to use. Work out your answers, and keep to time.

When I was learning to drive, I remember my instructor telling me to accelerate when overtaking. 'It reduces the time exposed to danger.' It's the same here – reduce the time exposed to danger. Do the interview once, and if you are happy with it, don't do it again. Make your excuses and leave. Remain in control of the time that you give. Keep clearly in mind what it is you are saying. You'll find all these points in the check lists – keep to the point, and stay on message.

THE TEN DOs OF BROADCAST INTERVIEWS

1 Do establish the type of programme and the name of the interviewer.
2 Do establish the story and the angle.
3 Do establish clearly why they want you.
4 Do find out what the first question will be – and the thrust of the interview.
5 Do take advice, but do your own homework.
6 Do an interview 'live' if at all possible; it's safer.
7 Do stick to the point.
8 Do keep it topical.
9 Do give examples.
10 Do show conviction and belief in what you are saying.

AND TEN DON'Ts ...

1 Don't be evasive.
2 Don't be long-winded or verbose.
3 Don't show doubt.
4 Don't try to bluff – if you don't know, say so.
5 Don't mumble.
6 Don't give one-word answers.
7 Don't use jargon or technical language that only the experts will understand.
8 Don't lose your temper.
9 Don't mislead, don't tell lies, don't be economical with the truth.
10 Don't lose control.

18

Hold the front page

Whereas everything in the world of the broadcast media is about time, and time measured in seconds and minutes, there is something much more leisurely about the world of print. It has its deadlines, it has its pressures, but it spends more time on the story – and especially the interview. The print journalist's not-so-secret weapon is lunch. Bernard Ingham, whom Lady Thatcher described as the greatest press secretary in the world, says in his book[48] about his time at Number Ten Downing Street that he gave some 5000 lobby briefings and about 30,000 other individual briefings: 'These figures include lunches and dinners with journalists. If these averaged only two a week, I chomped my way through at least 1000 meals with the fourth estate. (This makes me sound like the best fed Chief Press Secretary in the annals of government.) I certainly ate well.' But whereas Bernard Ingham seems to have welcomed rather than endured the eating for Britain process, his successor under Tony Blair, Alastair Campbell, sees nothing but danger in lunch. In a now famous leaked memo to the former ministers Harriet Harman and Frank Field, he says, 'I would urge extreme caution in relation to lunches.'

Anyway, before discussing the art of lunching successfully in the medium of print, you need first to appreciate how it differs from the media of electronics. In many respects you have more control over the outcome of radio and television interviews. They can only use what is on video or audio tape. If you've kept to the point and done those things that I have suggested it should be very hard for them to twist your words or take them out of context.[49] You agree to them turning on the tape recorder or camera on your terms. But the print medium is different. There are some brave reporters who never take a note, others who will have a little tape recorder to keep a record of the conversation; some have impeccable shorthand, some make squiggles and scrawls which serve as memory joggers. There's no reason why, in a formal interview with the print media, you shouldn't record it as well. Tony Benn even records broadcast interviews – partly to intimidate the interviewer, next to be used in his marvellous political diaries, and last to make sure that he is reported accurately. All very sensible precautions.

Yet there are still pitfalls, as I've said, because in the audio-visual media the audience can hear you speak, hear the exact inflection, hear the hesitation, the passion, the persuasiveness with which you have denied something. And in television they can look you in the eye, so to speak. In the print media, the impression you convey depends more on the writer or interviewer. A good writer can make all the difference. Journalists use the language in all its richness, they have an eye for detail, but most of all they won't come between you and the reader. Yet willy nilly, in the end, it is their impression of you that will suffuse the resulting article.

Let me quote the words of American author Janet Malcolm who wrote a fascinating account of how a journalist convinced a murderer on death row in the United States to talk to him. She relates the way in which both tried to exploit the other.[50] The actual story does not concern us here, but what she says in her very first paragraph describes more eloquently than I the challenge of the relationship between the journalist and the subject:

> Every journalist who is not too stupid or too full of himself to notice what is going on knows that what he does is morally indefensible. He is a kind of confidence man, preying on people's vanity, ignorance or loneliness, gaining their trust and betraying them without remorse. Like a credulous widow who wakes up one day to find the charming young man and all her savings gone, so the consenting subject of a piece of non-fiction learns – when the article or book appears – this hard lesson. Journalists justify their treachery in various ways according to their temperaments. The more pompous talk about freedom of speech and 'the public's right to know'; the least talented talk about art; the seemliest murmur about earning a living.

Now that is a pretty powerful indictment of the whole trade – and many would say, not one whit overstated. I used the phrase in the last chapter about minimising the 'time exposed to danger'. If you want to manage the message, you need to manage your time as well, when you meet the media. The more time you give them, the more you say. The more you say, the more they have to choose from, and the less you'll remember what you said. The more you say, the greater the chance that they will remember the one line you wish you hadn't used. You can fulminate and blame the 'bloody' media – but you said it, of your own free will. They were not burning you with hot irons, nor gouging out your eyes. It was your ego, you wanting to show off a little, feeling just rather too important talking to the journalist from a national newspaper. Like that widow in the paragraph I quoted from Janet Malcolm, you have been successfully chatted up, seduced, and you are the loser.

It is the reporter's stock in trade to get you to trust them and to get you to confide. It is not a trick, nor are they being devious. They have not lied about their identity nor their job; you can read what they do every day in the paper. Perhaps your colleagues have already dealt with them. A precaution would be to see who else they've talked to in your field – and then check them out. But at the end of the day, you agreed to the interview. If you are prepared to take the blame if it goes wrong, rather than blame the reporter, it may help to concentrate your mind on the job in hand.

Once again, it all comes down to preparation – about what you want to say and how you want to say it. You must decide what it is you don't want to talk about. You've got to do your homework here, every bit as much as you would if it were Jeremy Paxman and a Newsnight team arriving in your office. After all, the interview in this newspaper could well lead to Jeremy summoning you to his lair to answer a few questions. The difference between the broadcast interview and the press interview is that the press interviewer sets no time limit on the answers. In broadcast interviews you try to answer in up to 30 seconds – that's about 80 words. In a press interview, you can speak for, say, three or four minutes in answering the first question. You are less intimidated. Four minutes of speech at a normal speed would actually come to well over 600 words. You don't need to be a mathematical genius to see how much more information you have given.

Here are some more figures. As we've seen, there are five basic questions – the five Ws. A broadcast interview with 30-second answers would come to two and a half minutes, or 400 words. A four-minute answer to each question in print and you would have told your story in over 3000 words. I believe that makes a watertight case for discipline.

Whereas the broadcast journalist thinks in terms of time – minutes or seconds of air time – the print journalist has similar constraints – namely space. A full-length feature article in a newspaper rarely runs for more than 1250 words. So if we stay with the 3000 or so words you've delivered, the print journalist is still going to have to edit some out of the article. In actual fact, the writer will be putting in a lot of other information – about your career or your company, why the piece is being written, why you are in the news. So even though the medium is different, the journalistic process of collection, selection and rejection is still the same. The journalist selects the quotes that seem to help tell the story. In print, curiously, the quotes are shorter. The actual words are usually verbatim, but a précis of what you said; so your 600-word answer to a print journalist may in fact appear as a ten-word quote. In broadcast terms that is the equivalent of barely three seconds – much too short for radio or television, but normal in print. The editing process, or cutting-to-fit process, is more brutal, and much more selective, in print. Yet, ironically, people feel less threatened by the print journalist who laughs at your jokes, nods in agreement at everything you say, and praises your insight and intellect as you become more and more expansive, and begin to tell a few home truths about the competition. Sometimes I think a good press interviewer could be equally at home in the psychologist's consulting room – and indeed one psychologist, Anthony Clare, seems to have made the journey the other way with his radio programme.

You can meet people who will proudly show you the ten-word quote in The Times, and rail that they only got 30 seconds on television. In fact they will have said nine times as much in vision, with the added impact of seeing them say it. Which brings me to the last point. In much the same way that you must remember body language in vision, so you need to use it in the print interview. It's not a conversation, it's a sales job. Don't lounge, don't use bad language, don't drink, be polite, helpful and send out messages that are positive. The writer is as aware of body language as anyone, and it colours the way the piece is written.

Press conferences

Your dealings with the print media are not just about one-on-one interviews. They usually begin with the press conference. At the beginning you have total control. You have called the conference. You have distributed the statement or the press release. You make a short opening statement with background, or to introduce your colleagues. The problems can start when it is opened up for questions.

I've seen many a briefing for individuals giving a press conference which is extensive, to say the least. Their PR advisers seem to have tried to think of every possible question that might be asked, then they have drafted an answer which attempts to cover every possibility. They then hire tame interviewers to take the subject through his paces, asking all the questions. The plan is for the interviewee to know every single one of them by heart. I'm not convinced by this. First of all they are trying to get an extremely busy individual to learn the equivalent of Hamlet's part in the play. Even if you manage to memorise the 100 or so questions, the mind will be so cluttered that you might just use the wrong answer to a question, become worried that you can't remember all the answers, and look like a startled rabbit caught in the headlights of an oncoming car. Once again I come back to the idea that if you know what the messages are that you wish to communicate, then there should be no answer that you cannot tackle head on. It's knowing what you want to say, rather than worrying too much about a particular form of words.

The other problem is that if you get locked into a particular train of thought, you can become inflexible in response. Press conferences do not proceed in a logical fashion. Hands go up, and each questioner is more or less picked at random. Some will follow on from the previous question; others will start a whole new line of inquiry. Sometimes the same question will be asked in a different way over and over again if the media think that you are dodging the issue. After some press conferences you are like a damp rag, limp and useless. At other times you have hardly even got started before a kind of deafening silence descends and there are no more questions. Some reporters keep their best questions until after the formal open press conference, and seek a one-on-one interview; others will call later for 'more background'.

Much potential grief can be avoided if the press pack is thoroughly prepared. At the very least it should include individual biographies. By that I mean biographies that are relevant. We don't need every single interesting date in your life, and the title of every single paper that you have ever published. There should be a range of stills – 'mug shots' that are up-to-date, and possibly show you at work, rather than the heavily retouched 'studio portrait'. In a visual age, still pictures need much more imagination than merely the same boring old head-and-shoulders shot. There should be relevant information about the news you are giving – appointment, product, take-over; whatever it is, set out the facts and the background to it. Issue a statement in your name that sounds like you talking and is not full of such useless and meaningless phrases as 'It makes me very pleased to be able to announce today what I believe is one of the most momentous moments not only in my career but in the history of this company ...' If you need to talk up the 'news' like that, then probably you shouldn't have called a press conference. Let the event or whatever speak for itself.

Adequate background in the press pack ensures that during the press conference you can always refer to these facts when being questioned: 'You find that information on page 5, but obviously if you want more information on that, talk to me after the press conference.' Or you can indicate which of your colleagues is an expert in that field and who will be available afterwards. Give their phone numbers so that the media can call them later. A press conference should be about information not obstruction.

Of course there are press conferences that are forced upon you in a dispute of some sort. I've dealt with the press conference in a crisis on page 141. But much the same rules apply: know what you want to say rather than try to antic-ipate every query. It's rather like a batsman in cricket – you know roughly what the bowler is capable of, but you don't know exactly how the pitch is playing, or what the state of the game will be when you come to bat. But if you are a good batsman, you have confidence in your ability to see the ball and play it accordingly. So it is with media questions. There will be fast and slow balls, and a few googlies as well. You can never score a century every time you go out to bat – but you can aim for a good average. There are no certainties in this business.

The telephone interview

The telephone is another of the media's secret weapons – it allows them to get hold of you at the most unusual times and in the most unusual places. And if the media have your mobile number, heaven help you – they will call at the most inconvenient time. It never ceases to amaze me at what is in some reporters' books of contact numbers. Rather than talk to the PR person, all reporters prefer to talk to the principal character in a story. The odd fact is that as far as the BBC is concerned, such phone calls cannot be recorded unless you ask the person's permission. For the written media there are, as far as I know, no such rules; so they will get a verbatim copy of what is said.

You should treat phone calls in much the same way as the broadcast interview – keep to the point; don't volunteer too much information, only what is relevant; don't speculate; and retain control. On that last point, unless they have your mobile number, and you are sitting in your bath, try to win some time to think, by promising to call back within fifteen minutes. Instruct your PA or switchboard that all media calls should be treated this way; but make sure they at least establish why the media are calling and what they want to know. The extra time for preparation, getting your message right, will avoid most problems. But do call back – remember, silence smacks of guilt, fear or confusion. Of course they might be calling you to invite you to lunch. That, too, carries some basic rules.

The press lunch

Prime Minister Blair's press secretary may warn ministers about the perils of lunching – but he'll never be able to stop it. The problem with the press lunch is that you can be caught off guard, you can relax too much, and if the wine is very good, you may have just one glass too many. On the other hand, the advantage of the lunch is that you can get to know the media better, find out what they are interested in, what kind of story they are after. I firmly believe that the lunch – or dinner, come to that – should always be 'off the record', or for 'background purposes only'. And this should be stated right at the outset, so that there is absolutely no misunderstanding. If you are the host then you can hold it in your executive dining room – if you have one; or at your favourite restaurant. Always choose a place where you are most comfortable. It keeps you in charge. If you are the guest, and are given the choice, again go for somewhere you prefer.

As host, it is usual to say a very few words about the reason for the lunch and that it is off the record; as a guest, establish the ground rules as early as you can. I don't want to make too much of this. It all sounds Machiavellian enough. The simple point is that lunches last too long for the principal guest to be able to recall every twist and turn of the conversation – even though you may have done all the usual preparation. But the reporter or reporters around the table will be taking notes (quite openly) or will have trained themselves to recall those parts of the conversation that will be of use to them at a later date when they come to write a story about your organisation. You may find that not touching the rather excellent little Bordeaux the waiter keeps offering is also a useful ploy.

Finally, always remember the old saying: 'The pen is mightier than the sword'. What is written about you goes into the vaults of history – and can be retrieved at the most inconvenient moment. Do what you can to make sure that what goes into print is as accurate as possible, and make sure that inaccuracies are corrected promptly. In all my years in journalism, I never heard anyone say, 'Hold the front page', but I have heard them say, 'That's a good story – let's lead with it.' It could be your story.

TEN WAYS TO GET YOUR MESSAGE INTO PRINT

1   Always have a clear idea of what you want to say. Make sure the press release says it all.
2   Where possible, target the message. Every newspaper reinforces its readers' prejudices. Recognise them, and use them.
3   Give interviews. You can say more in a press interview – give more context and make an impression.
4   But don't say too much. Remember the message.
5   Why not tape the conversation? It helps concentrate the mind.
6   Everything should be on the record – for publication.
7   Talking 'off the record' is never helpful unless you know and trust the reporter extremely well.
8   If you don't know something, say so.
9   Follow up the interview with a letter – making any extra points you may have overlooked or which may be helpful. And if an article results, another letter shows you have read it. This is good for maintaining a relationship.
10   When a serious factual error has been made, always seek a printed correction – otherwise that error will stay in the cuttings for ever more.

19

Now is the time

Timing, as any investment guru will tell you, is everything. So it is in managing the message. Goldman Sachs postponed their much publicised public flotation when the markets started to fall in the wake of the Asian economic crisis. They could measure what it would have cost them to float – 40 per cent less than when they planned it. It was a big decision, but at least they could calculate the likely impact on the profit and loss account. The news business prides itself on its ability to react to the unexpected – re-jigging the programme or the paper at the last minute to take acount of a breaking story.

You need to be able to build in the same kind of flexibility and reaction time in managing the message. You may have worked for months on a new product launch. If this had coincided, say, with the sudden death of Diana, Princess of Wales, no one would have noticed anything – no matter what. So it is advisable to have a fall-back position planned should the day you inadvertently choose be the day that a major story breaks. Equally you ought to remember that some events might even work to your advantage, in which case you might plan to launch sooner than expected.

Let us assume a more normal news agenda. There are some broad guidelines about timing that can be of use. The first, and most obvious, is not to be late. If someone has asked you for a quote for the morning edition, and requested it by four o'clock, then get it to them by four o'clock – and as soon before four as possible But lateness can be defined in other ways. James Carville's 'rapid rebuttal' strategy works as long as the rapidity of the rebuttal is measured in minutes rather than hours. It's a case of striking while the iron is hot. The competition have made a great claim that puts your product in question. The longer you leave it, the more it'll look as if you don't know what to say;

or that they are right. When something like this happens out of the blue, it's hard to scramble like the World War Two fighter pilots and go out to strafe the enemy. But you should try.

There will be occasions when you can be prepared in advance, in the event, say, of a government report into your industry, a survey of your industry by a firm of consultants, or evidence being given to a government committee or a public inquiry. These days there is an ever-growing list of events which produce opportunities that you can exploit for your commercial advantage. Most of the news agencies can be accessed via the Internet, and they usually give a daily and weekly events diary. As we saw in the chapter on how the media works, the events that are in the news diary are often planned for in advance, and your contribution can be included in that forward planning. When the judge in the Louise Woodward case announced his decision, most comment had already been prepared by those hoping to exploit the situation. It's the same on Budget Day in Britain where all the pressure groups and trade associations who are likely to be involved in a tax change will want to get their two penn'orth in. Pre-planning is pre-armed.

A sound bite in time ...

... can save nine. 'Sound bite' has become the most used and yet misunderstood word in the language at the present time. It's a curious piece of media jargon that has now invaded the language and is usually used as a term of abuse.[51] 'Government by sound bite' is the current example of trying to counter what is often the effective presentation of policy. Yet in the world in which we live, where we are inundated with data, information and news, the sound bite is one way of getting the message out, quickly and accurately.

The original meaning of the phrase is self-evident. What the news programmes looked for, in both radio and television, were short pieces of what was sometimes known as 'actuality'. It meant 'clipping' the required sentence or two and inserting that into the report. It was the audio-visual equivalent of the 'direct' quote used by the print media. In sound and vision, of course, it had the added advantage that you heard and saw individuals making their own case, or putting across their point of view. These 'clips' could be taken from speeches or interviews. They usually required some editing to get them into the required length – ideally never more than 45 seconds.[52] Communications consultants in the political arena quickly began to study the device and train their politicians in its complexity; and it is quite a complex process even though it lasts less than a minute.

If we take the average British sound bite as around 30 seconds we are looking at about 80 words. Advanced sound biters may employ fewer words – using either the trick of repetition of a key phrase to drive the message home, the meaningful and dramatic pause to register emotions that range from shock or even revulsion at the suggestion made by the opposition to excitement at pulling off a big deal. Anger, too, can be registered in fewer words: 'I have never, repeat never, been so … angry, yes angry – at the suggestion made by that son …' Try saying that with passion, and a jabbing finger so that the body language reinforces the view – and you can see why you don't necessarily need all 80 words. If you are new to the business of sound bites, then keep it simple.

A good way to start is to take your message in all its complexity, and try to reduce it to no more than 80 words; and keep exactly to 80 words – not one more, nor one less. It forces you to edit out all the extraneous information. It makes you concentrate on the most relevant details. And if the resulting 80 words are constructed in such a way as to have a good beginning, necessary middle and essential conclusion – they cannot be shortened any further. They are, to all intents and purposes, edit proof. You will be surprised what you can say within this length. Yet a single sound bite will not work on all occasions. You should always have your target audience in mind when you construct it. And don't do what Tony Blair did when he announced sonorously: 'Now is not the time for sound bites. I feel the hand of history on my shoulder.'

The best and most controlled example I ever saw of sound bites in action was at a Republican convention in the United States. I was handed the TV script of one of the keynote speakers. He had written virtually every paragraph as a sound bite. Between each paragraph he would pause so that the editing process was easy. And since there are a number of key states in the Union, whose votes were crucial to the candidate, certain sound bites were addressed directly to them: 'So I say this to the voters of Virginia ...'; 'I have a message for the good people of California ...'; and ' Texas Republicans don't need me to tell them that the Lone Star State ...' Listening to the speech overall, you hardly noticed this device. Each message seemed to drop from his lips quite naturally; and to reinforce the message with a good picture, the various state delegations, who had also been warned what to expect, would start a 'spontaneous demonstration', waving the state flag and blowing whistles and toy trumpets. The regional media could help themselves; and that night each local station carried that clearly directed message to their viewers and listeners, complete with an over-the-top reaction by the crowds at the convention. The party spin doctors also helped the local TV stations by giving them advance copies of the speech. This meant that the local networks need only tape the sections that they were interested in. This saved them valuable time and made their correspondent on the spot look good with his instant reaction to the sound bite. In fact no one was the loser because the overall package helped garner votes for the speaker. Everyone was happy.

That's the set-piece sound bite. I happened to be one of the BBC 2 News-night presenters during the Falklands War. America media presence in London in vast numbers, plus the need to talk to the world to keep the Argentines isolated, led to the development of the Downing Street sound bite. The Americans, following their Secretary of State, had pretty well forced their way into Downing Street.[53] At first only the American visitors would stop and say something for the cameras and the folks back home. The British politicians just waved as if they were going to a cabinet meeting. Soon, though, the American visitors were stopping on their way out of Number Ten to make a statement. It took less than 24 hours before the British followed suit. Initially they were too wordy, a little naïve, and tended to agree with their American visitors. But soon they got the hang of it ... and there have been cameras and microphones in Downing Street ever since.

A good sound bite can do the most amazing job for you. When the then leading British industrialist Sir Michael Edwardes was given the hopeless task in the early 1980s of turning round what was then called British Leyland – Britain's last mass car manufacturer, he had one of the toughest PR jobs in the country. For a long time he kept his own counsel and said very little to the media. Meanwhile the unions were making all the running in the news, worrying about job losses and what the new boss was up to. They accused him of sidelining them and all sorts of other 'sins' in the industrial relations handbook.

Late one evening I got a call from Michael Edwardes's press adviser. Would I like to 'doorstep' him the next morning just after 7.30 at his offices. 'Doorstep', for the uninitiated, is media jargon for waiting at someone's home or office – on the doorstep – so as to get a few words from him. Rarely, if ever, is one invited to 'doorstep'. I turned up at the appointed time, complete with camera crew. Sure enough Michael Edwardes turned up in his company car, got out and came towards us. The hand-held camera light was turned on, and the camera started to film. Edwardes made as if to walk past us, but in best reporter style I asked him, 'Have you got a message for the unions about jobs?' Edwardes turned and issued a short snappy statement to the effect that if the unions stopped shouting and cared about the company they would talk to him in private so that a strategy for survival could be hammered out.

That sound bite ran on every news bulletin both on the BBC and on ITV. Later I heard that he had received a call from the chief negotiator who had agreed to secret talks. Later still I heard that when Michael Edwardes turned up to the meeting and the unions chided him on 'megaphone diplomacy', he replied, 'It was half past seven in the morning – look at the size of me [he's just over five feet tall], and look at the size of Hobday [I was then over twenty stone in weight] ...' I'm told the unions sympathised with him. 'Bloody media', one of them was heard to whisper.

What I like about this story is that Edwardes got his message out when he wanted, and he made sure the people to whom it was directed could not but fail to respond; and he seems to have built into the method of his delivery the excuse that he was bounced into it by the media. Game, set and match. When I related this story to a friend a few months later, he asked whether I was annoyed to have been used in this way. 'Annoyed?' I said. 'Don't be silly, I got an exclusive and a hero-gram from my editor.'

TEN KEY POINTS ABOUT TIMING THE MESSAGE

1 Don't be late, deadlines won't wait.
2 Be prepared – keep your messages under review and up-to-date.
3 Build a stockpile of ammunition – relevant arguments in case of need.
4 Keep a diary of key events in your world – e.g., an expected government decision.
5 React in minutes rather than hours.
6 A sound bite in time can save nine.
7 It's better to set the news agenda, rather than follow it.
8 Watch the competition – lead, don't follow.
9 Don't just cope with things now, think about the future.
10 But always make time to think before you act.

20

And finally ...

In the court of public opinion, you must promise to give the message, the whole message and nothing but the message. Yet on its own, the message will never be enough. It is part of an organisation's total image. That image is made up in a number of ways – the way the organisation is perceived, the behaviour of its people from the very top to the most lowly. It's in the ways in which it treats every one of its stakeholders – shareholders, employees, customers. It's to do with how it faces the competition. It's to do with how it treats its neighbours in the place where it is headquartered or has branches. In today's world every aspect of corporate behaviour is taken into account – every aspect is questioned. The slogans that you employ in an advertising campaign can be used to question your whole reputation, as the Campaign for Racial Equality found when it launched an advertising campaign showing ethnic minorities in a dubious light. The Advertising Standards Authority asked for the ads to be withdrawn because they broke the law. The defence was that they broke the law to make people aware of what they were tolerating – asking in the slogan 'Why didn't you complain?' There was a feeling that if you can do the very thing you would complain about in others, then the argument is weakened.

Another example was the High Street bank which had a campaign claiming it was 'The Listening Bank'. There were a number of press stories of occasions when the bank had obviously not listened to the customer. It's no use saying one thing in your advertising, and doing or saying something different in another context. So you have to be consistent in everything that you say and do. The bigger the organisation, the more difficult it is always to be consistent. I'm not calling for rigid control, but an awareness on the part of everyone that what they say and do constitutes part of the message that the organisation wants to put across. In this context actions can speak louder than words.

One of the curious facts about the management of the message is that almost the first executive decision taken when the message runs into trouble is to fire the messenger – not to look at the message. When the former German Chancellor Helmut Kohl got into difficulties and saw that he was losing public support, his head of information was asked to leave his post. Nor is it just the capitalist world that indulges in this form of public sacrifice. After the British handed back Hong Kong to China, the once glittering economy began to turn sour and there were a number of PR disasters. So Thomas Chan had to go. Yet these disasters, such as opening the airport before it was ready, were decisions taken by the political leadership against Mr Chan's advice. Whenever this happens it's almost certain that the situation will get much worse before it gets better.

Bernard Ingham, in his book Kill the Messenger, says that he knew that sometimes he had to act as a lightning conductor when storms were raging about government policy during Mrs Thatcher's days at Number Ten. But he argues that, as a professional press secretary, this was part of the assignment. He claims always to have managed to keep the trust of the media that he was doing a good job. Mrs Thatcher knew that she had the right man at her side. I remember any number of summit conferences that I covered for Newsnight or the Today programme seeing what had become a celebrated double act in the British press room. Whereas she often watched members of her cabinet like a hawk, she had total confidence in Bernard Ingham.

John Major, her successor, chose a career civil servant from the Foreign Office as his Press Secretary. He went on to become our ambassador to the United States, and a very successful one too. As the Prime Minister's press spokesman he was much more low-key than Ingham, yet pretty effective given the problems that the Conservative Party was having at the time as it began to split, tugged in opposing directions by the pro- and anti-European factions. Number Ten then welcomed a different type altogether in Alastair Campbell. Some see him as a bully, and very partisan. Most, though, even the most grudging, would accept that he is very effective. Outside government, too, certain press spokespeople have been amazingly compelling. Michael Cole served Mohamed Al Fayed extremely well despite the challenge of his boss's rather daunting image. Perhaps his greatest, albeit most undermining, moment came as he began the process of putting across Al Fayed's view that there had been a plot by the Establishment to kill his son and Diana Princess of Wales. You never believed that it was Cole's personal opinion, but at the same time, you did not know for sure that it was not. In other words, he managed perfectly to play the convincing role of his master's voice; and he always managed to present it more effectively than his master ever could.

So pick the person who is going to speak for you – if you don't do it yourself – with very great care. Take a lesson from the theatre and film world; they spend a great deal of time making sure they have the right leading lady or man to star in the production. When you are recruiting such people it's important to assess how they come across, and decide whether are they believable. How do you find out whether they have the presentation skills that are required? One of the best books I ever read on the subject was by David Bernstein, Put It Together and Put It Across, which he describes as the 'craft of business presentation'.[54] The process is explained in meticulous detail and ends up with you, at the podium, presenting to an audience. They can see you, hear you, even smell whether you had garlic for supper. In these circumstances you soon know whether the audience is with you or against you.

Bernstein puts his message across in a straightforward, no-nonsense way. Trust the American 'experts' to come up with language to sell their advice more expensively by making it sound scientific. It's a paradox – they want their clients to communicate better, but they know they must talk in a language that will encourage the client to trust them as real 'experts'. Richard Greene, the man who has advised Clinton, Blair, Princess Diana and even the House of Lords, distinguishes four types of communication:

1 **Visual:** thinking and communicating in pictures and images.
2 **Auditory:** the ability to use words to convey an idea.
3 **Auditory digital:** using language in an analytical or complex way.
4 **Kinesthenic:** the ability to convey feeling.

In an interview with The Times, Greene gave John Major as an example of someone who can communicate in the auditory way but is quite unskilled in the other forms and was thus perceived as boring. However you describe the communication process; whatever language you use, we all need to remember that it's not just the audience or the person in front of us we need to convince. There's another audience which is crucial, and indeed the most challenging. What I've been talking about is a vast unseen audience that reads newspapers and magazines, listens to the radio and watches television. Here you can never really know what they think – at least not while you are delivering the message. Get it wrong, and they may soon stop buying your product. Give them the slightest doubt about how safe a product is, and shelves and showrooms will be cleared of the allegedly dangerous article in next to no time.

Talking to an unseen audience presents a very special challenge to any communicator. The media pride themselves on knowing how to do it; but even they have to resort to focus groups, market research and a lot of crossed fingers. I've made a number of suggestions – listed at the end of each chapter – there are nearly two hundred of them – to help you shape your message, and get it out it in the form that makes it most acceptable to the media, and through them, most understandable to their audiences.

My son John, who works in the PR business in the corporate field, read this book and said, 'You've said a lot about the past, and the present, but what about the future?' Futurology, as far as I am concerned, is a load of crystal balls. But some future trends are beginning to make their impact. I'm certain that everything will speed up as better technology kicks in. So coping with a crisis or any new development will demand more staff rather than less, just to get the messages out. Information technology will also give us much more information, and many more sources for getting it. Thus information anxiety will grow, and people will feel overwhelmed by the amount of data available – the simpler, and more direct, your message, the more it will get through the fog of data. Global reach will mean that no company can confine its mistakes or its crimes within one jurisdiction or hide in another. There will be greater transparency – the law as well as the people will demand it. As President Clinton discovered, something done in an alcove off the Oval Office can become world news. Mind you, if you read an earlier futurologist, Nostradamus, the world is going to blow itself up in the end – so it doesn't really matter anyway.

Yet despite all the possibilities that technology can bring, some things will never change. History suggests that despite the progress that the human race has made down the centuries, despite mass communications and mass tourism, people have remained resolutely human in their needs, worries and expectations. People will always prefer peace to war, honesty to dishonesty. They will always want good to triumph over evil. They still believe in motherhood and apple pie.

There will be those who will argue that this displays a large degree of naïveté about the modern world where truth is relative, and cutting corners in pursuit of self-interest is the norm. I am not suggesting that everyone obey Nietsche's categoric imperative of telling the full unvarnished truth regardless of the consequences. I recognise that there are degrees of truth, and that truth can rarely be total – in that few of us will ever know the whole truth. But the Clintons of this world seriously damage public faith in authority with their lying, half-truths and semantic debates. Those in power – and here I mean the business world every bit as much as the political world – will have to work harder than ever to win respect and, most of all, trust. A reputation for honesty and fair dealing will do more for your image and your relations with the media and the public than anything else.

And remember the media in general have an image problem as well.[55] The public tends to be equally cynical about what they do, and how they do it. 'You can't believe all you see and hear in the media' is a thought that is rarely if ever contradicted. Time and again we've seen Fleet Street's finest hauled over the coals by the press watchdog, only to go on with the same vigour as before, invading people's privacy. David Mellor, when he was briefly Secretary of State at the Heritage Department, warned them, in a celebrated sound bite, that 'they were drinking in the last chance saloon'. It was ironic that when the media eventually brought him down, the audience seemed rather to enjoy the spectacle.

'Killing the messenger', to borrow from the title of Bernard Ingham's book, is always an attraction. The most uncomfortable fact about the media – and it is wise to remember it – is that they actually hold up a mirror to us, the public. They feed our appetite for gossip and drama. They ape our hypocrisy in spreading malicious stories about the rich and famous while claiming it's in 'the public interest'. The only public they are interested in, say their detractors, is the public that goes on watching, listening and reading the papers.

Into the New Millennium

The big story as we moved into the 21st century was to have been the chaos caused by the Millennium bug. It didn't happen, and those 'experts' who forecast it are still trying to explain why. Instead, the year 2000 began with an old-fashioned row over Britain's Millennium Dome at Greenwich. This story had everything – merging politics, industry and show business. There were larger-than-life characters in the drama: taking the lead role, none other than Tony Blair. In supporting roles were the project's political masters, Peter Mandelson, and his successor, Lord Falconer; the heroine (or is it villain?) was the pugnacious chief executive, Jennie Page, once described by an anonymous Labour minister as 'a cross between a porcupine and an armadillo'. In the role of white knight was the former television mogul Michael Grade, whose job was to make sure there was a 'wow' factor. Egos all. The Dome is destined to become a classic case study in how not to launch such a project. It's anybody's guess as to whether in time it will ever become a classic case study of how to snatch victory from the jaws of defeat. The Times, before the new century was a week old, explained the problem: 'The Dome is just a big exhibition with some good bits and a lot of ordinary ones. But it has been horribly oversold. Daylight has shone on the spin doctors' dark box of tricks. And it has shown that it is empty.'

Fuelling the story was the fact that there were pictures galore on file – still and video footage – to add impact to the coverage; what's more, many of the key players seemed keen to brief against everyone else. No one wanted to shoulder the blame. If you logged on to the Internet and initiated a search using the word 'Dome', you were soon awash with current and archive material. You even got the full text of a report on the Dome by the House of Commons Committee on Culture, Media and Sport. In other words, the news desks just needed to answer the phone, rather than hunt high and low for new things to say.

There's no doubting that on New Year's Eve the 10,000 VIPs in the Dome, including the Queen, were genuinely enthralled by the spectacle. Ominously, too many VIPs – among them Fleet Street editors – had had to queue for their tickets. Some observers suggested that this fact alone accounted for the negative press that followed. It didn't help, that's for sure. Peter Mandelson and Alastair Campbell began to accuse the media of an 'an anti-Dome vendetta'. This is never a good idea, since the media will want to prove their case with even more enthusiasm. Mandelson and Campbell quoted surveys of visitors which claimed that 85 per cent of them were happy. A Dome spokeswoman professed that the company was 'delighted' with attendance figures – but, when pressed, said the audited figures would not be revealed until later. Everyone understood this to mean that ticket sales were sharply down. It prompted The Mail on Sunday to estimate that the Dome could end up costing each and every Briton at least £5 a head to bail out the business. Corporate sponsors, such as Mars and Boots, were said to be so unhappy that they wanted a re-launch before they would pay the many millions they had pledged. Jennie Page, the chief executive, ran the risk of losing her £200,000 performance bonus if she couldn't pull the project round.

Opposition MPs had a field day. Even though the Dome at Greenwich had been originally a Tory idea, the Conservative Shadow Culture Secretary opined that 'it tries to be both bossy and frivolous. It is a perfect emblem of New Labour.' Scottish and Welsh politicians got in on the act, saying the project was a 'London-centric' operation and had no appeal to their constituents. If the Dome did fail to recoup its costs, they wanted a pledge that Scottish and Welsh electors would not have to put their hands in their pockets to meet any multi-million pound deficit.

The débâcle at the Dome seemed for a time to be a bigger story than the huge flu epidemic then raging across the nation – the worst for a decade. And even here, spin and counter-spin was the order of the day – with some saying the government was suggesting the flu epidemic was worse than in reality to hide problems in the National Health Service. Then a top doctor and Labour peer, Lord Winston, suggested the National Health Service was in trouble, only to be pressured into saying he had been misquoted. But his interview with the weekly journal The New Statesman had been recorded, and the reporter produced an audio tape of his remarks. The Government's spin doctor-in-chief was in trouble again. As The Daily Mail headlined it: 'Damned Lies and Labour.'

There were other noteworthy stories in the news, as we moved into the year 2000. Two of them make the very serious point for those few villains who think it doesn't matter what you say or do, you can lie your way out of trouble. Jonathan Aitken and Gary Glitter were released from short prison sentences in January with their reputations in tatters. Aitken, a former cabinet minister, had been found guilty of perjury; Glitter, a 'glam rock' star, had been found guilty of downloading child pornography on to his PC. Aitken's case demonstrates that no matter how high you rise in the world, you can always fall. Glitter's case shows that no matter how safe you feel behind closed doors, the new technology can find you out. Finally a rather frivolous story demonstrated that sometimes what seems to be a harmless joke can badly damage your public image. 'Posh' Spice, who had courted publicity at every turn, informed the public that her husband, the footballer David Beckham, liked wearing her underwear. One wonders whether he will ever recover his reputation. Will the crowds on the terraces ever let him forget? In his next game, he was given a red card and sent off after a very macho tackle on an opponent.

These are just some of the stories that ushered in the New Year in Britain. They show that any hopes of the new Millennium being a more caring, sensitive era would be dashed. In fact, any change has been one of magnitude over what went on before. The world's media are going to become even more probing and unforgiving. And more omnipresent. The announcement that AOL was merging with Time Warner (including CNN) really set the cat among the media pigeons, as old and new media joined forces. It's already put European media on its guard. What it all adds up to is that your messages are going to need better management than ever before. The only defence is honest dealing and a willingness to listen to, and then answer, one's critics. No amount of huffing and puffing, nor threats of legal action will make the problem go away. If you want to 'manage the message', you need to make sure it's one that can withstand constant and probing analysis by your enemies as well as by your friends.

William Shakespeare, one of the greatest creators of sound bites, put these words into the mouth of the old courtier Polonius, as he bade farewell to his son Laertes, who was about to set sail for England: 'This above all; to thine own self be true. And it must follow, as the night the day, that thou canst not then be false to any man.'

Notes

1 The question about 'hounding people' was given full vent when Princess Diana died in Paris. The main culprits were seen as the photographers and reporters who followed her everywhere – hounding her, it was said, to her untimely death in a high-speed car chase through the streets late at night. No one wanted to believe that perhaps it was the fault of her driver who had an excessive level of alcohol in his blood.

2 Yet the BBC itself offers media training videos, and has had many of its top executives media trained.

3 In a BBC 2 documentary on Alton Towers, in the series Modern Times, it was reported that the mission statement was 'where the magic never ends'. The general manager of the theme park was asked to define 'magic'. He replied, 'The magic is, it's magical. It's so different to anything else. It's almost as if it's unreal and it's actually happening to you.' This was certainly not a magic sound bite.

4 The phrases 'leaves on the track' and 'the wrong type of snow' were the result of the rail companies challenging a business school with a complex problem and asking them to present it in a way that would simply communicate the message (while making an apology for being late). In the end the use of these and similar phrases only served to make the rail companies look ridiculous. A prime example of trying to over-simplify a complex problem and getting it wrong. Finally the railway forum banned all such phrases from its lexicon of excuses – its communications co-ordinator (as he was grandly called) said that in future all staff would offer simpler expla-

nations. So never again will rail passengers be told that 'The delay has been caused because the driver's cab was inverse to the direction of travel'. Or will they?

5 If you would like to contribute to the next edition with your own experiences of 'Managing the Message' – mentioning its successes or failures, or your observations on what is written here, then e-mail me at **pjhobday@aol.com** If you want to go 'off the record', please say so. The reporter in me, though, would much prefer to be able to quote you directly.

6 In the end Frank Dobson kept his beard and won a seat in the cabinet. Harriet Harman soon lost favour because she could not communicate. She lost her cabinet job in the first reshuffle.

7 Campbell now earns more than the Prime Minister – which would suggest, say his critics both inside the party and outside, the importance that New Labour attaches to presentation as opposed to policy.

8 Both these individuals were among the first ministers to lose their jobs. Perhaps they went on lunching.

9 Greene told The Times, 'The peers suffer, like many Brits, from an excess of formality that stresses information at the expense of communication. It's an overly formal, somewhat pompous, erudite high-falutin' style which has been the historical way.'

10 The Central Office of Information, which employs a goodly number more, publishes a useful annual guide to who's who in the government information service. It provides names, telephone numbers and addresses in Whitehall. Recently I had an interesting assignment from the COI to

produce a 30-minute audio tape for distribution to MOD press officers and senior civil servants about the way the media worked – I interviewed editors in Fleet Street, from the Sun to the Telegraph; TV stations from the BBC to Sky and ITN, as well as the regional press and broadcast media. 'Tell us the truth' was the message from the journalists to the Whitehall press officer corps. The media also said 'Trust us to do a professional job.' But then they would say that, wouldn't they?

11 Most newspapers now give their web page address, so that via hypertext, one can go even more deeply into stories that interest or intrigue – which means that one's critics have access to even more information than appears in a single story. The ability to access newspaper back numbers via the net, and net research in general, means the public can be as well informed as the experts if it so wishes.

12 I should explain that I was working on this book at the time, hence my use of the net to explore just how in touch I could be, when I was in deepest Umbria in Italy with only my laptop and a GSM phone for company.

13 The Social Affairs Unit, a right-of-centre research and educational trust, recently commissioned a collection of essays looking at what it called 'The sentimentalisation of Society'. It examined the response of the public in many areas – education, work, play, and so on. The most celebrated of these pieces concerned what was seen as mass hysteria following the death of Diana, Princess of Wales. The theme of all the essays was the increasingly sentimental view of policy – we must care, feel, worry, love, hate – cold logic has little place. You may not believe it, but it's worth reading. It's published by Penguin Books, price £7.99. The title is Faking It.

14 Rejigging Radio Four schedules is always a tricky business. Here more than anywhere the audience believe they are the keepers of the flame. They hate change. Even so, it was quite a shock when the next round of audience figures were announced; it

seemed that about three-quarters of a million people had switched off or switched to other channels. Even the Today programme was said to have lost more than half a million. So much for consulting the audience. Happily the listeners are now returning.

15 Corporate Crime by Dr Gary Slapper and Professor Steve Tombs, published by Addison Wesley Longman at £13.99.

16 Maybe this explains the rising tide of complaints against lawyers themselves. The latest report from the Legal Services Ombudsman says that in the preceding twelve months complaints against solicitors have risen out of control – there is a backlog of 17,000 cases, rising by 350 a month. It can take a complainant three months to get even an acknowledgement. The Law Society is said to be planning to recruit 82 temporary case workers, and 23 extra permanent case workers.

17 The furore over the appointment of Greg Dyke to replace Sir John Birt as Director General of the BBC was partly about politics and the likely political bias a cash donor to the Labour Party might show in the job. But more importantly it was about whether the man who used Roland Rat to save TV AM might bring the same populist instincts to the BBC. Would Dyke go down-market in search of audiences? Dyke argued that that was not what he wanted to do – he aimed to bring back excellence and distinctive programming. In business-speak – go back to the BBC's core competencies.

18 'Language they'll understand' is a rather ambiguous phrase. What I mean is use plain and simple language. I left it in the text, though, so that I could use this footnote to point out the chapter on the uses and abuses of language. See page 153.

19 Estuary English is spoken by and large in the south-east of England by the general population – it's being said that it is now spreading to the detriment of other regional accents such as Scouse in and around Liverpool.

20 This was the perfect example of the dubious attractions of the ubiquitous

'photo-opportunity'. The belief is that one picture is worth a thousand words. But of course they may not be the thousand words you want to see. Some public figures think it's safer to be photographed than to be quoted. You need to take expert advice as to which is more appropriate.

21 According to the American communications expert Richard Greene, 'Diana's challenge was that she was visually talented and superb at the kinesthetic, empathetic part, but had no talent for auditory communications. She was not great with words and details. Prince Charles was the exact reverse. They had absolutely nothing in common.'

22 I could not find the word in my Shorter Oxford English Dictionary – I think it is an American import.

23 Information Anxiety was published by Doubleday in 1989. In the years since publication the numbers have grown, only to reinforce the main thesis in the book that data has replaced information and there is too much of it.

24 Microsoft, as I write, is said to be planning a Dictionary of World English to help people who get confused as to which English 'dialect' a person is using – American, British, Canadian, Australian, and so on.

25 Kalb was quoted in the New York Times on the web on 14 February 1999. Yet that same edition had nine articles on the post-impeachment mood in America, plus access, should the web site visitor want it, to additional articles, documents, video and audio, news polls, and so on. Thus, paradoxically, while the news is getting more sensational and more superficial, the dedicated researcher can get more detail and background than ever before, thanks to information technology.

26 And a British humorist, Alan Coren, once wrote that 'Television is more interesting than people. If it were not, we should have people standing in the corners of our rooms.'

27 It was at first nicknamed Chicken Noodle network.

28 In a statement the governors said that 'there was a role for well-produced and well-considered programmes which tackled family and personal issues in a responsible and enlightened way'. There was no place on the BBC for the sensational and voyeuristic.

29 According to the American architect, Frank Lloyd Wright, 'An expert is someone who has stopped thinking. Why should he think he is an expert?' Quoted in the Daily Express in 1959.

30 The hospitality suite is usually called 'The green room'. Why, I have no idea – perhaps someone can shed some light on the origin of the phrase?

31 I once covered a single story for all three media. I was then presenting the Money Programme on BBC. I had been sent to Uganda just after Idi Amin had fled the country. The story was how a society copes with the total collapse of the economy, and no real government in place. I made a 30-minute film for TV, a 20-minute report for BBC radio and wrote 2500 words for the BBC's weekly newspaper The Listener. Just one event shows the difference in coverage depending on the medium in question. My 2500 words were as good a summary as I could make of the main issues, with lots of descriptive prose and lots of pithy quotes. The real difference came in radio and TV. I was in the marketplace of the second city, Jinja, when some remnants of Amin's troops were spotted and a firefight started. The cameraman, sound man and I dropped to the floor. The camera was switched off, but the sound continued running. Radio therefore had the most dramatic start to the story – gunfire, screams and a scared reporter breathlessly explaining what was happening. TV had no mention of the incident at all – we had no pictures.

32 Still pictures of both these events were on every front page – and the use of pictures in newspapers is driven by competition from TV. Increasingly, I believe, managing the message means managing the visual image every bit as skilfully as well. Think about where you want to be interviewed

when a TV crew comes to see you. Think where the reporter might do the stand-up.

33 Those metallic characters in the BBC TV science fiction programme Dr Who. Their only lines were 'Exterminate, exterminate' and 'You will obey'. They had no brains, only a recorded message.

34 It was called European Business Weekly and was subsequently acquired by the Financial Times. The use of corporate footage gave what was a low-budget production a very expensive look without damaging my small editorial allowance.

35 Rebuttal is not to be confused with what is sometimes called the 'pre-buttal'. This technique was used with some success by the Clinton White House. The President's spin doctors would leak sensitive information to spark debate and then have rapid rebuttals ready and plans to control it.

36 His co-author is Leighton Andrews, some-time head of Public Affairs at the BBC. The book is published by Hawksmere.

37 Product recall isn't always a PR disaster. A recent example of a very effective product recall was Bass. They took all the product off the shelves, and were strongly supported in the media for their action. In some cases there is not only praise but profit in such a decision. Zanussi, the domestic appliance group, found that a recall can lead to increased awareness of a product which in turn produces higher levels of sales.

38 It is said that there was quite a battle waged inside the British cabinet between the then Secretary of Defence George Robertson and Foreign Secretary Robin Cook as to who should give the morning briefing at the Ministry of Defence. In the end we had Cook standing at a podium with the MOD logo displayed everywhere – somewhat confusing to the casual viewer. The emergence of the story didn't help either.

39 e.g. They think the 'media are a bunch of conniving little sh*ts'.

40 The Way We Live Now is published by Chatto & Windus at £18.

41 De Oratore (On the Orator) is published with the Latin and English texts side-by-

side in the Loeb Classical Library by the Harvard Press at £12.95.

42 The problem, however, is that the Labour government seems to want to call every-thing 'The People's ...' They are the People's Party, so the overuse of the term somewhat debases the coinage.

43 See Chapter Four.

44 The satirical magazine Private Eye has a column which collects some of the nonsense that appears in the press. And William Safire, of the New York Times, writes regularly on language and how the press mangles it. He has published a number of books. Two of my favourites are Take My Word for It and You Could Look It Up. If you can't find them in Britain, then Amazon.com, the Internet bookshop, will surely locate and send them to you.

45 An even more up-market name for the job is 'barrista', with the stress on the second syllable.

46 Try not to ask the media to fax it to you – it gives the impression that you are not up-to-date with the news that concerns your industry. If it's a minister, the minister's press office will help; if it's a pressure group, they will be happy to send you a copy. Check with the news agencies; these days you may find it if you search the net.

47 I did discuss some isolated examples of media distortion on pages 72–3. But those who were discovered have paid a heavy price – with their careers.

48 Kill the Messenger by Bernard Ingham is published by HarperCollins at £17.50.

49 See 'A word about editing', page 200.

50 The Journalist and the Murderer by Janet Malcolm, published by Vintage Books, a division of Random House, 1990.

51 According to Richard Hoggart in his book The Way We Live Now (Chatto & Windus, £18), 'sound bites are the semantic equiv-alent of "chicken nuggets"'.

52 In the United States research shows that the average sound bite is not less than 12 seconds – or about 30 words. That's believed to be the attention span of the audience brought up on TV commercials.

53 I don't know how they did it, but they had won the concession from the police. We Brits were allowed into Downing Street as well – and we've been there ever since. So much so that the reporter's stand-up in front of Number Ten is now a visual cliché.

54 Published by Cassell, 1988.

55 In October 1998 New Yorker magazine carried out a nationwide survey of public attitudes to the American media following its intensive coverage of the Clinton impeachment story. Some 79% thought the media rearranged and distorted the facts to make up a good story; 71% believed legitimate news outlets were sinking to the level of the tabloids with gossip and unsubstantiated rumours as their main diet; 48% thought the media had a negative effect on society.

Index

A

A-Z of Public Advocacy (Des
  Wilson), 138
advertising, 51, 221
Aitken, Jonathan, 15, 43,
  133
Al Fayed, Mohamed, 33,
  136–7, 162, 223
alcohol, avoiding, 102–4, 174,
  209
ambiguity, avoiding, 130, 136,
  157–9
anchors. see presenters
angles, on stories, 83–6
local, 123–4
Archer, Lord and Lady, 102
attention
  getting public's, 65
  shortness of span, 15, 16,
    35, 129, 195–8, 217,
    233(n52)
audiences
  addressing, 48–50, 61, 196
  attracting, 73–4
  controlling media, 35–7, 47
  disappearing, 58–9
  knowing as people, 59
  'minority,' 69
  reaction, monitoring, 35–6
  satisfying wants of, 83
  talking to unseen, 224
  targeting, 84–5, 115, 123,
    182
  understanding agenda of,
    55

B

Bashir, Martin, 180
BBC, 74, 106, 230(n28)
  accused of bias, 191

appointment of Director
  General, 229(n17)
ban on media training,
  13–14, 227(n2)
centralisation of news
  operation, 76, 92
investing in new technology,
  76
News Guide for reporters,
  158
use of market research, 51,
  229(n14)
Bell, Sir Tim, 28
Benn, Tony, 206
Birt, Sir John, 229(n17)
Blair, Cherie, 186
Blair, Tony
  and spin doctors, 21–9
  and use of language, 59,
    156, 217
body language, 16, 19, 28,
  188
  on camera, 179–87, 201
  of Diana, Princess of Wales,
    179–80
  when talking to reporters,
    209
Bosanquet, Reginald, 103
Boyle, James, 51
Bradbury, Grace, 180
Branson, Richard, 59–60
Breaking the News: How the
  Media Undermine American
  Democracy (James
  Fallows), 72
briefing, of media, 146–9,
  232(n38)
briefs, for press conferences,
  131, 209
broadcast interviews. see

interviews, broadcast
broadcast journalism, 34–5
Brown, Gordon, 170
Brunson, Michael, 109
Buchanan, Elizabeth, 28
Bush, George, 65, 71
business
  and battle for public
    opinion, 31–2, 39–40,
    42
  lessons from politics, 19,
    29, 32, 45
  media as, 16, 68–9
  media training, 13–14,
    196
  public relations function
    (see public relations,
    function)
  relationship with media, 39,
    54, 72–3

C

Callaghan, James, 141
campaigning, principles for
  success, 138–9
Campbell, Alastair, 22–9,
  44–5, 191, 205, 222,
  228(n7)
Campbell, Nicky, 51
Carter, President Jimmy, 167
CEEFAX, 98
Central Office of Information,
  125, 228(n10)
Chamberlain, Neville, 155
Chan, Thomas, 222
Charles, Prince, 28, 40, 183,
  184, 230(n21)
Church of England
  and spin doctors, 27–8
Churchill, Winston

and use of language,
155–6, 199
Clare, Anthony, 208
clichés, 164, 168, 169. see
also language
visual, 183
Clinton, Bill, 14, 35–7, 47–8,
68, 156–7, 179, 184,
233(n55)
clothes, and image, 59–60,
156, 186–7, 188
CNN, 35, 70–1, 97, 111,
230(n27)
Cole, Michael, 223
columnists, job of, 104–5
communication
non-verbal (see body
language)
types of, 223–4
communications technology,
advances in, 67
computers. see information
technology
'confessional' programmes, 74
consumer programmes, 72–3
control
of interviews, 199–200
issue of, 26
of knowledge, 37, 38–9
of media by audience,
35–7, 47
of messages, 135–9
staying in, 132, 133,
144–5, 146–9, 193
Cook, Robin, 23, 24,
232(n38)
Coren, Alan, 230(n26)
corporate
crime, 53–4
jargon, 15, 17, 50, 129,
130, 153–4, 168–9,
196, 227(n3, n4)
videos, using, 126
Corporate crime (Dr. Gary
Slapper), 229(n15)
correspondents, specialist
job of, 105
credibility, of the powerful,
47–8, 52–61, 156–7
crime, corporate, 53–4
crises, 152, 194

briefing the media during,
146–9, 232(n38)
choosing a spokesman, 149
co-operating with the
media, 144–5
media drivers in, 143–4
planning for, 141–3
staying in control of, 145
'croneyism,' history of
word, 169–71
Curry, Edwina, 25, 160

D

Daily Mail, 104, 105
Daily Mirror, 74
Daily Telegraph, 105
data, 18, 63, 64. see also
knowledge
Davies, Mandy Rice, 45
Davies, Ron, 18
De Oratore (Cicero), 155,
232(41)
delaying tactics, in interviews,
145
di Manio, Jack, 103
Diana, Princess of Wales, 28,
60, 102, 136, 156,
179–80, 184
digital technology, 12, 35
Dimbleby, Jonathan, 112, 184
disclaimers, to press releases
avoiding need for, 119–20
distortion, of messages, 15,
17, 72–3, 200, 227(n3,
n4)
Dobson, Frank, 23
docu-dramas, 34–5
documentary programmes,
honesty of, 74
Draper, Derek, 24
'dumbing down,' 58, 68–9,
78–9, 166, 191
Dyke, Greg, 229(n17)

E

editing, process of, 72
in broadcast media, 108,
202
in news management,
82–3, 92–3, 193
in newspapers, 205, 208

editors, job of
broadcast media, 109–10
print media, 104
Edwardes, Sir Michael,
218–19
English. see also language
Estuary, 59, 229(n19)
'Plain English' campaign,
167
Standard, 158–9
as world language, 68,
230(n24)
European, The, 181
examples, using to illustrate
points, 176–7, 197–8
exclusives, (stories), 91, 106,
132, 148
myth of, 83–4
experts, being wary of, 29,
41, 95–6, 97, 146,
230(n29)

F

'factoids,' 63, 65
Faking It (Social Affairs Unit),
229(n13)
feature writers, job of, 105–6
Field, Frank, 27, 228(n8)
figures (statistics), as
hindrance to messages,
176
Financial Times, 84, 132
Financial World Tonight, 9,
192
flexibility, importance of, 135
food industry, and media, 40,
159–60
Ford, Anna, 51

G

global culture, as created by
media, 67–8
'global village,' concept of, 33,
37
Goebbels, Dr., 41
government
and battle for public
opinion, 31–4
and control of knowledge,
37–9
Guardian, 27–8, 84, 85, 98

H

Hague, William, 57, 170–1
Harman, Harriet, 27, 228(n8)
headlines, 109, 141
  writing, 106–8
Healey, Denis, 161
Hidden Persuaders, The
  (Vance Packard), 51
Hoddle, Glen, 18, 63, 135
honesty
  being 'economical with the
    truth,' 156–7
  as best policy, 14, 16,
    145–6, 225
  of media, 200
  of programmes, 73
Howard, Michael, 161
Howe, Lord, 125, 161
human angle, in news stories,
  35, 42–3, 85, 93, 105
Humphrys, John, 13, 112, 191

I

If They Haven't Heard It, You
  Haven't Said It (Harvey
  Thomas), 196
image
  and clothes, 59–60, 156,
    186–7, 188
  versus language, 184–5
  of media, 225
  and message, 221
  of self, 180–8
images
impact of, 109, 150,
  231(n32)
  moving, 180, 182
  still, 182–4
  as weapons, 11–12
imitation, in the media, 69–71
immediacy, aiming for, 130,
  198
impressions, managing, 127–8
individuals
  in news stories, 35, 42–3,
    85, 93, 105
  rights championed by
    media, 78
information, 66. see also
  knowledge
  need for, 63–4

overload, 64–5
Information Anxiety (Richard
  Saul Wurman), 64, 75,
  230(n23)
information technology, 12,
  18, 33, 89, 98, 224
Ingham, Sir Bernard, 26, 205,
  222
insults, using to advantage,
  133, 160–3
Internet
  and control of knowledge,
    38–9
  explosive growth of, 12
  global reach of, 36–7
  for news summaries, 35
  for research, 132,
    228(n11), 230(n25)
interviewers
  'hostile,' 13, 191–2
  press, 208
  skills of, 112 (see also
    presenters)
interviews
  addressing the audience,
    196
  broadcast, 16, 50,
    189–203, 205–9
  choosing language for,
    195–8
  confrontational, 192
  controlling, 199–200
  and crisis management,
    145
  dealing with questions,
    127–34
  fears about, 191–2
  live versus pre-recorded,
    124–6, 189–90, 193–4,
    202
  newspaper, 205–9
  as performances, 179–80
  preparing for, 145, 173–8,
    192–5, 197, 207
  telephone, 211
Irvine, Lord, 25, 107

J

jargon. see corporate, jargon
jibes, using to advantage,
  133, 160–3

Jones, Paula
  and Bill Clinton, 184–5
'journalese,' 158
journalism
  broadcast, 34–5
  process of, 82
Journalist and the Murderer,
  The (Janet Malcolm), 206,
  232(n50)
journalists
  as information processors,
    98
  relationship with subjects,
    206–7

K

Kennedy, President, 167,
  185–6
Kill the Messenger (Bernard
  Ingham), 205, 222,
  232(n48)
Kinnock, Neil, 25
knowledge. see also
  information
  versus data, 18, 63, 64
  democratising control of,
    37
  hunger for, 60, 66
Kohl, Chancellor Helmut, 222

L

Lamont, Norman, 43, 161
language, 108, 127, 130,
  172. see also corporate,
  jargon; English
  appropriateness for
    audience, 59
  avoiding ambiguity, 136,
    140, 157–9
  damaging phrases, 159–63
  fashionable phrases, 165–6,
    167–8
  versus image, 184–5
  in interviews, 195–8
  'journalese,' 158
  oratory, skills of, 154–6
  overuse of '-gate' suffix,
    164–5
  in personal vendettas,
    162–3
  political correctness, 163–4

in print media, 158–9,
232(n44)
verbal imports, 166–7
words as weapons, 11–12,
162–3
lawyers, complaints against,
229(n16)
leader writers, job of, 105
Lewinsky, Monica, 36, 37, 68,
98, 156–7
Listener, The, 7
Livingstone, Ken, 54
local angle, using, 123–4
lunches, press, 211–12
Lynam, Des, 192

M
Macgregor, Sue, 112, 164
Macmillan, Harold, 33
Madonna, 84–6, 186
Major, John, 161, 186, 224
Major, Norma, 186
make-overs, being wary of,
186
Mandela, Nelson, 183
Mandelson, Peter, 22–9, 44,
157, 170
market forces, as media
driver, 58
market research, 116
reliance on, 50–1
marketing, 47, 81, 92
Maxwell, Robert, 17, 156, 181
media
American, 72, 233
as business, 16, 68–9
commonly asked questions
about, 10
exponential growth of, 67,
76
future of, 224
as hostile environment, 11,
13–14, 102
hounding of individuals by,
106, 227(n1)
and lying, 10, 200
people in, 101–4, 113
broadcast, 108–12
print, 104–8
perception of, 101
ubiquity of, 12, 70

media training, 13–14, 196,
227(n2)
Megatrends (John Naisbitt),
70
Mellor, David, 160, 225
memory, tricks for, 173–7
messages
contextualising, 194–5,
232(n46)
controlling, 135–9
defining, 115–26, 194, 209
distorting, 15, 17, 72–3,
200, 227(n3, n4)
managing government's,
32–3
as marketable products, 22
'spinning' of, 21–9, 36 (see
also spin doctors)
targeting, 84–5, 115, 123,
182
testing, 131–4
timing, 93, 215–20
messengers
choosing with care, 149,
222–3
firing, 222, 225
Minogue, Kylie, 186
mission statements, 17,
115–16
mistrust, climate of, 14, 101,
145
Money Box, 9
Money Programme, 9, 174,
231(n31)
Murdoch, Rupert, 12, 97

N
nerves, dealing with, 174–5
news
as 24-hour operation,
89–97, 100, 144, 148
business of, 89
definition of, 70, 81, 82
financial, 192
future of, 96–8
growth of local and
regional, 75–6
management of, 82–3
as show business, 99
news media, what it wants,
81–7, 193

Newsnight, 23, 55, 96, 112,
132, 218
presenting, 9
newspaper interviews. see
interviews, newspaper
newspapers
cost pressures of, 77–8
electronic, 98
future of, 75
Nixon, Richard, 185–6
non-verbal communication.
see body language

O
Observer, 24, 106, 162
obsessiveness, power of,
137–8
opinions, versus facts, 130,
134
oratory, science of, 154–6

P
Panorama, 179–80, 184
Parker Bowles, Camilla, 28
passion, power of, 136–7
Paxman, Jeremy, 13, 23, 112,
191, 207
perception
importance of, 26
of media, 101
of powerful people, 52–4
of presenters, 111
Percival, Alan, 25
persistence, power of, 137–8
persuasion, in interviews, 127
'photo-opportunities,' 102,
230(n20)
photographers, choosing with
care, 183
pictures, impact of, 109, 150,
231(n32)
moving, 180, 182
still, 182–4
'Plain English' campaign, 167
political correctness, 163–4
politicians, 54
interviews with, 191–2
politics
and language of jibes, 161–2
lessons for business, 19,
29, 32, 45

'prebuttals,' 135, 231 (n35)
preparing
    for interviews, 133, 173–8
    for press conferences, 210
Prescott, John, 24–5
presentation
    of self, 180–8
    skills, 47, 48–50, 223
    tailoring for medium,
        108–9, 123, 231 (n31)
presenters, job of, 111–12
Press Association, 92
Press Complaints Commission,
    106
press conferences, 93–4, 122
    briefs for, 131, 209
    managing, 209–11
press lunches, 211–12
press releases, analysis of
    example, 117–23
pressure groups, 53, 93, 159,
    163
    as effective message
        managers, 40–3, 44
    persistence of, 137
    and personal vendettas,
        162–3
    use of Internet, 36, 40
print, getting into, 205–13
Private Eye, 33
producers, job of, 110
production, radio and
    television, 77
Profumo, John, 157
propaganda, 41
public, as informed electorate,
    44–5
public opinion
    battle for, 11, 31–46
polls, 36
public relations
    function, 131, 132–3
        business need for, 29
        in crisis management,
            146–8
        limitations of, 138–9
    industry, 12
        growing power of, 76–7
        role in news making, 95
    and Prince Charles, 28
public speaking, 48–50

public voice, encouragement
    of, 57–8
Put it together and put it
    across (David Bernstein),
    223

Q
Queen, the
    and spin doctors, 28, 107,
        169–70
questions
    avoiding awkward, 145–6
    dealing with in interviews,
        127–34
quotes, use in news, 95–6

R
racism, avoiding, 164, 221
Radio Five, morning show, 91
Ratner, Gerald, 56
Rayner, Claire, 95
rebuttals, rapid
    technique of, 135–6, 215
Redhead, Brian, 91, 190, 191
repetition, use of, 170
reporters, job of, 106
research, 92
    market, reliance on, 50–1
    for targeting appropriate
        audience, 85
researchers, job of in broad-
    cast media, 110, 195
responses, to statements
    drawing, 93
rhetoric, 155
Rhys Jones, Sophie, 10
rights, of public, 56
risks, minimising, 34–5
Robinson, Ann, 72
Rowland, Tiny, 162
Royal Family, 18, 28

S
Saddam Hussein, 38, 71
scare tactics, using, 42
self-image, creating and
    controlling, 180–8
sensationalism, 68–9
sexism, avoiding, 164
Short, Clare, 24, 25
silence

as admission of guilt, 144,
    146, 163
    disadvantages of, 132
    simplicity, importance of,
        118, 157, 175
Simpson, O. J., trial of, 35,
    97, 107, 150, 185
Sky, 35, 71, 97
Sky News, 71, 82, 97
slogans, use of, 41–2, 129,
    221
society, sentimentalisation of,
    228 (n13)
sound bites, 43–4, 65, 83,
    94, 130, 195, 196–9,
    216–19, 225, 233 (n52)
sources, of stories, 82–3
    finding, 194, 232 (n46)
specialist correspondents, job
    of, 105
speculation, avoiding, 130
spin doctors, 30
    Carville, James ('king of
        spin'), 136, 138, 215
    New Labour's, 21–9, 44–5,
        171
    origin of term, 21
    power of, 76–7
spokesmen, choosing with
    care, 149, 222–3
Standard English, 158–9
stories (news), 81–6, 193,
    194
    angles on, 83–6, 123–4
    crises as, 149–50
    mileage of, 93, 94
    phases of, 94–5
    visibility of, 89–90
sub-editors, job of, 106–8
Sun, 84, 107, 141, 180

T
Take My Word For It (William
    Safire), 232 (n44)
Talk Radio, 91
targeting
    audiences, 84–5, 115, 123,
        182
    messages, 84–5, 115, 123,
        182
Tatchell, Peter, 162

technology
  communications, advances
    in, 67
  digital, 12, 33, 35, 73, 97,
    98
  information, 12, 18, 33,
    89, 98, 224
  investing in, 76
Telegraph, 85
telephone interviews, 211
television
  future of, 74–5
  news coverage, 70–2
testing, of messages, 131–4
'textual analysis,' and motives,
  156
Thatcher, Margaret, 21, 34,
  38, 43, 186, 222
time, as driving force in
  media, 130
Times, 98, 105, 132, 153,
  169

timing of messages, 93,
  215–20
Timpson, John, 190
Today, 83, 91, 105–6, 107,
  110, 132, 164, 173, 199,
  229(n14)
presenting, 9–10
travel industry, crises in,
  141–2
Tusa, John, 171

U
United States Information
  Service, 126

V
vendettas, personal, 162–3
visiting cards, 128
voice
  making yours heard, 32–4
  public, encouragement of,
    57–8

W
Wark, Kirsty, 112
Watchdog, 72–3
Way We Live Now, The
  (Richard Hoggart), 153,
  232(n40), 233(n51)
Webb, Justin, 51
websites, use of, 36
Whelan, Charlie, 24, 26
Widdecombe, Ann, 133,
  161–2, 186
Wilson, Des, 138
Woodward, Louise, trial of,
  97, 107, 180, 216
words. see language

Y
You Could Look It Up (William
  Safire), 232(n44)
Young, Kirsty, 111